Power Programming with

MICROSOFT®
MACRO
ASSEMBLER

Power Programming with
MICROSOFT®
MACRO
ASSEMBLER

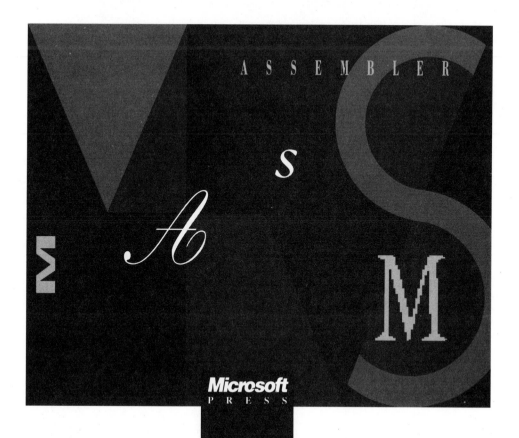

Ray Duncan

PUBLISHED BY
Microsoft Press
A Division of Microsoft Corporation
One Microsoft Way
Redmond, Washington 98052-6399

Library of Congress Cataloging-in-Publication Data
Duncan, Ray, 1952–
    Power programming with Microsoft Macro Assembler / Ray Duncan.
        p.   cm.
    Includes bibliographical references and index.
    ISBN 1-55615-256-6
    1. Assembler language (Computer program language)   2. Microsoft
Macro Assembler (Computer program)   I. Title.
QA76.73.A8D84   1991
005.265--dc20   91-21617
                                                 CIP

Printed and bound in the United States of America.

1 2 3 4 5 6 7 8 9   MLML   6 5 4 3 2 1

Distributed to the book trade in Canada by Macmillan of Canada, a division of
Canada Publishing Corporation.

Distributed to the book trade outside the United States and Canada by Penguin Books Ltd.

Penguin Books Ltd., Harmondsworth, Middlesex, England
Penguin Books Australia Ltd., Ringwood, Victoria, Australia
Penguin Books N.Z. Ltd., 182-190 Wairau Road, Auckland 10, New Zealand

British Cataloging-in-Publication Data available.

Acquisitions Editor: Dean Holmes
Project Editor: Mary Renaud
Technical Editor: Jeff Carey

For Rachel

Ray Duncan is a contributing editor to *PC Magazine* and *Dr. Dobb's Journal*. He is also the author of *Advanced MS-DOS Programming* and *Advanced OS/2 Programming,* both published by Microsoft Press. He currently works as a staff neonatologist at Cedars-Sinai Medical Center in Los Angeles, California.

Contents

Acknowledgments

My heartfelt thanks to all the folks at Microsoft Press who have managed to maintain their patience and good humor throughout this book's long gestation. Special thanks to my friends at Microsoft, *PC Magazine,* and elsewhere who made this book possible: Jeff Carey, Claudette Moore, Trudy Neuhaus, Tony Rizzo, and Mary Renaud.

Introduction

This book does not attempt to teach the rudiments of assembly-language programming, Microsoft MASM syntax, MS-DOS function calls, or the Intel 80x86 architecture. Plenty of introductory books on these subjects have already been published; a list of my personal recommendations can be found in the Bibliography. Nor is this book directed to the veteran assembly-language programmer who constructs device drivers or crafts high-performance video games for a living. Instead, my objective lies somewhere between these two extremes: to provide useful building blocks for the programmer who has learned the basic tricks of the trade but is not yet experienced at putting together serious, nontrivial assembly-language applications.

The first and last chapters of this book address global MASM programming issues—code structure and code optimization. The remaining chapters are oriented toward various categories of application tasks that are frequently encountered during MS-DOS-based MASM program development, with each chapter presenting generalized routines that perform these tasks. With rare exceptions, the chapters do not depend on one another and can be read somewhat in isolation. The companion disk contains all of the procedures from the book in source code form and also includes, for almost every procedure, an interactive demonstration program that allows you to exercise the procedure. These demonstration programs are provided both in source code and as pre-linked executable files. (Information about the companion disk is on page 372.)

The most beneficial way to use this book is not by reading it from beginning to end. Rather, I recommend that you turn to a specific chapter as a need for its contents arises in the course of your own work. First, browse the chapter and try to imagine how the routines it contains could fit into your own program. Next, copy the entire directory for that chapter from the companion disk to a directory on your hard disk, and run the executable versions of the various demonstration programs. Finally, load the demonstration programs under the control of a debugger such as CodeView and step through the procedures until you understand exactly how they work. You will then be able to alter and improve the routines and make them a permanent part of your own programming toolkit.

The listings in this book and the additional programs on the companion disk have been tested with Microsoft MASM 5.1, Microsoft LINK 5.1, Microsoft MAKE 4.06, and CodeView 3.0. To keep the source code compatible with the widest possible range of commercial and shareware assemblers, linkers, and debuggers, I have refrained from using the simplified segment directives of MASM version 5 and the many syntactic changes introduced in MASM version 6. (If you own MASM 6, you should assemble these programs using the MASM 5.1 compatibility switch, /Zm.) Additionally, in order to keep the routines straightforward and easy to understand, I have made no attempt to optimize the code for either size or speed or to include robust error handling.

Much of the text in the book has appeared in one form or another in my Power Programming column in *PC Magazine*. Most of the routines have been extensively overhauled since their original publication, however, and several of the more complex modules (such as the linked list and binary tree managers in Chapter 11) were written especially for this book and have not been published elsewhere. If you discover a conflict between the *PC Magazine* version of a routine or its documentation and the version you find here, you should assume that this book contains the later, improved incarnation.

I've tried to ensure that the listings and information in this book are reliable and accurate, but I'm also confident—human nature being what it is—that the programs contain the usual quota of obscure errors. I welcome your comments, questions, and bug reports at any of the following electronic mail addresses:

PC MagNet: 72241,52
BIX: rduncan
MCI Mail: RDUNCAN, 373-8337

I wish you the best of luck in all your assembly-language programming endeavors.

Ray Duncan
Los Angeles
December 1991

1

Thoroughly Modular MASM

Assembly-language programs are written in symbols that an assembler (such as the Microsoft Macro Assembler, referred to as MASM) translates directly into the computer's machine instructions—the bits in memory that tell the computer where to go, when to go there, and what to do when it arrives. In high-level languages such as C, Pascal, and Basic, each line of source code can correspond to many machine operations; but the ratio of assembly-language statements to machine instructions, in contrast, is typically less than 1 to 1—a result of the many directives that assembly-language programs must include to control the grouping of machine code and data and the relationships between modules.

As compilers for modern, structured languages have become more efficient and less expensive, fewer and fewer situations arise in which coding in assembly language is mandatory or even desirable. The benefits of using a high-level language and an integrated development environment are clear: increasing your productivity; giving you access to powerful source-oriented profilers, debuggers, and other tools; and allowing you to concentrate on programming problems rather than on machine dependencies. Writing applications for modern graphical user interfaces such as Microsoft Windows essentially demands the use of a high-level language; these graphical environments are so complex that you need the leverage provided by a compiler's support for function prototyping, parameter type-checking, complex data structures, and so on.

Nevertheless, assembly language will always be needed in some situations—for example, because a compiler is not efficient enough or because it does not allow adequate access to machine-level resources. And there will always be some people (like me) who simply enjoy programming in assembly language and having complete control of the machine. Whichever category you find yourself in, paying careful attention to your program's logical and physical structure and conservatively using the assembler's support for modularization and information hiding (such as it is) can make your life easier and your job more enjoyable. For example, you can think of the source code for an assembly-language program as being structured at several levels (two of which are illustrated in Figure 1-1):

■ The module level

■ The segment level

■ The procedure level

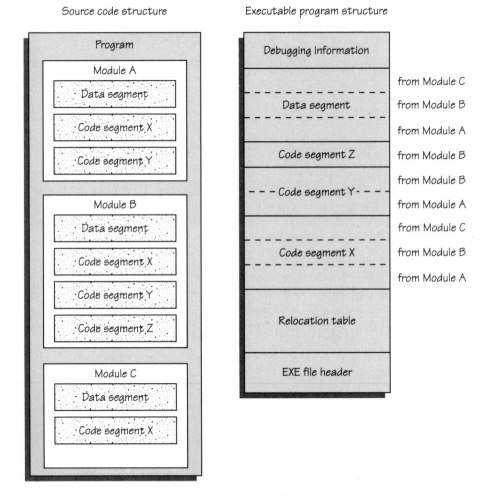

Figure 1-1.
The levels of structure in a MASM program's source code module and segment compared to the executable file for the same program.

Each level has its own special considerations, which can work either for or against your goal of a fast, compact, bug-free MASM application. MASM facilities for macros and data structures can also be beneficial when they are used with discretion. In this chapter, we'll survey these concepts and features briefly before moving on to practical examples of their use throughout the rest of the book.

Factoring Programs into Procedures

Procedures are the functional units of a program that carry out a particular job. They are declared and delimited within your source code with the PROC and ENDP directives, using this general form:

```
name PROC attribute
      .
      .
      .
      RET
name ENDP
```

This form is basically a fancy guise for the conceptual entity you know as a subroutine. The scope of the PROC and ENDP directives has some effect on the meaning of certain labels, as you'll see later, and also some effect on code generation. In particular, the *attribute* carried by a PROC declaration, which is either NEAR or FAR, tells the assembler what type of call you expect to use to enter the subroutine—that is, whether the subroutine will be called from other routines in the same segment or from routines in other segments. The assembler uses this information to generate the right opcode for any occurrence of the RET instruction within the procedure.

The most recent versions of MASM contain additional modifiers that you can add to the PROC directive. These include USES, which specifies which registers should be saved and restored, and "local names" and data types for parameters that are being passed to the routine on the stack. In MASM version 6.0, you can even declare function prototypes for your procedures with the PROTO keyword and create calls to prototyped procedures that push the right variables onto the stack with the INVOKE keyword. These directives are most useful when you are writing MASM routines that will be called from a high-level language; they are used less frequently when you are programming totally in assembly language (mainly because parameters are rarely passed on the stack in a pure MASM program, for reasons of efficiency).

The "main" procedure, which receives control when the program is loaded, calls other procedures within the program in an orderly way, depending on the user's input, the command-line parameters, and other factors. (Of course, second-level procedures can in turn call third-level procedures, and so on.) The main procedure can have any name; you can simply call it "main," as in a C program. The name is designated by including it in the END statement at the end of the file containing that procedure. Because a program returns control to MS-DOS by a function call rather than by executing a subroutine return (RET), the main procedure's attribute is not important, although it is usually assigned the FAR attribute by convention.

Within a procedure, structured programming in the computer scientist's sense of the term ("*goto*-less programming") is out of the question. The flow of control is usually governed by explicit comparisons and conditional jumps, and a MASM program without such branch points would be a useless program indeed. MASM version 6.0, however, has several new directives that allow you to think about the flow of execution at a somewhat higher level:

```
.IF         .WHILE      .REPEAT        .REPEAT
 .           .           .              .
 .           .           .              .
 .           .           .
.ELSE       .ENDW       .UNTIL         .UNTILCXZ
 .
 .
 .
.ENDIF
```

For example, the statements

```
.IF         AX = 0
mov         ax,-1
.ELSE
mov         ax,1
.ENDIF
```

will generate actual code as follows:

```
              cmp       ax,0
              jne       label1
              mov       ax,-1
              jmp       label2
label1:  mov       ax,1
label2:
```

I personally am wary of using such high-level control constructs in assembly-language programs; when I'm willing to give away authority over code generation in my program, I prefer to use a C compiler. But you can follow other guidelines when writing procedures that will facilitate your program's debugging and maintenance. For example, a useful rule of thumb is that a procedure should not exceed one page in length; a longer procedure is probably too complex, and some of its function should be delegated to subsidiary procedures. Ideally, a procedure should perform a single well-defined function, have only one entry point and one exit point, invoke other procedures only by CALLs, always exit via a RET instruction, and avoid any action that might have unexpected global effects on the behavior of other procedures. Documentation discipline is extremely important as well. Each procedure should be prefaced in the source code with a detailed comment that states the procedure's calling sequence, the results returned, the registers affected, and any data items accessed or modified.

Factoring Programs into Segments

Segment directives give you the power to group similar or related procedures or data items together in the executable program, regardless of where those procedures or data items appear in the program's source code. Segments are declared with the SEGMENT and ENDS commands, using this general form:

```
name SEGMENT attributes
    .
    .
    .
name ENDS
```

The attributes of a segment include its *alignment type* (byte, word, or paragraph), *combine type* (public, private, common, or stack), and *class name*. The segment attributes are used by the Linker when it is collecting segments of the same name or the same class name to build the executable program image. Most of the time, you can get by with using a small selection of attributes in a rather stereotyped way—as I will demonstrate. If you want to know more about the intricacies of segment attributes, however, a full elaboration can be found in your MASM manual.

Whereas the procedural level of structure in your program is almost entirely conceptual, the segment level of structure has both a logical representation in the source code and a physical counterpart in the final executable program (specifically, in MS-DOS EXE programs, the executable programs discussed in this book). The Intel 80x86 microprocessors have four (or more) segment registers, which are essentially used as base pointers. When the processors are running in real mode, as they do under MS-DOS, each segment register can point to a different 64-KB area within the first megabyte of memory. Thus, by manipulating the segment registers, a program is able to address any memory location, although it can address only 256 KB simultaneously.

A minimum of three segments must be declared in an EXE program: a code segment, a data segment, and a stack segment. Organizing your program's segment structure becomes especially important when the program has more than 64 KB of code or data. In such a case, you'll want to put the most frequently used routines or data into the primary code and data segments (for reasons of speed) and put the less frequently used routines and data structures into secondary (FAR) code and data segments. If you have more than two code segments, you might also assign procedures and data to segments in such a manner that procedures that call each other frequently are in the same segment (because "near calls" are faster) and procedures that call each other infrequently are in separate segments.

Programs are classified into a particular *memory model* by the number of their code and data segments. The memory model most commonly used for assembly-language programs is the *small* model, which has one code and one data segment, but several others can also be used. Figure 1-2 lists the most common memory models. You should also be aware that two additional models exist: the *tiny* model, which consists of intermixed code and data in a single segment (an MS-DOS COM file, for example); and the *huge* model, which is supported by the Microsoft C Compiler and allows use of data structures larger than 64 KB.

Memory Model	Code Segments	Data Segments
Small	One	One
Medium	Multiple	One
Compact	One	Multiple
Large	Multiple	Multiple

Figure 1-2.
Terminology for memory models commonly used in assembly-language and C programs.

For each memory model, Microsoft has established certain segment and class names that are used by all its high-level language compilers (Figure 1-3). These naming conventions have been adopted by virtually all other vendors of MS-DOS-based assemblers, linkers, and compilers. The Microsoft conventions will make it easier for you to integrate your assembly-language subroutines into programs written in high-level languages such as C or, conversely, to use routines from high-level language libraries in your assembly programs.

Another important Microsoft language convention specifies that the program's primary or NEAR data segment—the segment that the program expects to address with offsets from the DS register—and its stack segment should be named with the *group* directive as members of DGROUP. DGROUP is sometimes referred to as the "automatic data group," and it has a special significance in Microsoft Windows, OS/2, and assembly-language modules that are linked with C or other high-level language programs. (In C programs, DGROUP also contains the *local heap,* which is used by the C runtime library for dynamic allocation of small amounts of memory.)

You also need to consider segment order when writing EXE programs. The high-level language compilers assume that code segments always come first, followed in order by FAR data segments, the NEAR data segment, and the stack. (Refer to Figure 1-4 on page 8.) The Linker builds the executable file by putting segments in the order in which it first encounters them. Consequently, you can force the segment order you need by declaring all the segments that you will use, in the desired order, in the first module that you specify to the Linker (even if some or most of those segments are empty in that particular module).

Memory Model	Segment Name	Align Type	Combine Class	Class Name	Group
Small	_TEXT	Word	Public	CODE	
	_DATA	Word	Public	DATA	DGROUP
	STACK	Para	Stack	STACK	DGROUP
Medium	module_TEXT	Word	Public	CODE	
	.				
	.				
	.				
	_DATA	Word	Public	DATA	DGROUP
	STACK	Para	Stack	STACK	DGROUP
Compact	_TEXT	Word	Public	CODE	
	data	Para	Private	FAR_DATA	
	.				
	.				
	_DATA	Word	Public	DATA	DGROUP
	STACK	Para	Stack	STACK	DGROUP
Large	module_TEXT	Word	Public	CODE	
	.				
	.				
	data	Para	Private	FAR_DATA	
	.				
	.				
	_DATA	Word	Public	DATA	DGROUP
	STACK	Para	Stack	STACK	DGROUP

Figure 1-3.
Segments, classes, and groups for the standard memory models as used with assembly-language programs. Microsoft C and other high-level language compilers use a superset of these segments and classes.

In MASM versions 5.0 and later, directives have been added that allow you to segment your program and abide by all the Microsoft conventions in a much less laborious fashion. The DOSSEG instruction causes the Microsoft segment order to be used. The .MODEL directive defines the number and types of segments, assigns the correct default attribute for procedures, and generates implicit ASSUME and GROUP statements. The .CODE, .DATA, and .STACK directives automatically produce the proper segmentation declarations and assign each their proper attributes.

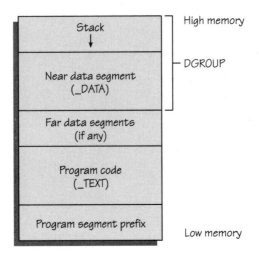

Stack ↓	High memory
Near data segment (_DATA)	DGROUP
Far data segments (if any)	
Program code (_TEXT)	
Program segment prefix	Low memory

Figure 1-4.
A memory image of a program just after loading. This program follows the Microsoft high-level language conventions for segment order and naming.

Factoring Programs into Modules

Under MS-DOS, the module level of organization is implemented in terms of files; assembly-language source code files are translated by MASM one at a time into relocatable object modules. An object module can reside in an individual (OBJ) file, or many object modules can be indexed and stored together in a library (LIB) file using the Librarian utility (LIB.EXE). The Linker (LINK.EXE) combines one or more OBJ files (optionally with additional object modules extracted from libraries) into an executable program (EXE) file by collecting like segments together, collecting unlike segments of like class together, resolving intermodule references, and adding a relocation table and other information. The structure of an executable program has some correspondence to the structure of its source code, but the module level of organization disappears. (Refer to Figure 1-1 on page 2.)

When you first get started with MASM programming, you might be tempted to ignore the concept of modules. Each time you need a particular subroutine, you are usually writing and debugging it for the first time, and thus it might seem easier to put all the source code for each program in a single file so that you can edit and assemble it as a unit. But you should try to resist this temptation. A great many tasks recur in every nontrivial assembly-language program, and if you take the trouble to properly generalize the subroutines that solve these recurring needs, separate them into individual source code modules, put the resulting OBJ modules into a library, and exploit the Linker's ability to extract the modules from the library when they are needed, you will reap many benefits.

Use of such a modular style reduces the size of each application source file because the file does not need to contain the source code for subroutines it has in common with other programs. You can also maintain the subroutines more easily because the subroutine source code is centralized instead of existing in many copies in different applications. When you improve (or fix) one of these routines, you can simply re-assemble it, stuff the OBJ file into the library, relink all the programs which use that routine, and, *voilà*—instant upgrade. The MAKE.EXE utility, which goes hand in hand with LIB.EXE and LINK.EXE, can help you automate this entire process. Much of the remainder of this book is devoted to giving you a "jump start" on a modular style of programming by providing subroutines for many common MASM programming problems.

Let's put all this procedure, segment, and module discussion in perspective by look-ing at the skeleton listing for a MASM program in Figure 1-5. The procedure that receives control from MS-DOS is called *main*. It uses CALLs to invoke other pro-cedures within the program and uses Int 21H Function 4CH to exit to MS-DOS when the program's work is done. The segment names, order, and attributes; the declara-tion of DGROUP; and the use of ASSUME in this skeleton all follow the Microsoft conventions. Note that this is a *small-model* program, with one code segment, one data segment, and one stack segment. Figure 1-6 (which follows on page 10) is the equivalent of the listing in Figure 1-5, but it uses the simplified segment directives that are available in MASM versions 5.0 and later. The rest of the example code in this book will use explicit segment directives for compatibility with the widest pos-sible range of commercial and shareware assemblers, but I encourage you to use the simplified directives in your own work.

```
              .                        ; miscellaneous equates,
              .                        ; structures, and other
              .                        ; declarations go here

DGROUP   group    _DATA,STACK          ; declare automatic data group

_TEXT    segment word public 'CODE'

         assume  cs:_TEXT,ds:DGROUP,ss:STACK

main     proc    far                   ; routine that initially
                                       ; receives control

         mov     ax,DGROUP             ; set DS = our data segment
         mov     ds,ax
              .
              .
              .
```

Figure 1-5. *(continued)*
A skeleton for a MASM small-model program that uses the traditional directives for segments, groups, and ASSUME.

Figure 1-5. *continued*

```
        mov     ax,4c00h        ; main routine terminates
        int     21h             ; and passes return code

main    endp

        .                       ; other procedures needed by
        .                       ; program go here
        .

_TEXT   ends

_DATA   segment word public 'DATA'

        .                       ; all read/write or static
        .                       ; data goes in this segment
        .

_DATA   ends

STACK   segment para stack 'STACK'

        db      256 dup (?)     ; program stack

STACK   ends

        end     main            ; defines entry point
```

```
        dosseg                  ; use Microsoft segment order
        .model  small           ; create small-model program

        .                       ; miscellaneous equates,
        .                       ; structures, and other
        .                       ; declarations go here

        .code                   ; begin code segment

main    proc                    ; routine that initially
                                ; receives control

        mov     ax,@data        ; set DS = our data segment
```

Figure 1-6.   *(continued)*

A skeleton for a MASM small-model EXE program that uses the simplified segment directives of MASM versions 5.0 and later. Note that the .MODEL directive eliminates the need for the GROUP and ASSUME directives and that the .CODE, .DATA, and .STACK directives automatically declare segments with names and attributes that follow the Microsoft conventions.

Figure 1-6. *continued*

```
        mov     ds,ax
        .
        .
        .
        mov     ax,4c00h        ; main routine terminates
        int     21h             ; and passes return code

main    endp

        .                       ; other procedures needed by
        .                       ; program go here
        .

        .data                   ; begin data segment

        .                       ; all read/write or static
        .                       ; data goes in this segment
        .

        .stack  256             ; program stack

        end     main            ; defines entry point
```

Using Macros

The macro capability of MASM is essentially a sophisticated text substitution mechanism. Although a detailed discussion of macros is beyond the scope of this book, we can look at two simple ways you can take advantage of macros to make your programs easier to read and maintain.

First, you can use macros to synthesize instructions that don't actually exist, in order to reduce the need for special-case coding. For example, the conditional jumps supported by the Intel 80x86 processors in real mode have a range of only −128 through 127 bytes, whereas the unconditional JMP instruction has a range of −32,768 through 32,767 bytes. If you are writing a procedure that contains many tests for error conditions and correspondingly many conditional jumps to a central error exit point, you will eventually find that adding a few more lines of code to the procedure causes the assembler to generate the error message "jump out of range" for some of the conditional jumps. You can fix these errors by going into the code, inverting the sense of the conditional jump instruction, and replacing the simple conditional jump with a "jump around a jump"—for example, changing the instruction

```
        jz      error
```

to this sequence of instructions:

```
        jnz     label1  ; continue if not zero
        jmp     error   ; jump if zero
label1:
```

Unfortunately, you will often find that the addition of this new code puts still other conditional jumps out of range and causes even more errors. If your code is not performance sensitive, you can eliminate out-of-range errors completely by writing macros for "long" conditional jumps and using these macros throughout your code instead of the native Intel 80x86 conditional jumps. For example, the macro for a "long jump if zero" instruction named JMPZ looks like this:

```
jmpz    macro   p1    ; this macro builds a
        local   p2    ; "long" conditional jump
        jnz     p2    ; if zero flag is set and
        jmp     p1    ; avoids out-of-range errors
p2:
        endm
```

Once defined, JMPZ can be used just like JZ:

```
jmpz    error
```

The *p1* parameter for this macro is the destination of the long conditional jump. The *p2* parameter is a label internal to the macro and unknown to the rest of the application; the *local* instruction tells the assembler to generate a unique label for the *p2* parameter each time the macro is expanded.

The second instance in which macros might be useful involves short sequences of specialized code that are duplicated many times throughout the application. You don't want to put that code in a subroutine, for reasons of performance, but you don't want to type the same code over and over. For example, when you are writing characters directly into the video refresh buffer of the now-archaic IBM Color Graphics Adapter, you must wait for a video retrace interval if you don't want the display cluttered up with "snow." You can write a macro that will generate the proper waiting code as follows:

```
waitcga macro          ; wait for CGA retrace interval
        local p1
        mov   dx,03dah ; DX = CGA status port address
        cli            ; disable interrupts
p1:     in    al,dx    ; read status port
        and   al,1     ; retrace bit on yet?
        jz    p1       ; loop if not in retrace
        endm
```

Then simply insert the *waitcga* instruction in your code wherever it's needed.

Although macros can be very helpful, they can also be dangerous when overused. Macros that are too long or too complex can obscure optimization opportunities, cause difficulties during debugging (because source-oriented debuggers don't understand and display macros as they appear in the source code), and make programs much more difficult to modify later—especially if the code must be given to a programmer other than the one who invented the macros. Over the years, I've reached a middle ground where I tend to avoid macros except for the short, simple types described in this section.

Using Data Structures

We've talked about structuring your code—but what about structuring your data? Although MASM's support in this area is not very elaborate, you might find two MASM facilities useful. First, it's perfectly legal to write macros that are expanded into data statements rather than machine instructions, and several special MASM directives—REPT, IRP, and IRPC—are particularly well suited to generating tables of values and other static data structures with macros. Because you won't need to use these directives very often, we won't discuss them here; but you should remember that they exist and that they are explained in detail in your MASM manual.

Second, MASM allows you to define templates for multi-item data records much as you do with the C language's *struct* keyword. The general format for declaring a data structure is similar to the format used for procedures and segments:

```
name    STRUC
... data statements
name    ENDS
```

(In MASM 6.0, STRUCT can be used instead of STRUC.) Each data statement in the body of the STRUC can have its own identifier and initial value. An initial value can also be specified when the structure is "instantiated" to allocate named storage. For example, you could create a *pixel* data structure, which contains a pixel's x and y coordinates and current color as uninitialized values:

```
pixel   struc
x       dw      ?
y       dw      ?
color   dw      ?
pixel   ends
```

You can then allocate memory for three pixel structures named *pixelA*, *pixelB*, and *pixelC*, giving each a different initial value, with the following statements:

```
pixelA  pixel   <0,0,0>   ; location (0,0), color = 0
pixelB  pixel   <0,0,1>   ; location (0,0), color = 1
pixelC  pixel   <20,20,0> ; location (20,20), color = 0
```

You can access values within the pixel variables with code such as this:

```
mov     ax,pixelA.color  ; load color of pixelA
```

When you have a number of records with the same format in an array or buffer, you can put a pointer to the record of interest into a register and then use the field identifiers from the STRUC as offsets, as shown here:

```
mov     bp,offset buffer ; point to pixel record
mov     ax,[bp].color    ; load color of pixel
```

Unfortunately, although MASM's STRUC bears a strong family resemblance to the C language *struct*, two crippling differences exist in versions of MASM prior to 6.0.

First, in earlier versions of MASM, STRUCs cannot be nested, which means that you can't build complex data structures using smaller, more easily understood STRUCs as building blocks. For example, the following pair of structure declarations is illegal:

```
point2D struc           ; structure for 2-D points
x         dw      ?
y         dw      ?
point2D ends

point3D struc           ; structure for 3-D points
          point2D       ; declare x and y coordinates
z         dw      ?     ; add z coordinate
point3D ends
```

The second problem with earlier MASM STRUCs is that the names of the member data items must be unique in the source file—in other words, no "scoping" of structure members is allowed. For example, the following two structure declarations cause an error message if they occur in the same file:

```
point2D struc
x         dw      ?
y         dw      ?
point2D ends

point3D struc
x         dw      ?
y         dw      ?
z         dw      ?
point3D ends
```

In spite of these shortcomings, STRUCs, like macros, can be extremely helpful if they are used judiciously. And if you update to MASM version 6.0, STRUCs can be a very powerful tool indeed.

2

Processing Command Lines

If you write programs that will be run via MS-DOS's command-line interpreter, COMMAND.COM, the concepts of command lines and command tails are vital to you. With programs such as utilities and filters, the command line might constitute the user's only interaction with the program. Command-line processing is an especially crucial subject for programmers because the tools we write for our own use are often invoked from a batch or MAKE file and thus must be able to work in a non-interactive mode.

The *command line* is the line the user enters to run a program. It begins with the name of the program (optionally followed by other parameters, separated by spaces, tabs, or other delimiters) and is terminated with a carriage return (the Enter key on IBM PCs). The *command tail* is what remains of the command line after the program name and any redirection or piping parameters are removed. Each filename, switch, or other parameter in the command tail is called a *command-tail argument*.

MS-DOS presents command-tail information to a program as part of a larger structure called the program segment prefix (PSP), which typically lies just below the program's code, data, and stack. (See Figure 2-1 on the following page.) The command tail begins at offset 80H in the PSP and consists of, first, a byte containing the length of the command tail; second, the text of the command tail itself; and, third, a carriage return (0DH), which is not included in the count. The PSP also contains other information, including the address of another block of information called the environment (discussed in Chapter 3).

COM programs are entered with all segment registers (CS, DS, ES, and SS) pointing to the base of the PSP. Because these registers typically remain unchanged throughout the execution of a COM program, access to the command tail is easy for such a program. In contrast, an EXE program is passed the segment address of the PSP in registers DS and ES at entry, but it usually resets these registers quickly to get at the variables and constants in its own data segment. Thus, the program either must store the PSP address if it expects to look at the command tail later or must copy the command tail to another buffer within its data segment. (In MS-DOS versions 3.0 and later, Int 21H Function 62H can be called at any time to get the PSP address, but it's usually not worth the trouble of including special code simply to use this function when it's available.)

Offset

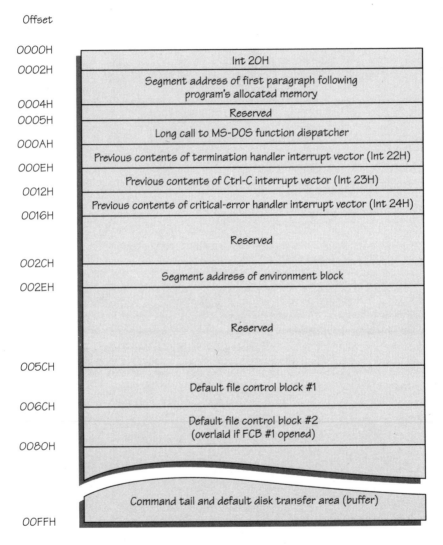

Offset	
0000H	Int 20H
0002H	Segment address of first paragraph following program's allocated memory
0004H	Reserved
0005H	Long call to MS-DOS function dispatcher
000AH	Previous contents of termination handler interrupt vector (Int 22H)
000EH	Previous contents of Ctrl-C interrupt vector (Int 23H)
0012H	Previous contents of critical-error handler interrupt vector (Int 24H)
0016H	Reserved
002CH	Segment address of environment block
002EH	Reserved
005CH	Default file control block #1
006CH	Default file control block #2 (overlaid if FCB #1 opened)
0080H	
	Command tail and default disk transfer area (buffer)
00FFH	

Figure 2-1.
The structure of the program segment prefix (PSP).

Parsing Command-Tail Arguments

When you look at the command tail shown in Figure 2-2, for example, you can immediately see that parsing command-tail arguments can develop into a rather messy job. You must be able to handle any number of white-space characters (either blanks or tabs) between any two arguments, allow arguments of any size, and cope with as many arguments as MS-DOS might allow the user to cram onto a single command line. Clearly, you'll want to solve this kind of problem only once and then encapsulate the solution in a library routine so that you can forget about the many details.

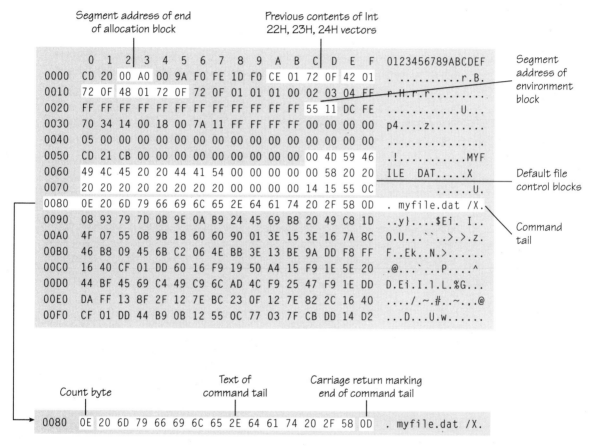

Figure 2-2.
An example of a program segment prefix under MS-DOS version 5.
The program that owns this PSP was started with the command
`C>forth myfile.dat /X <Enter>`.

Rather than reinventing the wheel, let's take a look at the approach to command-line parsing used by the C language's runtime library. The runtime library provides a mechanism that makes it very simple to inspect command-tail arguments within a program. Before the body of an application program begins to execute, the startup code (which is inserted into every C application program by the Linker) inspects the command tail, counts the arguments, and converts each argument into an ASCII string terminated with a null, or zero, byte (usually called an *ASCIIZ string*). The startup code then passes the argument count and an array containing the addresses of the ASCIIZ strings to the *main()* routine of the C program as the integer *argc* and the pointer array *argv[]*, respectively.

As a further convenience (when the host operating system makes the information available), the startup code provides the filename of the program itself in the form of an ASCIIZ string as command-line argument *argv[0]*. The program can use *argv[0]* to find its data files, overlays, and the like in cases where the current directory is not the directory from which the program was loaded. If the name of the program is not known, *argv[0]* usually points to a dummy string of some kind. Thus, the value of *argc* is always 1 or greater, even if the command line used to load the program contains no arguments.

To see how this works, consider the program TRYARGS.C, shown in Figure 2-3. When TRYARGS is executed, it displays the number of command-line arguments

```
/*
    TRYARGS.C -- Demo of C runtime library command-line argument processing.
    Copyright (C) 1991 Ray Duncan
*/

#include <stdio.h>

main(int argc,char *argv[])
{
    int x;

    printf("\nThe command line contains %d arguments", argc);

    for (x=0; x<argc; x++)
        printf("\nArgument %d is:   %s ", x, argv[x]);

    puts("");
}
```

Figure 2-3.
TRYARGS.C, which demonstrates how the C runtime library parses command-line arguments.

and then lists each argument by number on a separate line. For example, if you type the command line

```
C>TRYARGS FOO BAR  <Enter>
```

you see the following:

```
The command line contains 3 arguments
Argument 0 is:  C:\TRYARGS.EXE
Argument 1 is:  FOO
Argument 2 is:  BAR
```

A subtle but handy feature of the C runtime library's command-line processing is that it allows you to create an argument with embedded white space by enclosing the argument in quotation marks. For instance, the command

```
C>TRYARGS "FOO BAR"  <Enter>
```

results in this output:

```
The command line contains 2 arguments
Argument 0 is:  C:\TRYARGS.EXE
Argument 1 is:  FOO BAR
```

Note that the quotation marks are discarded.

MASM Command-Tail Routines

Now that you've seen the parsing tricks of the C language masters, let's put together a pair of routines that deliver the same sort of functionality for MASM programs. Figures 2-4 and 2-5 contain the source code for general-purpose MASM modules called ARGC.ASM and ARGV.ASM. The first returns the number of command-tail arguments, and the second returns the address and length of a specific command-tail argument. Both work just as you would expect from your introduction to the TRYARGS.C program.

```
;
; ARGC.ASM -- Returns number of command-tail arguments.  Treats blanks
;             and tabs as white space, carriage return as terminator,
;             text enclosed in quotation marks as a single argument.
;
; Copyright (C) 1991 Ray Duncan
;
; Call with:    ES:BX = command-tail address
;
; Returns:      AX    = argument count (always >= 1)
;
; Destroys:     Nothing
```

Figure 2-4. *(continued)*
ARGC.ASM, a routine that returns the number of command-tail arguments.

Figure 2-4. *continued*

```
cr      equ     0dh                     ; ASCII carriage return
lf      equ     0ah                     ; ASCII linefeed
tab     equ     09h                     ; ASCII tab
blank   equ     20h                     ; ASCII space character
quote   equ     22h                     ; ASCII quote character

_TEXT   segment word public 'CODE'

        assume  cs:_TEXT

        public  argc
argc    proc    near

        push    bx                      ; save original BX and CX
        push    cx                      ; for later
        mov     ax,1                    ; force count >= 1

argc1:  mov     cx,-1                   ; set flag = outside argument

argc2:  inc     bx                      ; point to next character
        cmp     byte ptr es:[bx],cr
        je      argc5                   ; exit if carriage return
        cmp     byte ptr es:[bx],quote
        je      argc3                   ; beginning of quoted argument
        cmp     byte ptr es:[bx],blank
        je      argc1                   ; outside argument if ASCII blank
        cmp     byte ptr es:[bx],tab
        je      argc1                   ; outside argument if ASCII tab

                                        ; not blank, tab, or quote
        jcxz    argc2                   ; jump if already inside argument

        inc     ax                      ; else found argument, count it'
        not     cx                      ; set flag = inside argument
        jmp     argc2                   ; and look at next character

argc3:  inc     ax                      ; quote found, count argument

argc4:  inc     bx                      ; point to next character
        cmp     byte ptr es:[bx],quote  ; found end of quoted argument?
        je      argc1                   ; yes, jump
        cmp     byte ptr es:[bx],cr     ; found end of command tail?
        jne     argc4                   ; no, keep looking

argc5:  pop     cx                      ; restore original BX and CX
        pop     bx
        ret                             ; return AX = argument count
```

(continued)

continued

```
ndp
ds
```

```
;
; ARGV.ASM -- Returns address and length of command-tail argument
;             or fully qualified program name.  Treats blanks and tabs
;             as white space, carriage return as terminator,
;             text enclosed in quotation marks as a single argument.
;
; Copyright (C) 1991 Ray Duncan
;
; Call with:    ES:BX = command-tail address
;                       (implicit: ES = PSP segment)
;               AX    = argument number (zero-based)
;
; Returns:      ES:BX = argument address
;               AX    = argument length
;                       (0 = argument not found)
;
; Destroys:     Nothing
;
; Note: If ARGV is called with AX = 0 (argv[0]) and if the host
; system is MS-DOS version 3.0 or later, ARGV returns ES:BX =
; address and AX = length of the fully qualified program filename
; at the end of the program's environment block.  When ARGV is
; called with AX = 0 under MS-DOS versions 1.x and 2.x, it returns
; ES:BX unchanged and AX = 0.

cr      equ     0dh                     ; ASCII carriage return
lf      equ     0ah                     ; ASCII linefeed
tab     equ     09h                     ; ASCII tab
blank   equ     20h                     ; ASCII space character
quote   equ     22h                     ; ASCII quote character

_TEXT   segment word public 'CODE'

        assume  cs:_TEXT

        public  argv
argv    proc    near
```

Figure 2-5. *(continued)*

ARGV.ASM, a routine that returns the address and length of a specified command-tail argument.

Figure 2-5. *continued*

```
        push    cx                          ; save original CX and DI
        push    di

        or      ax,ax                       ; is it argument 0?
        jz      argv12                      ; yes, jump to get program name

        xor     ah,ah                       ; initialize argument counter

argv1:  mov     cx,-1                       ; set flag = outside argument

argv2:  inc     bx                          ; point to next character
        cmp     byte ptr es:[bx],cr
        je      argv9                       ; exit if carriage return
        cmp     byte ptr es:[bx],quote
        je      argv7                       ; beginning of quoted argument
        cmp     byte ptr es:[bx],blank
        je      argv1                       ; outside argument if ASCII blank
        cmp     byte ptr es:[bx],tab
        je      argv1                       ; outside argument if ASCII tab

                                            ; if not blank, tab, or quote
        jcxz    argv2                       ; jump if already inside argument

        inc     ah                          ; else count arguments found
        cmp     ah,al                       ; is this the right one?
        je      argv4                       ; yes, go find its length
        not     cx                          ; no, set flag = inside argument
        jmp     argv2                       ; and look at next character

argv4:                                      ; found argument, calc length
        mov     ax,bx                       ; save param starting address

argv5:  inc     bx                          ; point to next character
        cmp     byte ptr es:[bx],cr
        je      argv6                       ; found end if carriage return
        cmp     byte ptr es:[bx],blank
        je      argv6                       ; found end if ASCII blank
        cmp     byte ptr es:[bx],tab
        jne     argv5                       ; found end if ASCII tab

argv6:  xchg    bx,ax                       ; set ES:BX = argument address
        sub     ax,bx                       ; and AX = argument length
        jmp     argv14                      ; return to caller

argv7:                                      ; start of quoted argument
        inc     ah                          ; count this argument
        cmp     ah,al                       ; is this the one we need?
        je      argv10                      ; yes, go find its length
```

(continued)

Figure 2-5. *continued*

```
argv8:  inc    bx                        ; no, scan over it
        cmp    byte ptr es:[bx],quote    ; reached trailing quote?
        je     argv1                     ; yes, found end of argument
        cmp    byte ptr es:[bx],cr       ; end of command tail?
        jne    argv8                     ; no, keep looking

argv9:  xor    ax,ax                     ; set AX = 0, argument not found
        jmp    argv14                    ; return to caller

argv10: inc    bx                        ; point to actual argument
        mov    ax,bx                     ; save its starting address

argv11: inc    bx                        ; point to next character
        cmp    byte ptr es:[bx],cr
        je     argv6                     ; found end if carriage return
        cmp    byte ptr es:[bx],quote
        je     argv6                     ; found end if quote mark
        jmp    argv11                    ; keep looking

argv12:                                  ; special handling for parameter 0
        mov    ax,3000h                  ; check if MS-DOS 3.0 or later
        int    21h                       ; (force AL = 0 in case MS-DOS 1)
        cmp    al,3
        jb     argv9                     ; MS-DOS 1 or 2, return nothing

        mov    es,es:[2ch]               ; get environment segment from PSP
        xor    di,di                     ; find program name by
        xor    al,al                     ; first skipping over all
        mov    cx,-1                     ; environment variables
        cld

argv13: repne scasb                      ; scan for double null (can't use
        scasb                            ; SCASW since might be odd addr)
        jne    argv13                    ; loop if it was single null
        add    di,2                      ; skip count word in environment
        mov    bx,di                     ; save program name address
        mov    cx,-1                     ; now find its length
        repne scasb                      ; scan for another null byte
        not    cx                        ; convert CX to length
        dec    cx
        mov    ax,cx                     ; return length in AX

argv14:                                  ; common exit point
        pop    di                        ; restore registers
        pop    cx
        ret                              ; return to caller

argv    endp

_TEXT   ends

        end
```

The ARGC routine is passed the address of the command tail in registers ES:BX, and it returns the number of command-tail arguments in register AX. Multiple tabs or blanks are treated as a single separator between arguments, and any text enclosed in quotes is treated as a single argument. For symmetry with the C language *argc*, the value returned is always at least 1 (that is, ARGC counts the program name as an argument, even though that name is not present in the PSP command-tail data).

The ARGV routine is passed the address of the command tail in registers ES:BX and a zero-based argument number in AX. It returns the address of the argument in ES:BX and the length of the argument in AX. If the argument is not present (that is, if ARGV is called with AX greater than or equal to the value returned by ARGC), AX is returned as 0. The ARGV routine contains special code for a parameter of 0 and returns a pointer to the program name from the environment block if the host system is MS-DOS version 3.0 or later.

Internally, the ARGC and ARGV routines are not very interesting. They consist mostly of brute-force comparisons of characters in the command tail to detect all the possible delimiters—spaces, tabs, quotes, and carriage returns—mingled among conditional jumps and register increments. This style of programming, sometimes characterized as "spaghetti code," should ordinarily be avoided. But in these cases, where the programming problems are small and well defined, it helps us keep the routines tiny and fast.

PROCEDURES INTRODUCED IN THIS CHAPTER

Procedure Name	Action	Parameters	Results
ARGC	Returns number of command-tail arguments (including program name)	ES:BX = segment:offset of command line	AX = argument count (always >= 1)
ARGV	Returns address and length of specific command-tail argument	ES:BX = segment:offset of command line AX = argument number (zero-based)	ES:BX = argument address AX = argument length (0 = argument not found)

Companion Disk

The companion disk directory \CH02 contains the programs and modules that are listed below.

Routines Presented in This Chapter

ARGC.ASM	Returns the number of command-tail arguments
ARGV.ASM	Returns the address and length of a specific command-tail argument

Demonstration Program

TRYARGS	MAKE file for TRYARGS.EXE
TRYARGS.ASM	Demonstration program

The program TRYARGS.ASM demonstrates use of the routines ARGC and ARGV. To build TRYARGS.EXE, enter this command:

```
C>MAKE TRYARGS   <Enter>
```

When you run TRYARGS.EXE, it displays the total number of command-line arguments (including the name of the program) and then formats and displays each argument. Text enclosed within quotation marks is processed as a single argument, regardless of embedded blanks or other delimiters.

3

Using the Environment

Many MS-DOS users—and programmers, for that matter—regard the environment as an enigma. Some are mystified about why it exists and what it is good for. Others are puzzled about how to get at or change the information in the environment once they think of something to do with it.

To understand why the environment exists, let's take a look at UNIX system software. When a new user is assigned a password for a UNIX system, a profile file is created for that person defining the user's type of terminal, the preferred shell or command processor, the name of the user's home directory, and other items. This file is an ordinary ASCII text file and can be edited by the user or the system manager at any time.

When the user logs in, UNIX locates the individual profile file, starts up a new copy of the specified shell and attaches it to the terminal, and then creates for that user a block of memory called the environment. The environment contains one or more strings, called *environment variables,* of the following form:

```
name=value
```

Most of the environment variables are derived from the contents of the profile file. Programs the user runs can inspect the environment to figure out what command-line options to use as defaults or how to control the user's terminal. For example, the environment might contain this variable:

```
TERM=VT52
```

A variable of this form indicates that the user's terminal is a VT52 CRT. A general-purpose text editor could search for this environment variable and could then look up VT52 in an internal table that tells the program which escape sequence to use to clear the screen or to position the cursor.

In short, the term *environment* stems from the notion of an in-memory block of information that defines each user's preferences and working conditions—a block of information that might be different for each user logged onto the system at any given time. By editing the profile file or using other commands to change or add strings to the environment, the user can customize the behavior of the various utility programs to make work easier or to accommodate the special needs of a particular terminal.

Environments Under MS-DOS

MS-DOS environments are conceptually derived directly from UNIX environments. In MS-DOS, an environment is a block of memory containing one or more environment variables, each consisting of a null-terminated ASCII string (an ASCIIZ string). As in UNIX, each environment variable takes this form:

```
name=value
```

An environment block is always aligned on a paragraph boundary (that is, its beginning memory address is always evenly divisible by 16), and it can be as large as 32 KB. The entire set of ASCIIZ strings in an environment block is terminated by an extra null byte. (Under MS-DOS 3.0 or later, the fully qualified pathname of the file from which the program was loaded follows the two zero bytes that terminate the environment.) Figure 3-1 shows an example of a typical MS-DOS environment block.

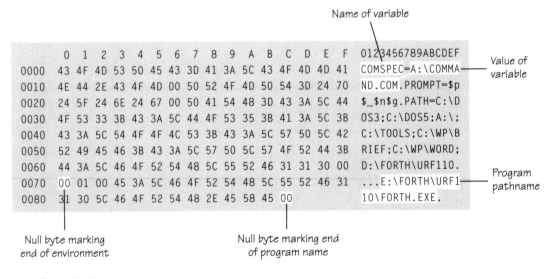

Name of variable

Value of variable

Program pathname

Null byte marking end of environment

Null byte marking end of program name

Figure 3-1.
Hex and ASCII dump of a typical MS-DOS 5.0 environment block. The segment base address of the environment for a particular program is found at offset 002CH in the program segment prefix (PSP). Note the fully qualified pathname of the program following the last environment variable.

The original, or master, environment for the MS-DOS operating system is owned by the command interpreter that is loaded when the system is turned on or when it is restarted (usually COMMAND.COM). COMMAND.COM places strings into the system's master environment block as a result of PATH, SHELL, PROMPT, and SET directives. Default values for the environment variables PATH and COMSPEC are always present.

For example, if an MS-DOS 3.2 system is booted from drive C with neither a PATH command in the AUTOEXEC.BAT file nor a SHELL command in the CONFIG.SYS file, COMMAND.COM's environment will contain these two strings:

```
PATH=
COMSPEC=C:\COMMAND.COM
```

COMMAND.COM uses these two environment variables to search for executable external commands and to find its executable file on the disk so that it can reload its transient portion when necessary. When the PROMPT string is present (as a result of a previous PROMPT or SET PROMPT= command), COMMAND.COM uses it to tailor the prompt displayed to the user.

Other strings in the environment simply provide information to transient programs and do not affect how the MS-DOS system operates. For example, the Microsoft C Compiler and Linker look for LIB, INCLUDE, and TMP strings that tell them where to find C header files and object module libraries and where to build temporary working files. At any time, you can display the current contents of COMMAND.COM's environment block by entering a SET command without parameters.

Understanding the environment can be difficult in part because each program has its own copy. The address of a program's environment is stored (as a segment, or paragraph address) at offset 002CH in its program segment prefix (PSP). When one program (the *parent*) uses the MS-DOS EXEC function to launch another program (the *child*), it must provide as one of the EXEC parameters a pointer to an environment block. If the parent supplies a zero pointer for this parameter, the child simply inherits an identical copy of the parent's environment. Alternatively, the parent can provide a pointer to an expanded, altered, or empty block of ASCIIZ strings.

As a result, any changes a program makes to its own environment block are visible (potentially) to its own children but vanish when it exits. Similarly, a child program cannot affect the environment of its parent in any "well-behaved" way, because no documented method exists by which a program can know the address of any memory block allocated before the program was loaded. This limitation is called *scoping*. This is why, for example, launching a secondary copy of COMMAND.COM to execute SET, PROMPT, or PATH commands is a fruitless enterprise—the master environment owned by the original copy of COMMAND.COM is not changed.

We should also mention, especially for those interested in programming terminate-and-stay-resident (TSR) utilities, that the environment block owned by each program is static after it is created. Thus, the environment belonging to a TSR will not be updated by SET, PATH, or PROMPT commands entered after the TSR is first loaded. For this reason, most TSR programs ignore the environment or even (if they are extremely conservative in their use of system resources) release the memory block allocated for their environment before "going resident."

Despite these limitations, you can utilize SET commands and the environment to make your programs more flexible. One of the enhancements introduced in Microsoft MASM 5.0 provides a good illustration. MASM versions 5.0 and later allow you to define a MASM= string in the environment containing the default switches used for each program assembly. For example, if you place the command

```
SET MASM=/L /Zi /T
```

in your AUTOEXEC.BAT file, MASM will use its "terse" message mode, generate a listing, and include symbolic debugging information in the resulting object file each time you invoke it.

Extracting Information from the Environment

Because the histories of the C language and UNIX are closely intertwined, you might surmise—correctly—that the C runtime library provides convenient ways to extract strings from a program's environment. A C program can either receive environment information passively or obtain it actively by calling a library function.

As discussed in Chapter 2, the C startup module passes to the *main()* routine of a C program two parameters related to the command line: *argc*, the number of arguments in the command line; and **argv[]*, an array of pointers to the individual arguments. The C program startup code also provides *main()* with a third parameter, *envp*, which is an array of pointers to the ASCIIZ strings in the program's environment. The last address in the array points to a null string (a string consisting only of a zero byte).

A C program can use the *envp* pointer or simply ignore it. Most programmers don't bother to declare *envp* as a formal parameter for *main()* because they prefer to use the standard C library function *getenv()*. *Getenv()* is called with a pointer to the *name* of an environment variable and returns a pointer to the *value* associated with *name*—the part of the environment variable following the equal sign (=). If *name* is not found, the function returns a pointer to a null string.

From a MASM programmer's point of view, extracting information from the environment block is an unpleasant and messy process. First, although MS-DOS provides a program with a pointer to the environment block in the form of a segment address at offset 002CH in the program segment prefix, access to the PSP is inconvenient, at best, for EXE programs (which need DS and ES to access their data segment). Second, although ASCIIZ strings are fine for C programs, they are painful to manipulate in MASM programs. When a program wants to copy or alter an ASCIIZ string, it must first scan the entire string for a null byte, to determine the length of the string.

The source listing GETENV.ASM (Figure 3-2) contains a MASM procedure analogous to the C runtime library function *getenv()*. GETENV is called with the segment of the program segment prefix in register ES and the address of the *name* of an ASCIIZ environment variable in registers DS:SI. It returns the address and length of the *value* associated with *name* in registers ES:DI and AX, respectively, or returns 0 in AX if the specified environment variable is not found.

```
;
; GETENV.ASM -- Returns address and length of variable
;               portion of environment string.
;
; Copyright (c) 1991 Ray Duncan
;
; Call with:    DS:SI = ASCIIZ name of environment variable
;               ES    = segment of program segment prefix (PSP)
;
; Returns:      ES:DI = address of value of environment variable
;               AX    = length (0 = not found)
;
; Destroys:     Nothing

psp_ptr equ     002ch                   ; offset of environment
                                        ; pointer within PSP


_TEXT   segment word public 'CODE'

        assume  cs:_TEXT

        public  getenv
getenv  proc    near

        push    cx                      ; save registers
        push    si

        mov     es,es:[psp_ptr]         ; get pointer to environment

        mov     cx,8000h                ; assume max env = 32 KB
        xor     di,di                   ; initial env offset
        xor     ax,ax                   ; default length result

get1:   cmp     byte ptr es:[di],0      ; check for end of environment
        je      get4                    ; end reached, return AX = 0

        pop     si                      ; initialize address of target
        push    si                      ; variable to be found
```

Figure 3-2.   *(continued)*

GETENV.ASM, a procedure that returns a pointer to the value portion of the specified environment string.

Figure 3-2. *continued*

```
        repe  cmpsb                        ; compare target and env strings
        cmp   byte ptr [si-1],0
        jne   get2                         ; jump if incomplete match
        cmp   byte ptr es:[di-1],'='
        je    get3                         ; jump if match was complete

get2:                                      ; match was incomplete
        repne scasb                        ; scan for end of env string
        jmp   get1                         ; and try again to match

get3:   push  di                           ; save address after equal sign
        repne scasb                        ; look for end of this string
        pop   ax                           ; get back starting address
        xchg  di,ax                        ; find string length
        sub   ax,di
        dec   ax                           ; don't include null byte

get4:                                      ; common exit point
        pop   si                           ; restore registers
        pop   cx
        ret                                ; return to caller

getenv  endp

_TEXT   ends

        end
```

The internal operation of GETENV is straightforward: It simply hops from one environment variable to another, making a character-by-character comparison of the supplied name with the *name* portion of each variable until it either finds a match or reaches the extra null byte that marks the end of the block. GETENV uses the 80x86's special string instructions in several places, however, so you might want to review it again after you've read Chapter 5.

Changing the Environment

Given that each program's environment is static and that a program can't touch the system's master environment block or even the environment of its immediate parent in any documented and portable way, why would a program want to alter its own environment?

Clearly, the main reason for changing the environment is to affect the behavior of a child program. Consider an application program, such as a word processor, that starts up a secondary copy of COMMAND.COM in order to allow the user to enter

MS-DOS commands without losing the working context. The word processor might want the child COMMAND.COM to display a special prompt format reminding the user that the application is still active, or it might want to limit the programs that can be run from the child command processor by modifying or removing the environment's PATH variable.

A C programmer can use the runtime library function *putenv()* to change the *value* of any environment variable. The same function can also be used to add a new variable to the environment or to delete one. *Putenv()* is called with a pointer to a string of this familiar form:

```
name=value
```

The function returns 0 if the operation is successful or −1 if the operation fails.

More is going on in this seemingly simple C library function than meets the eye. For example, if *name* does not already exist in the environment—or if *name* exists, but the new *value* is longer than the old one—a space crunch results. The memory block that holds a program's environment typically sits just below the program itself and is only big enough to hold the environment passed to it from its parent. Thus the existing environment cannot usually be expanded or "grown" in place.

Consequently, *putenv()* must allocate a new block of memory to hold the modified environment, copy the unchanged strings from the old environment into the new, and append the new or modified variable passed to it. *Putenv()* must then update all the pointers in the *envp* array originally passed to the *main()* function of the C program, because it cannot predict when or if that program will use *envp*. The pointer at offset 002CH of the program's PSP must be updated to reflect the new environment's address. Finally, *putenv()* can release the memory block holding the original environment back to the system's free memory pool so that the block can be reused on future allocation calls.

A complicated process indeed! Obviously, *putenv()* can fail unexpectedly if the system doesn't have enough free memory. This is not a major problem, though, because you would ordinarily use *putenv()* only before starting up a child program—and if the system lacks the memory to change the environment, it probably also lacks the memory to run the child program.

To duplicate the same capability in a MASM program, you must do everything the hard way. PUTENV.ASM (Figure 3-3 on the following pages) is a procedure that can be called from a MASM application to add, delete, or change an environment variable. It relies in part on the GETENV.ASM procedure. An important prerequisite for using the PUTENV subroutine is that your MASM program must release any extra memory with Int 21H Function 4AH when it first gets control. Otherwise, PUTENV has nothing to allocate.

```
;
; PUTENV.ASM -- Adds or modifies MS-DOS environment variable.
;
; Copyright (C) 1991 Ray Duncan
;
; Call with:     DS:SI = new ASCIIZ environment variable
;                        in the form name=value
;                ES    = segment of program segment prefix (PSP)
;
; Returns:       AX    =  0 if successful
;                      = -1 if failed
;
; Destroys:      ES

psp_ptr equ     002ch                   ; offset of environment
                                        ; pointer within PSP


DGROUP  group   _DATA

_TEXT   segment word public 'CODE'

        assume  cs:_TEXT
        extrn   getenv:near

                                        ; names for working storage
oldenv  equ     [bp-2]                  ; segment of old environment
envlen  equ     [bp-4]                  ; length of old environment
newenv  equ     [bp-6]                  ; segment of new environment
pspseg  equ     [bp-8]                  ; segment of PSP
oldlen  equ     [bp-10]                 ; length of existing variable
newlen  equ     [bp-12]                 ; length of new env variable
newname equ     [bp-14]                 ; offset of new name portion
newvar  equ     [bp-16]                 ; offset of new param portion


        public  putenv
putenv  proc    near

        push    bp                      ; set up stack frame for
        mov     bp,sp                   ; working storage
        sub     sp,16

        mov     newname,si              ; save offset of new variable
        mov     pspseg,es               ; save PSP segment
        mov     es,es:[psp_ptr]         ; pick up segment of old
        mov     oldenv,es               ; environment and save it

        push    cx                      ; save other registers
```

Figure 3-3.   (continued)

PUTENV.ASM, a procedure that modifies an existing environment variable
in the environment block or adds a new environment variable.

Figure 3-3. *continued*

```
        push    si
        push    di

                                ; find old environment length
        mov     cx,8000h        ; assume max = 32 KB
        xor     di,di           ; ES:DI = environment base
        xor     al,al
put1:   repne scasb             ; scan for double null (can't use
        scasb                   ; SCASW since might be on odd addr)
        jne     put1

        mov     envlen,di       ; save length of old environment

        mov     di,si           ; find length of new env variable
        mov     ax,ds           ; ES:DI = addr of new variable
        mov     es,ax
        mov     cx,-1
        xor     al,al
        repne scasb             ; scan for terminating null byte
        not     cx              ; now CX = length including null
        mov     newlen,cx       ; save length of new variable

                                ; attempt to allocate memory
                                ; block for new environment
        mov     bx,cx           ; length of old environment
        add     bx,envlen       ; + length of new variable
        mov     cl,4            ; divide by 16 and round
        shr     bx,cl           ; up to find paragraphs to
        inc     bx              ; allocate for new environment
        mov     ah,48h          ; fxn 48h = allocate memory block
        int     21h             ; transfer to MS-DOS
        jnc     put2            ; jump if allocation succeeded
        mov     ax,-1           ; otherwise, return error flag
        jmp     put6

put2:   mov     newenv,ax       ; save new environment segment

        mov     di,offset envar ; copy name portion of new
                                ; variable to local storage

put3:   movsb                   ; copy characters up to =
        cmp     byte ptr [si],'='
        jne     put3            ; loop until end of name found
        xor     al,al           ; append null byte to name
        stosb

        inc     si              ; save address of parameter
        mov     newvar,si       ; portion of new variable
```

(continued)

Figure 3-3. *continued*

```
            mov     si,offset envar      ; check if new environment
            mov     es,pspseg            ; variable has a previous value
            call    getenv               ; in old environment
            mov     oldlen,ax            ; save length of value, if any

            or      ax,ax                ; was it present in old block?
            jnz     put4                 ; yes, PUTENV the hard way

            push    ds                   ; no, just copy existing environment
                                         ; and add new variable

            mov     ds,oldenv            ; DS:SI = old environment block
            mov     es,newenv            ; ES:DI = new environment block
            mov     cx,envlen            ; CX = length of old environment
            dec     cx                   ; less the extra null byte
            xor     si,si
            xor     di,di
            rep movsb                    ; copy old stuff

            pop     ds                   ; DS:SI = address of new variable
            mov     si,newname           ; ES:DI = end of new environment
            mov     cx,newlen            ; CX = length of new variable
            rep movsb                    ; append new variable
            xor     al,al                ; and extra null byte
            stosb                        ; marking end of environment
            jmp     put5                 ; go update PSP env pointer

put4:                                    ; come here on the messy case
                                         ; env variable already exists
                                         ; ES:DI = offset + 1 of = in
                                         ;     old variable from GETENV

            push    ds                   ; copy old environment to new
            mov     ax,es                ; up through = of
            mov     ds,ax                ; variable we are changing
            mov     cx,di                ; DS:SI = old environment
            mov     es,newenv            ; ES:DI = new environment
            xor     si,si                ; CX = offset + 1 of =
            xor     di,di                ;     in old variable
            rep movsb

            pop     ds                   ; now let DS:SI = offset + 1
            push    si                   ; of = in new variable
            mov     si,newvar            ; and CX = length of portion
            mov     cx,newname           ; following =
            add     cx,newlen
            sub     cx,newvar            ; copy new parameter portion
            rep movsb                    ; to new environment
```

(continued)

Figure 3-3. *continued*

```
        pop     si                      ; skip over parameter portion
        add     si,oldlen               ; of old variable
        inc     si                      ; and its null byte

        push    ds                      ; now copy remainder of
        mov     ds,oldenv               ; old environment to new one
        mov     cx,envlen               ; total length less portion
        sub     cx,si                   ; already copied and length
        rep movsb                       ; of old environment variable
        pop     ds

put5:                                   ; PUTENV function successful
        mov     es,oldenv               ; release old environment block
        mov     ah,49h
        int     21h                     ; transfer to MS-DOS

        mov     es,pspseg               ; update pointer to new
        mov     ax,newenv               ; environment in caller's PSP
        mov     es:[psp_ptr],ax

        xor     ax,ax                   ; return success code

put6:   pop     di                      ; restore registers
        pop     si
        pop     cx
        mov     sp,bp                   ; discard stack frame
        pop     bp
        ret                             ; back to caller

putenv  endp

_TEXT   ends


_DATA   segment word public 'DATA'

envar   db      80 dup (0)              ; name of new environment var
                                        ; for call to GETENV
_DATA   ends

        end
```

PUTENV must be called with the address of the new or modified environment variable in registers DS:SI and the segment of the program's PSP in register ES. The logic of PUTENV is straightforward: First, it saves the PSP address, picks up the base address of the program's current environment block, and scans the existing environment to find its length. Next, it calls GETENV to see whether the environment variable currently exists. PUTENV then has the information necessary to attempt to allocate a memory block large enough to hold the new environment. If the allocation fails, PUTENV returns to the calling program with an error code. Otherwise, PUTENV copies the old environment block to the new (without the previous instance of the variable, if any), appends the new environment variable, and tacks on an extra null byte to mark the end of the environment. Finally, PUTENV updates the pointer at PSP:002CH, releases the original environment block with a call to Int 21H Function 49H, and returns a success code to the calling program.

PROCEDURES INTRODUCED IN THIS CHAPTER

Procedure Name	Action	Parameters	Results
GETENV	Returns address and length of value of specified environment variable	DS:SI = segment:offset of ASCIIZ name of environment variable ES = segment of program segment prefix	ES:DI = segment:offset of value of environment variable AX = length of value string (0 = not found)
PUTENV	Adds environment variable or modifies value of existing environment variable	DS:SI = segment:offset of ASCIIZ environment variable in the form *name=value* ES = segment of program segment prefix	If function successful: AX = 0 If function unsuccessful: AX = −1

Companion Disk

The companion disk directory \CH03 contains the programs and modules that are listed below.

Routines Presented in This Chapter

GETENV.ASM   Returns the address and length of the value of a specified environment variable

PUTENV.ASM   Adds an environment variable or modifies the value of an existing environment variable

Demonstration Program

TRYENV   MAKE file for TRYENV.EXE

TRYENV.ASM   Interactive demonstration program

The interactive program TRYENV.ASM demonstrates use of the routines GETENV and PUTENV. To build TRYENV.EXE, enter this command:

```
C>MAKE TRYENV  <Enter>
```

When you run TRYENV.EXE, it prompts you for the name of an environment variable, calls GETENV to find the variable, and displays the variable's current value, if any. TRYENV then prompts you for a new value for the environment variable, calls PUTENV to modify the environment block, and displays the complete contents of the environment block. The cycle is then repeated. To exit the demonstration program, press the Enter key at the first prompt.

4

Converting Numbers for Input and Output

The two previous chapters discussed the noninteractive ways that a user can pass information to a MASM program: the command line and the environment. Now let's turn our attention to some basic tools for interactive input and output. In this chapter, we'll examine routines for conversion and formatting of ASCII numeric strings; in the next chapter, we'll move on to more generalized string handling.

Converting ASCII Numeric Strings to Binary Values

Let's start with a fundamental problem: converting ASCII numeric strings to their equivalent binary values. Imagine that your program prompts the user for a numeric value and then issues a request to MS-DOS to read a string from the keyboard. When the program regains control from the read operation, its buffer will contain a sequence of ASCII characters, terminated by a special character (depending on the input function). The program must translate the values of the ASCII characters into binary data that can be combined with or compared to other such data, using the computer's arithmetic and logical instructions.

Suppose, for example, that your program uses MS-DOS's Int 21H Function 3FH to read a string from the keyboard. If the user types

```
100 <Enter>
```

the program's buffer will contain the following sequence of bytes after returning from the MS-DOS function call:

```
31H  30H  30H  0DH  0AH
```

This sequence corresponds to the ASCII characters 1, 0, and 0, followed by a carriage return (0DH) and linefeed (0AH). Before the program can work with the user's entry, it must convert this string of bytes to the binary value 0064H, or 100. Fortunately, the ASCII codes for the characters 0 through 9 are assigned consecutively, as shown in the following table:

Character	*ASCII Code*
0	30H
1	31H
2	32H
3	33H
4	34H
5	35H
6	36H
7	37H
8	38H
9	39H

Consequently, converting a decimal number represented as an ASCII string to a binary value is a straightforward process:

1. Initialize the result to zero.

2. Get the next character. If it is not in the range 30H through 39H, the conversion is finished.

3. Subtract 30H from the character (or use a logical AND operation with a mask value of 0FH), leaving a binary value in the range 0 through 9.

4. Multiply the previous result by 10, and then add the newly obtained value (0 through 9).

5. Return to step 2 and proceed.

Usually, of course, you'll also want to allow for the possibility of a leading plus or minus sign, but the extra logic required to handle signed numbers is trivial.

Figures 4-1 and 4-2 contain source code for ATOI and ATOL, two MASM functions that convert signed decimal ASCII strings to signed integers using the general procedure just described. Both require the address of an ASCII string of the form

[*white space*][*sign*][*digits*]

in registers DS:SI, and both terminate on the first invalid character. ATOI returns a 16-bit result in register AX, whereas ATOL returns a 32-bit result in registers DX:AX (with the most significant half in DX).

```
;
; ATOI.ASM -- Converts decimal ASCII string to 16-bit signed integer.
;
; Copyright (C) 1991 Ray Duncan
;
; Call with:    DS:SI = address of string in the form
;                       [white space][sign][digits]
;
; Returns:      AX    = result
;               DS:SI = address + 1 of terminator
;
; Destroys:     Nothing
;
; Like the C runtime library function 'atoi', this routine gives no
; warning of overflow and terminates on the first invalid character.

blank    equ     20h                    ; ASCII blank character
tab      equ     09h                    ; ASCII tab character

_TEXT    segment word public 'CODE'

         assume  cs:_TEXT

         public  atoi
atoi     proc    near

         push    bx                     ; save registers
         push    cx
         push    dx

         xor     bx,bx                  ; initialize result
         xor     cx,cx                  ; initialize sign flag

atoi1:   lodsb                          ; scan off white space
         cmp     al,blank               ; ignore leading blanks
         je      atoi1
         cmp     al,tab                 ; ignore leading tabs
         je      atoi1

         cmp     al,'+'                 ; if plus sign, proceed
         je      atoi2
         cmp     al,'-'                 ; is it minus sign?
         jne     atoi3                  ; no, test if numeric
         dec     cx                     ; was minus sign, set flag
                                        ; for negative result

atoi2:   lodsb                          ; get next character
```

Figure 4-1. *(continued)*

ATOI.ASM, a routine that converts a decimal ASCII string to a 16-bit signed integer.

Figure 4-1. *continued*

```
atoi3:  cmp     al,'0'          ; is character valid?
        jb      atoi4           ; jump if not in range 0-9
        cmp     al,'9'
        ja      atoi4           ; jump if not in range 0-9

        and     ax,0fh          ; isolate lower 4 bits

        xchg    bx,ax           ; previous answer * 10
        mov     dx,10
        mul     dx

        add     bx,ax           ; add this digit

        jmp     atoi2           ; convert next digit

atoi4:  mov     ax,bx           ; put result into AX
        jcxz    atoi5           ; jump if sign flag clear
        neg     ax              ; make result negative

atoi5:  pop     dx              ; restore registers
        pop     cx
        pop     bx
        ret                     ; back to caller

atoi    endp

_TEXT   ends

        end
```

```
;
; ATOL.ASM -- Converts decimal ASCII string to long (32-bit) signed integer.
;
; Copyright (C) 1991 Ray Duncan
;
; Call with:    DS:SI = address of string in the form
;                       [white space][sign][digits]
;
; Returns:      DX:AX = result (high word in DX)
;               DS:SI = address + 1 of terminator
;
; Destroys:     Nothing
;
```

Figure 4-2. (continued)

ATOL.ASM, a routine that converts a decimal ASCII string to a 32-bit signed integer.

Figure 4-2. *continued*

```
; Like the C runtime library function 'atol', this routine gives no
; warning of overflow and terminates on the first invalid character.

blank    equ     20h                     ; ASCII blank character
tab      equ     09h                     ; ASCII tab character

_TEXT    segment word public 'CODE'

         assume  cs:_TEXT

         public  atol
atol     proc    near

         push    bx                      ; save registers
         push    cx
         push    di

         xor     bx,bx                   ; initialize result
         xor     dx,dx                   ; in DX:BX
         xor     cx,cx                   ; initialize sign flag

atol1:   lodsb                           ; scan off white space
         cmp     al,blank                ; ignore leading blanks
         je      atol1
         cmp     al,tab                  ; ignore leading tabs
         je      atol1

         cmp     al,'+'                  ; if plus sign, proceed
         je      atol2
         cmp     al,'-'                  ; is it minus sign?
         jne     atol3                   ; no, test if numeric
         dec     cx                      ; was minus sign, set flag
                                         ; for negative result

atol2:   lodsb                           ; get next character

atol3:   cmp     al,'0'                  ; is character valid?
         jb      atol4                   ; jump if not in range 0-9
         cmp     al,'9'
         ja      atol4                   ; jump if not in range 0-9

         and     ax,0fh                  ; isolate lower 4 bits
         push    ax                      ; and save digit value

         mov     ax,bx                   ; previous answer * 10
         mov     di,dx                   ; DI:AX = copy of DX:BX
         add     bx,bx                   ; * 2
         adc     dx,dx
         add     bx,bx                   ; * 4
```

(continued)

Figure 4-2. *continued*

```
            adc     dx,dx
            add     bx,ax               ; * 5
            adc     dx,di
            add     bx,bx               ; * 10
            adc     dx,dx

            pop     ax                  ; add this digit
            add     bx,ax               ; to result
            adc     dx,0

            jmp     atol2               ; convert next digit

atol4:      mov     ax,bx               ; result low half to AX
            jcxz    atol5               ; jump if sign flag clear

            not     ax                  ; take two's complement
            not     dx                  ; of DX:AX
            add     ax,1
            adc     dx,0

atol5:      pop     di                  ; restore registers
            pop     cx
            pop     bx
            ret                         ; return to caller

atol        endp

_TEXT       ends

            end
```

The source code for ATOL contains a couple of useful tricks. The lines between the labels ATOL3 and ATOL4 demonstrate how to multiply a 32-bit quantity by 10 by adding copies together. This is special-case code; the general solution on an 8086/88 requires that you perform the multiplication in 8-bit or 16-bit pieces and then add the intermediate results or use a shift-and-add algorithm. The lines between ATOL4 and ATOL5 illustrate one way to find the negative value of a 32-bit quantity on a 16-bit machine: The two's complement is obtained by first taking the one's complement of each half and then adding 1 to the result. (Multiple-precision arithmetic is discussed in more detail in Chapter 12.)

When you write programming tools and utilities, remember that it's more convenient for the user to enter addresses and bit masks in hexadecimal instead of decimal. A routine that converts hexadecimal ASCII strings to binary values follows the same general strategy as the ATOI and ATOL procedures, but it requires several special considerations. The routine must be able to handle ASCII codes for the characters A through F, which are themselves consecutive but are not contiguous to the ASCII codes for the characters 0 through 9, as shown in the following table:

Character	ASCII Code	Character	ASCII Code
0	30H	8	38H
1	31H	9	39H
2	32H	A	41H
3	33H	B	42H
4	34H	C	43H
5	35H	D	44H
6	36H	E	45H
7	37H	F	46H

The conversion routine must therefore test for two distinct ranges of character values. When a character is in the alphabetic range, the routine must use a correction factor in order to end up with the linear range of binary values 0 through 0FH.

In addition, the user should be allowed to enter the alphabetic characters in either lowercase or uppercase. And, finally, explicit use of multiplication is unnecessary in hexadecimal conversion because you can multiply the result by 16 by shifting it left 4 bits; this makes up for the increased complexity introduced by the need to test for two ranges of character codes.

The procedure HTOI (Figure 4-3) converts a hexadecimal ASCII string to a 16-bit integer. Its use of registers is symmetric with the ATOI routine shown in Figure 4-1 on page 43. (The routines HTOL and HTOQ, which convert hexadecimal ASCII strings to 32-bit and 64-bit integers, are included on the companion disk but are not reproduced here.)

```
;
; HTOI.ASM -- Converts hexadecimal ASCII string to 16-bit (short) integer.
;
; Copyright (C) 1991 Ray Duncan
;
; Call with:    DS:SI = address of string
;
; Returns:      AX    = result
;               DS:SI = address + 1 of terminator
;
; Destroys:     Nothing
;
; Like the C runtime library function 'atoi', this routine gives no
; warning of overflow and terminates on the first nonconvertible character.
```

Figure 4-3.   *(continued)*

HTOI.ASM, a routine that converts a hexadecimal ASCII string to a 16-bit unsigned integer.

Figure 4-3. *continued*

```
_TEXT     segment word public 'CODE'

          assume  cs:_TEXT

          public  htoi
htoi      proc    near

          push    cx                  ; save register
          xor     cx,cx               ; set result to zero

htoi1:    lodsb                       ; get next char, be sure
                                      ; it is 0-9 or A-F

          cmp     al,'0'
          jb      htoi3               ; exit if char < '0'
          cmp     al,'9'
          jbe     htoi2               ; proceed if char 0-9
          or      al,20h              ; fold char to lowercase
          cmp     al,'f'
          ja      htoi3               ; exit if > 'F' or 'f'
          cmp     al,'a'
          jb      htoi3               ; exit if < 'A' or 'a'
          add     al,9                ; fudge factor for A-F

htoi2:                                ; add digit to result
          shl     cx,1                ; first shift current result
          shl     cx,1
          shl     cx,1
          shl     cx,1
          and     ax,0fh              ; isolate binary value 0-F
          or      cx,ax               ; add to result
          jmp     htoi1               ; get next character

htoi3:    mov     ax,cx               ; return AX = value
          pop     cx                  ; restore register
          ret                         ; back to caller

htoi      endp

_TEXT     ends

          end
```

Converting Binary Values to ASCII Strings

After your program has prompted the user to type in numbers, converted those numbers to binary values, and calculated the results, it must be able to convert the binary result back to an ASCII string that can be printed or displayed on the screen.

Suppose, for example, that you have the number 100 as a 16-bit integer. This value is represented in memory as the following 2-byte sequence:

64H 00H

(In the Intel series of processors, the less significant byte lies at the lower address.) In terms of ASCII codes, these 2 bytes represent a lowercase *d* and a null character, so you can't simply ship the 2 bytes to the screen driver or a list device directly and expect the user to make sense of them. Instead, you must first transform the value into this 3-byte sequence:

31H 30H 30H

These bytes are the ASCII codes for the characters 1, 0, and 0.

Follow these basic steps to convert an unsigned binary value to an ASCII string for a given radix or base:

1. If the working value is zero, go to step 8.

2. Divide the working value by the radix.

3. Add the remainder from step 2, which is in the range [0 ... radix − 1], to the value 30H (the ASCII code for the character 0).

4. If the result of step 3 is greater than 39H (the ASCII code for the character 9), add a correction factor (the difference between the ASCII code for A and the ASCII code for 9, minus 1).

5. Store the ASCII code produced in steps 3 and 4 in the developing output string. Note that the characters in the string are being produced in reverse order.

6. The quotient from step 2 becomes the new working value.

7. Return to step 1.

8. If no characters have been generated, force storage of a single 0 character.

Conversion of signed values is only a little more complicated. You must first test the sign of the value, save the sign somewhere, and then force the number positive before beginning step 1 above. At the end of the conversion, test the sign flag and store a minus-sign character at the beginning of the output string if the original value was negative.

Figures 4-4 and 4-5 on the following pages contain the MASM source code for procedures named ITOA and LTOA, which convert 16-bit and 32-bit signed integers to ASCII strings. These routines accept a binary value, a radix, and the address of a buffer, and they return the address of the resulting ASCII string. Both assume that the supplied buffer will be of adequate size.

The logic of ITOA closely follows the procedure outlined above. The 16-bit binary number is converted to its absolute value and then is repeatedly divided by the radix in order to extract the digits of the developing string. At the end, the sign of the original value is recalled, a minus-sign character is stored at the head of the string (if necessary), and the length of the string is calculated.

The routine LTOA resembles ITOA but is necessarily more complex because the Intel 80x86 family does not have a divide instruction that returns a 32-bit quotient and a 16-bit remainder—which are necessary to fully convert a 32-bit binary value. Therefore, such an operation is synthesized from the usual unsigned divide instruction in the subroutine DIVIDE.

```
;
; ITOA.ASM -- Converts 16-bit signed integer to ASCII string.
;
; Copyright (C) 1991 Ray Duncan
;
; Call with:     AX   = 16-bit integer
;                DS:SI = buffer to receive string,
;                        must be at least 6 bytes long
;                CX   = radix
;
; Returns:       DS:SI = address of converted string
;                AX   = length of string
;
; Destroys:      Nothing
;
; Because the test for value = 0 is made after a digit
; has been stored, the resulting string will always
; contain at least one significant digit.

_TEXT   segment word public 'CODE'

        assume  cs:_TEXT

        public  itoa
itoa    proc    near

        add     si,6                    ; advance to end of buffer
        push    si                      ; and save that address
        or      ax,ax                   ; test sign of 16-bit value
        pushf                           ; and save sign on stack
        jns     itoa1                   ; jump if value was positive
        neg     ax                      ; find absolute value

itoa1:  cwd                             ; divide value by radix to extract
        div     cx                      ; next digit for result
        add     dl,'0'                  ; convert remainder to ASCII char
        cmp     dl,'9'                  ; in case converting to hex ASCII
        jle     itoa2                   ; jump if in range 0-9
        add     dl,'A'-'9'-1            ; correct char if in range A-F
```

Figure 4-4. *(continued)*

ITOA.ASM, a routine that converts a 16-bit signed integer to an ASCII string in any radix.

Figure 4-4. *continued*

```
itoa2:  dec     si                      ; back up through buffer
        mov     [si],dl                 ; store this character in string
        or      ax,ax
        jnz     itoa1                   ; no, convert another digit

        popf                            ; was original value negative?
        jns     itoa3                   ; no, jump
        dec     si                      ; yes, store sign in output
        mov     byte ptr [si],'-'

itoa3:  pop     ax                      ; calculate length of string
        sub     ax,si
        ret                             ; back to caller

itoa    endp

_TEXT   ends

        end
```

```
;
; LTOA.ASM -- Converts 32-bit (long) signed integer to ASCII string.
;
; Copyright (C) 1991 Ray Duncan
;
; Call with:    DX:AX = 32-bit integer
;               DS:SI = buffer to receive string,
;                       must be at least 11 bytes long
;               CX    = radix
;
; Returns:      DS:SI = address of converted string
;               AX    = length of string
;
; Destroys:     BX, DX
;
; Because the test for value = 0 is made after a character
; has been stored, the resulting string will always
; contain at least one significant digit.

_TEXT   segment word public 'CODE'

        assume  cs:_TEXT

        public  ltoa
```

Figure 4-5. *(continued)*

LTOA.ASM, a routine that converts a 32-bit signed integer to an ASCII string in any radix.

Figure 4-5. *continued*

```
ltoa        proc    near

            add     si,11                   ; advance to end of buffer
            push    si                      ; and save that address
            or      dx,dx                   ; test sign of 32-bit value
            pushf                           ; and save sign on stack
            jns     ltoa1                   ; jump if value was positive
            not     dx                      ; it was negative, take two's
            not     ax                      ; complement of the value
            add     ax,1
            adc     dx,0

ltoa1:      call    divide                  ; divide value by radix
            add     bl,'0'                  ; convert remainder to ASCII char
            cmp     bl,'9'                  ; in case converting to hex ASCII
            jle     ltoa2                   ; jump if in range 0-9
            add     bl,'A'-'9'-1            ; correct char if in range A-F

ltoa2:      dec     si                      ; back up through buffer
            mov     [si],bl                 ; store this character in string
            mov     bx,ax                   ; is value = 0 yet?
            or      bx,dx
            jnz     ltoa1                   ; no, convert another digit

            popf                            ; was original value negative?
            jns     ltoa3                   ; no, jump
            dec     si                      ; yes, store minus sign in output
            mov     byte ptr [si],'-'

ltoa3:      pop     ax                      ; calculate length of string
            sub     ax,si
            ret                             ; back to caller

ltoa        endp

;
; General-purpose 32-bit by 16-bit unsigned divide.  This routine must
; be used instead of the machine's usual unsigned divide for cases
; where the quotient might overflow 16 bits (for example, 100,000 / 2).
; If called with a zero divisor, this routine returns the dividend
; unchanged and gives no warning.
;
; Call with:  DX:AX = 32-bit dividend
;             CX    = divisor
;
; Returns:    DX:AX = quotient
;             BX    = remainder
;             CX    = divisor (unchanged)
;
```

(continued)

Figure 4-5. *continued*

```
; Destroys:     Nothing
;
divide proc    near

        jcxz    div1                    ; exit if divide by zero
        push    ax                      ; 0:dividend_hi/divisor
        mov     ax,dx
        xor     dx,dx
        div     cx
        mov     bx,ax                   ; BX = quotient1
        pop     ax                      ; remainder1:dividend_lo/divisor
        div     cx
        xchg    bx,dx                   ; DX:AX = quotient1:quotient2

div1:   ret                             ; BX = remainder2

divide endp

_TEXT  ends

       end
```

The routine ITOH (Figure 4-6) is derived directly from ITOA but is more special-ized. It always converts the binary value to a hexadecimal ASCII string, and it always produces a string of exactly four ASCII characters. Note also that ITOH doesn't need to use the divide instruction because it can extract each successive character by shifts and logical AND instructions.

```
;
; ITOH.ASM --   Converts 16-bit unsigned integer
;               to hexadecimal ASCII string.
;
; Copyright (C) 1991 Ray Duncan
;
; Call with:    AX    = value to convert
;               DS:SI = address to store four-character string
;
; Returns:      DS:SI = address of converted string
;
; Destroys:     Nothing

_TEXT  segment word public 'CODE'
```

Figure 4-6. *(continued)*

ITOH.ASM, a routine that converts a 16-bit unsigned integer to a hexadecimal ASCII string.

Figure 4-6. *continued*

```
        assume  cs:_TEXT

        public  itoh
itoh    proc    near

        push    ax                          ; save registers
        push    cx
        push    dx
        push    si

        mov     dx,4                        ; initialize char counter

itoh1:  mov     cx,4                        ; isolate next 4 bits
        rol     ax,cl
        mov     cx,ax
        and     cx,0fh
        add     cx,'0'                      ; convert to ASCII
        cmp     cx,'9'                      ; is it 0-9?
        jbe     itoh2                       ; yes, jump
        add     cx,'A'-'9'-1                ; add correction for A-F

itoh2:  mov     [si],cl                     ; store this character
        inc     si                          ; bump string pointer
        dec     dx                          ; count characters converted
        jnz     itoh1                       ; loop, not four yet

        pop     si                          ; restore registers
        pop     dx
        pop     cx
        pop     ax
        ret                                 ; back to caller

itoh    endp

_TEXT   ends

        end
```

Advanced Numeric Formatting

The simple routines ITOA and LTOA illustrate the basic strategies used in conversion, but they are not suitable for "production-quality" programs. Both routines require the calling program to produce an output buffer of adequate size or risk the consequences; both require the calling program to clear the output buffer of any previous ASCII string by filling the buffer with ASCII blanks or some other suitable padding character; and neither allows the caller to control the length or alignment of the generated ASCII string.

The LTOA routine can, however, be used as a stepping-stone to a more powerful routine called LCVT (Figure 4-7). LCVT converts a double-precision (32-bit) signed integer to a formatted ASCII string, always using decimal base (radix = 10). It is capable of right or left justification, padding the output field with a special character, and inserting a decimal point at a specified location in a number, among other options.

```
;
; LCVT.ASM --   Converts 32-bit (long) signed integer
;               to formatted decimal ASCII string.
;
; Copyright (C) 1991 Ray Duncan
;
; Call with:    BH    = decimal places
;               BL    = field width
;               CH    = conversion flags
;                       bit meaning
;                         7 = 0 if left-justify
;                             1 if right-justify
;                         6 = 0 fill field with '*'
;                                 if number too large
;                             1 truncate to fit
;                         5 = 0 prefix with '-' only
;                             1 prefix with '+' or '-'
;                         4 = 0 pad with blanks
;                             1 pad with char in CL
;                       0-3 = reserved
;               CL    = pad character
;                       (if bit 4 of CH is set)
;               DX:AX = 32-bit signed integer
;               DS:SI = buffer to receive string
;
; Returns:      If successful:
;               Carry = clear
;               DS:SI = formatted string
;               AX    = output field length
;
;               If error (number too large,
;               and bit 6 of CH was not set):
;               Carry = set
;               and output buffer filled with '*'
;
; Destroys:     DX
;
; At least one significant digit is always stored. Calling this
; function with field width = 0 results in an error return.
```

Figure 4-7.   *(continued)*

LCVT.ASM, a routine that converts a 32-bit signed integer to a formatted decimal ASCII string.

Figure 4-7. *continued*

```
DGROUP   group    _DATA

flags    equ      [bp-1]                  ; formatting flags
fpad     equ      [bp-2]                  ; pad character, if any
fdecpl   equ      [bp-3]                  ; decimal places in output
fwidth   equ      [bp-4]                  ; width of output field
fseg     equ      [bp-6]                  ; segment of output field
foffs    equ      [bp-8]                  ; offset of output field
fsign    equ      [bp-10]                 ; sign of original number

_DATA    segment word public 'DATA'

buflen   equ      16                      ; length of working buffers

buf1     db       buflen dup (?)          ; LTOA builds string here
buf2     db       buflen dup (?)          ; formatted string built here

_DATA    ends

_TEXT    segment word public 'CODE'

         assume   cs:_TEXT

         extrn    LTOA:near

         public   lcvt
lcvt     proc     near

         push     es                      ; save registers
         push     di
         push     bp
         push     cx
         push     bx

         mov      bp,sp                   ; set up local variables
         sub      sp,10
         mov      fpad,cx                 ; save flags and pad char
         mov      fwidth,bx               ; save width and dec places
         mov      fseg,ds                 ; save output field segment
         mov      foffs,si                ; save output field offset
         mov      fsign,dx                ; save sign of number

         or       bl,bl                   ; is output width 0?
         jnz      lcvt01                  ; no, proceed
         jmp      lcvt15                  ; error if width = 0

lcvt01:  cmp      bh,(buflen+2)           ; too many decimal places?
         jbe      lcvt02                  ; no, proceed
         jmp      lcvt14                  ; error if buffer too small
```

(continued)

Figure 4-7. *continued*

```
lcvt02: or      dx,dx                   ; test sign of number
        jns     lcvt03                  ; jump if number positive

        neg     dx                      ; negative, take abs value
        neg     ax                      ; of number so we can control
        sbb     dx,0                    ; sign placement

lcvt03: mov     cx,10                   ; use decimal base
        mov     si,DGROUP               ; set DS:SI = local buffer
        mov     ds,si
        mov     si,offset DGROUP:buf1

        call    LTOA                    ; convert DX:AX to ASCII
                                        ; returns DS:SI -> string,
                                        ;         AX = length

                                        ; now format the string
        add     si,ax                   ; point to end of string
        dec     si                      ; returned by LTOA
        mov     cx,ax                   ; let CX = string length

        push    ds                      ; point to end of buffer
        pop     es                      ; for formatted string
        mov     di,offset DGROUP:buf2+buflen-1

        std                             ; prepare for backward move
        xor     bx,bx                   ; init places counter

lcvt04: movsb                           ; transfer one char
        inc     bx                      ; count characters
        cmp     bl,fdecpl               ; need decimal point now?
        jne     lcvt05                  ; no, jump
        mov     al,'.'                  ; yes, store it
        stosb

lcvt05: loop    lcvt04                  ; until all chars transferred
        cmp     bl,fdecpl               ; decimal taken care of?
        ja      lcvt08                  ; yes, jump
        je      lcvt07                  ; well, partially

lcvt06:                                 ; no, need decimal point
        mov     al,'0'                  ; store zeros up to
        stosb                           ; decimal point
        inc     bx
        cmp     bl,fdecpl
        jne     lcvt06
        mov     al,'.'                  ; store decimal point
        stosb
```

(continued)

Figure 4-7. *continued*

```
lcvt07: mov     al,'0'                      ; force leading zero
        stosb


lcvt08: test    word ptr fsign,-1           ; was number negative?
        jns     lcvt09                      ; no, jump
        mov     al,'-'                      ; yes, store minus sign
        stosb
        jmp     lcvt10


lcvt09: test    byte ptr flags,20h          ; is plus sign needed?
        jz      lcvt10                      ; no, jump
        mov     al,'+'                      ; yes, store plus sign
        stosb


lcvt10: cld                                 ; string now formatted
                                            ; with dec point and sign
        mov     si,di                       ; copy address
        inc     si                          ; calc length of string
        mov     ax,offset DGROUP:buf2+buflen
        sub     ax,si                       ; now AX = length
        mov     es,fseg                     ; set ES:DI = address and
        mov     di,foffs                    ; CX = length of user's
        mov     cl,fwidth                   ; output buffer
        xor     ch,ch
        jcxz    lcvt15                      ; return error if width = 0
        cmp     cx,ax                       ; string too big for field?
        jae     lcvt11                      ; no, jump
        test    byte ptr flags,40h          ; OK to truncate string?
        jz      lcvt14                      ; no, return error
        mov     ax,cx                       ; truncate formatted length


lcvt11: push    ax                          ; save formatted length
        mov     al,' '                      ; default pad char = blank
        test    byte ptr flags,10h          ; test special padding flag
        jz      lcvt12                      ; jump if use ASCII blank
        mov     al,fpad                     ; else use special char


lcvt12: rep stosb                           ; flood field with pad character
        mov     di,foffs                    ; restore output buffer address
        pop     cx                          ; length of formatted string
        test    byte ptr flags,80h          ; left- or right-justify?
        jz      lcvt13                      ; jump if left-justify
        mov     al,fwidth                   ; right-justify, length of
        xor     ah,ah                       ; user's output buffer
        sub     ax,cx                       ; minus formatted string length
        add     di,ax                       ; = offset into output field


lcvt13: rep movsb                           ; transfer formatted string
```

(continued)

Figure 4-7. *continued*

```
        clc                         ; success signal: clear carry
        jmp     lcvt16              ; go clean up and exit

lcvt14:                             ; error encountered, fill
                                    ; output field with asterisks
        mov     es,fseg             ; ES:DI -> output field
        mov     di,foffs
        mov     cl,fwidth           ; CX = output field length
        xor     ch,ch
        mov     al,'*'              ; character = asterisk
        rep stosb                   ; flood output buffer

lcvt15: stc                         ; error signal: set carry

lcvt16: mov     ds,fseg             ; return DS:SI = address
        mov     si,foffs            ; of output field
        mov     al,fwidth           ; AX = output field width
        mov     ah,0                ; (protect carry flag)
        mov     sp,bp               ; discard local variables

        pop     bx                  ; restore registers
        pop     cx
        pop     bp
        pop     di
        pop     es
        ret                         ; back to caller

lcvt    endp

_TEXT   ends

        end
```

Unlike ITOA and LTOA, LCVT requires quite a few different parameters. It is called with the registers set up as follows:

BH	= decimal places
BL	= field width
CH	= conversion flags
CL	= pad character
DX:AX	= 32-bit signed integer
DS:SI	= address of buffer to receive formatted string

■ The *decimal places* parameter controls where a decimal point is inserted into the formatted string. Leading zeros are added to the output string if necessary to accommodate the number of decimal places requested. If the decimal places parameter is zero, no decimal point will appear.

- The *field width* parameter specifies the number of character positions available in the caller's buffer to accept the output string. The output field is first initialized, and then the formatted numeric string is left-justified or right-justified in the field according to the conversion flags.

- The *conversion flags* parameter controls justification, sign insertion, truncation, and padding of the output field. The bits of register CH have the following meanings:

Bit	Value	Significance
7	0	Left-justify
	1	Right-justify
6	0	Fill field with asterisks if formatted number is too large for field
	1	Truncate number if necessary to fit within field
5	0	Prefix number with minus sign if negative, no sign if positive
	1	Always prefix number with plus sign or minus sign
4	0	Use ASCII blank as pad character
	1	Use character in register CL as pad character
0–3		Not used

- The *pad character* in register CL is used only if bit 4 of the conversion flags in register CH is set. Otherwise, the pad character defaults to an ASCII blank, and register CL is ignored. The pad character is used to initialize the positions of the output field (addresses DS:SI through DS:SI + *width* − 1) that are not occupied by the formatted numeric string.

Upon return from the LCVT routine, the carry flag is clear if the conversion was successful. If an error was encountered, the carry flag is set. Errors are usually caused by a number that is too large to fit into the output field after it has been converted to ASCII. Registers DS:SI are returned unchanged—that is, pointing to the beginning of the output field—and register AX contains the length of the output field (for symmetry with the routine LTOA).

Notice that the registers and the flags are arranged so that a zero value (except for the output field width) results in the simplest, most common numeric format: left-justified, padded with blanks, no decimal point, and no truncation allowed. For example, the following code sequence converts the value 10 to an ASCII string and then left-justifies the string in an output field eight characters wide:

```
        .
        .
        .
mov     ax,10           ; number to convert
cwd                     ; make it into double
```

```
mov     si,seg buffer       ; address of output field
mov     ds,si
mov     si,offset buffer
mov     bx,8                ; field width = 8
                            ; decimal places = 0
mov     cx,0                ; flags = 0
                            ; pad char not used
call    LCVT                ; request formatting
jc      error               ; jump if conversion error
    .
    .
    .
```

How LCVT Works

LCVT first saves all affected registers. It then creates a stack frame of local variables where it can place copies of the various formatting parameters and the sign of the number to be converted. In this instance, we are using a stack frame not to make the routine re-entrant but simply for addressing convenience: Because the local variables are accessed through SS:BP, we can easily use the DS and ES segment registers for other purposes.

LCVT then performs some elementary error checking on the formatting parameters. If the width of the output field is zero or if the number of decimal places is such that the resulting number will not fit into LCVT's local working buffer, the routine exits with an error condition. If you are inclined to make the routine more idiot-proof, you can add further error checking for field widths that are negative or too large, illegal conversion flags, unprintable pad characters, and so on.

After the parameters have been validated, LCVT checks the sign of the number to be converted and takes the absolute value of the number if it is negative. This prevents LTOA from attempting to insert a sign into the string and allows LCVT to keep complete control over the sign placement. LCVT then calls LTOA with the positive 32-bit number, which LTOA converts to an ASCII string in LCVT's working buffer.

With the primitive ASCII string produced by LTOA, LCVT can proceed to apply the formatting requested by the calling program. It first inserts the decimal point into the string at the requested location (adding leading zeros to the string if necessary) and ensures that at least one character precedes the decimal point. LCVT then adds a minus sign in front of the string if the original number was negative. If the original number was positive, LCVT adds a plus sign only if bit 5 of the conversion flags (register CH) was set.

At this point, the length of the formatted string (including the decimal point and the sign) is known, and the string is ready to be copied to the calling program's buffer.

First, LCVT initializes the caller's buffer with ASCII blanks or with the specified pad character, depending on bit 4 of the conversion flags. This relieves the calling program of the need to worry about any characters remaining in the field from previous output operations.

61

Next, LCVT checks the length of the formatted string against the caller's field width. If the string fits into the field, LCVT tests bit 7 of the conversion flags to determine whether to right-justify or left-justify the numeric string and copies the formatted string to the user's buffer with the appropriate offset.

If the formatted string does not fit into the caller's field, LCVT tests bit 6 of the conversion flags to determine whether the number can be truncated. If the bit is zero, LCVT fills the caller's field with asterisks to indicate an overflow. If bit 6 is set, LCVT simply copies as many characters as will fit, starting with the most significant digits.

Finally, LCVT discards the local variables on the stack frame, restores the affected registers, and returns with DS:SI and AX containing the address and length of the output field. The carry flag can be tested by the calling program to determine whether an overflow or some other conversion error occurred.

PROCEDURES INTRODUCED IN THIS CHAPTER

Procedure Name	Action	Parameters	Results
ATOI	Converts decimal ASCII string to 16-bit signed integer	DS:SI = segment:offset of ASCII string	DS:SI = segment:offset + 1 of terminator AX = binary value
ATOL	Converts decimal ASCII string to 32-bit signed integer	DS:SI = segment:offset of ASCII string	DS:SI = segment:offset + 1 of terminator DX:AX = binary value
HTOI	Converts hex ASCII string to 16-bit unsigned integer	DS:SI = segment:offset of ASCII string	DS:SI = segment:offset + 1 of terminator AX = binary value
ITOA	Converts 16-bit signed integer to ASCII string	DS:SI = segment:offset of buffer to receive string AX = binary value CX = radix	DS:SI = segment:offset of converted string AX = length of string
ITOH	Converts 16-bit unsigned integer to hex ASCII string	DS:SI = segment:offset of buffer to receive string AX = binary value	DS:SI = segment:offset of converted string

(continued)

PROCEDURES INTRODUCED IN THIS CHAPTER *continued*

Procedure Name	Action	Parameters		Results
LCVT	Converts 32-bit signed integer to formatted decimal ASCII string	DS:SI =	segment:offset of buffer to receive string	If function successful: Carry = clear
		DX:AX =	binary value	DS:SI = segment:offset of formatted string
		BH =	decimal places	AX = length of formatted string
		BL =	field width	If function unsuccessful:
		CH =	conversion flags	Carry = set
		CL =	pad character	
LTOA	Converts 32-bit signed integer to ASCII string	DS:SI =	segment:offset of buffer to receive string	DS:SI = segment:offset of converted string
		DX:AX =	binary value	AX = length of string
		CX =	radix	

Companion Disk

The companion disk directory \CH04 contains the programs and modules that are listed below.

Routines Presented in This Chapter

ATOI.ASM   Converts a decimal ASCII string to a single-precision (16-bit) signed integer

ATOL.ASM   Converts a decimal ASCII string to a double-precision (32-bit) signed integer

HTOI.ASM   Converts a hexadecimal ASCII string to a single-precision (16-bit) unsigned integer

ITOA.ASM   Converts a single-precision (16-bit) signed integer to an ASCII string in any radix

ITOH.ASM   Converts a single-precision (16-bit) unsigned integer to a hexadecimal ASCII string

LCVT.ASM   Converts a double-precision (32-bit) signed integer to a signed, formatted ASCII string

LTOA.ASM   Converts a double-precision (32-bit) signed integer to an ASCII string in any radix

Additional Conversion Routines
Not Shown in This Chapter

HTOL.ASM   Converts a hexadecimal ASCII string to a double-precision (32-bit) unsigned integer

HTOQ.ASM   Converts a hexadecimal ASCII string to a quad-precision (64-bit) unsigned integer

Demonstration Programs

TRYITOA   MAKE file for TRYITOA.EXE

TRYITOA.ASM   Interactive demonstration program

TRYLCVT   MAKE file for TRYLCVT.EXE

TRYLCVT.ASM   Interactive demonstration program

The interactive program TRYITOA.ASM demonstrates use of the routines ATOI and ITOA. To build TRYITOA.EXE, enter this command:

```
C>MAKE TRYITOA  <Enter>
```

When you run TRYITOA.EXE, it prompts you for a number, calls ATOI to convert the ASCII string to a binary value, calls ITOA to convert the binary value back to an ASCII string, and displays the string. The cycle is then repeated. You can press the Enter key at the prompt to exit the demonstration program.

Although TRYITOA is a simple program, it lets you step through the routines with your favorite debugger and examine the conversion process. You can easily modify TRYITOA to work with other pairs of conversion routines, such as HTOI and ITOH or ATOL and LTOA, allowing you to trace execution through hexadecimal and long-integer conversion.

The interactive program TRYLCVT.ASM demonstrates use of the routines LCVT, HTOL, ATOL, and LTOA and lets you experiment with the various formatting options LCVT supports. To build TRYLCVT.EXE, enter this command:

```
C>MAKE TRYLCVT  <Enter>
```

When you run TRYLCVT.EXE, it prompts you for a number and for the formatting parameters, converts your entries to binary values with HTOL and ATOL, calls LCVT to convert the binary number back to a formatted string, and then displays the result, as shown in this example:

```
C>TRYLCVT

LCVT Demonstration Program

Enter a number:            1234
Enter output width:        10
Enter decimal places:      2
Enter flags (hex):         30
Enter pad character:       #

You entered:               +12.34####

Enter a number:            1234
Enter output width:        15
Enter decimal places:      8
Enter flags (hex):         90
Enter pad character:       #

You entered:               #####0.00001234

Enter a number:

C>
```

To exit TRYLCVT, simply press the Enter key at the *Enter a number:* prompt.

5

Manipulating Strings

In addition to converting numbers, programs must also be able to manipulate arbitrary streams of text in order to cope with free-form entries by the user and to create aesthetically pleasing, easily understood output. The Intel 80x86 family of processors provides a good foundation for text handling with its repertoire of specialized string instructions:

LODS	LOaD String
CMPS	CoMPare String
MOVS	MOVe String
SCAS	SCAn String
STOS	STOre String

Each instruction's mnemonic can be followed by a B, W, or D suffix, indicating whether the instruction is to operate on bytes, words, or (in the case of the 80386 or 80486) doublewords. With ASCII text, the B suffix is most common.

A string instruction used alone processes a single byte, word, or doubleword. Used in combination with a *repeat* prefix, a string instruction can also efficiently process a series of bytes, words, or doublewords. The repeat prefixes come in three flavors:

REP	Repeat while CX not zero
REPNZ or REPNE	Repeat while CX not zero and Z flag not set
REPZ or REPE	Repeat while CX not zero and Z flag not clear

The machine instruction, or *opcode,* for each string instruction occupies only 1 byte of memory, and the prefix (if any) uses only 1 additional byte. This is possible because no register or address information needs to be encoded in the machine instructions—all the string instructions are "hardwired" for the register use shown in Figure 5-1 on the next page. Furthermore, the string instructions automatically increment or decrement the SI and DI registers according to the CPU's direction flag (controlled with the STD and CLD instructions) as each item of data is processed.

Register(s)	Used By	Significance
DS:SI	LODS CMPS MOVS	Contains the address of the source string operand
ES:DI	CMPS MOVS SCAS STOS	Contains the address of the destination string operand
CX	REP REPE REPNE	Contains the number of items to be loaded, compared, moved, scanned, or stored
AL, AX, or EAX	LODS SCAS STOS	Receives data or contains data to be scanned for or stored

Figure 5-1.

"Hardwired" use of registers by the string instructions and repeat prefixes. Two of the string instructions—CMPS and MOVS—are the only two-memory-operand instructions supported by the Intel CPUs.

Using the Basic String Instructions

In MASM programming, common string operations can be (and usually are) coded in-line because the opcodes for the five string instructions listed above (even combined with a repeat prefix) are shorter than a CALL instruction. For example, the following code copies a string of *length* bytes from *string1* to *string2* (resembling the C function *memmove*):

```
mov   si,seg string1
mov   ds,si
mov   si,offset string1
mov   di,seg string2
mov   es,di
mov   di,offset string2
mov   cx,length
cld
rep movsb
```

The B suffix used with the MOVS mnemonic tells the assembler to generate the opcode for a byte move rather than a word or doubleword move. Note that although the CLD (clear direction flag) instruction is included here for clarity, the direction flag stays clear (or set) until you change it; most applications simply clear the direction flag once in their initialization code and leave it alone thereafter.

On 8086, 80286, or 80386 machines, if the source and destination addresses are word-aligned, you can copy a string more quickly with the MOVSW instruction, which takes advantage of the CPU's 16-bit data path. If the string's length is odd, the remaining single byte can be copied with a final MOVSB:

```
mov   si,seg string1
mov   ds,si
mov   si,offset string1
mov   di,seg string2
```

```
mov   es,di
mov   di,offset string2
mov   cx,length
cld
shr   cx,1
rep movsw
rcl   cx,1
rep movsb
```

On 80386 or 80486 machines, even better performance results if the source and destination addresses are doubleword-aligned and the MOVSD instruction is used.

What about comparing strings? The following code compares the first *length* bytes of *string1* to *string2*, setting the CPU flags appropriately (equivalent to the C function *memcmp*):

```
mov   si,seg string1
mov   ds,si
mov   si,offset string1
mov   di,seg string2
mov   es,di
mov   di,offset string2
mov   cx,length
cld
repz cmpsb
```

After the comparison, the CPU's zero (Z) flag is set (1) if the strings were identical or clear (0) if the strings were different. In the latter case, the sign (S) flag is set (1) if *string1* was less than *string2* or clear (0) if *string1* was greater than *string2*. The CMPSB mnemonic is typically followed by a conditional jump instruction that tests the Z and S flags and takes the appropriate action.

Want to initialize an array? The code below (like the C function *memset*) stores *length* copies of *char* in memory starting at the address *string1*:

```
mov   di,seg string1
mov   es,di
mov   di,offset string1
mov   cx,length
mov   al,char
cld
rep stosb
```

Need to search for the first occurrence of a character? The following code (like the C function *memchr*) scans *length* bytes of *string1* for *char*:

```
mov   di,seg string1
mov   es,di
mov   di,offset string1
mov   cx,length
mov   al,char
cld
repnz scasb
```

69

After the scan, the Z flag is clear (0) if no matching characters were found in *string1*. If a matching character was found, the Z flag is set (1), and ES:DI points 1 byte past the character.

Here's a trick that comes in handy when you mix MASM routines with C programs. The code finds the length of the ASCIIZ *string1* (not including the terminal null byte) and leaves the length in register CX:

```
mov   di,seg string1
mov   es,di
mov   di,offset string1
xor   al,al              ; look for null
mov   cx,-1
cld
repnz scasb              ; CX = -length - 2
not   cx                 ; CX = length + 1
dec   cx                 ; CX = length
```

If you want to include the null byte in the length, simply remove the DEC CX instruction from the sequence. (The CX register is used in an original way here. I have no idea who devised this clever snippet; I picked it up along the way in the last few years and have used it hundreds of times.)

The examples given here are rather simple: They don't check for overlapping regions during string moves, they don't allow for case insensitivity during string compares, and so forth. But you can use them to build a set of more powerful and general subroutines. This chapter divides these routines into three packages so that you can include them in your applications selectively. Figure 5-2 lists the complete arsenal of string functions presented in this chapter. Examples of usage are provided only for the functions in the first string package because all the routines in all the modules work in a similar manner.

Function	Description	Module
STRBRK	Searches for character	STRINGS1.ASM
STRCAT	Concatenates strings	STRINGS2.ASM
STRCMP	Compares strings (case sensitive)	STRINGS1.ASM
STRCMPI	Compares strings (case insensitive)	STRINGS3.ASM
STRDUP	Duplicates string	STRINGS2.ASM
STRLWR	Lowercases string	STRINGS2.ASM
STRNDX	Searches string (case sensitive)	STRINGS1.ASM

Figure 5-2. *(continued)*

Alphabetic list of string functions presented in this chapter.

Figure 5-2. *continued*

Function	Description	Module
STRNDXI	Searches string (case insensitive)	STRINGS3.ASM
STRSPN	Validates string	STRINGS1.ASM
STRUPR	Uppercases string	STRINGS2.ASM
STRXLT	Translates string	STRINGS2.ASM
STRXTR	Extracts string	STRINGS2.ASM

MASM String Package #1

The listing STRINGS1.ASM (Figure 5-3) is the source code for our first string package. It contains four public routines for string comparisons, searching, and validation: STRCMP, STRNDX, STRSPN, and STRBRK. These four routines are relatively low-level: They are case sensitive, written for maximum performance, and do not carry out any error checking. Although their names were chosen with an eye toward the names used in the C runtime library, the arguments and results of these routines are oriented toward a MASM programmer's needs, and they are not exactly equivalent to any apparent C counterparts.

```
;
; STRINGS1.ASM -- MASM String Package #1
;               contains STRCMP, STRNDX, STRSPN, STRBRK.
;
; Copyright (C) 1991 Ray Duncan

_TEXT   segment word public 'CODE'

        assume  cs:_TEXT


;
; STRCMP:       String comparison routine
;
; Call with:    DS:SI = address of string1
;               BX    = length of string1
;               ES:DI = address of string2
;               DX    = length of string2
;
; Returns:      Z     = true  if strings are equal
;               or
;               Z     = false if strings are not equal, and
;               S     = true  if string1 < string2
;               S     = false if string1 > string2
```

Figure 5-3.   *(continued)*

STRINGS1.ASM, the source code for MASM string package #1.

Figure 5-3. *continued*

```
;
; Destroys:     BX, CX, SI, DI
;
        public  strcmp
strcmp  proc    near

        mov     cx,dx                   ; set length to compare

        cmp     bx,dx                   ; use shorter of two lengths
        ja      scmp1                   ; jump if string1 longer

        mov     cx,bx                   ; string1 is shorter

scmp1:  repz cmpsb                      ; now compare strings
        jz      scmp2                   ; jump, strings equal so far

        ret                             ; return Z = F, strings not equal

scmp2:  sub     bx,dx                   ; compare original string lengths
        ret                             ; return with S and Z flags set

strcmp  endp


;
; STRNDX:       String search routine
;
; Call with:    DS:SI = pattern address
;               BX    = pattern length
;               ES:DI = address of string to be searched
;               DX    = length of string to be searched
;
; Returns:      CY    = true if no match
;               or
;               CY    = false if match, and
;               ES:DI = pointer to match for pattern
;                       string within searched string
;
; Destroys:     CX, DX, SI, BP
;
        public  strndx
strndx  proc    near

        mov     bp,si                   ; save pattern offset
        dec     bx                      ; decr pattern length by 1
        cld

sndx1:  mov     si,bp                   ; AL = first char of pattern
        lodsb
```

(continued)

Figure 5-3. *continued*

```
        mov     cx,dx                   ; remaining searched string length
        repnz scasb                     ; look for match on first char

        jnz     sndx3                   ; searched string exhausted, exit

        mov     dx,cx                   ; save new string length
        mov     cx,bx                   ; get pattern length minus 1
        repz cmpsb                      ; compare remainder of strings

        jz      sndx2                   ; everything matched

        add     di,cx                   ; no match, restore string addr
        sub     di,bx                   ; advanced by one char

        cmp     dx,bx                   ; searched string exhausted?
        ja      sndx1                   ; some string left, try again
        jmp     sndx3                   ; no match, jump to return

sndx2:  sub     di,bx                   ; match found, let
        dec     di                      ; ES:DI = matched string addr
        clc                             ; and return CY = false
        ret

sndx3:  stc                             ; no match, return CY = true
        ret

strndx  endp

;
; STRSPN:         String validation routine
;
; Call with:      DS:SI = text string to be validated
;                 BX    = length of text string
;                 ES:DI = validation string
;                 DX    = length of validation string
;
; Returns:        CY    = false if text string valid
;                 or
;                 CY    = true if text string invalid, and
;                 DS:SI = pointer to invalid character
;                           within text string
;
; Destroys:       AX, BX, CX, SI
;
        public  strspn
strspn  proc    near

        mov     cx,bx                   ; CX = length of text string
        jcxz    sspn5                   ; exit if no text string
```

(continued)

Figure 5-3. *continued*

```
           or      dx,dx                    ; exit if no validation string
           jz      sspn3

sspn1:     lodsb                            ; get next text string char
           xor     bx,bx                    ; BX is validation string index

sspn2:     cmp     al,es:[bx+di]            ; compare to validation string
           je      sspn4                    ; this character is OK

           inc     bx                       ; bump validation string addr
           cmp     bx,dx                    ; end of validation string yet?
           jne     sspn2                    ; no, check next position

           dec     si                       ; yes, point to bad character

sspn3:     stc                              ; return CY flag true and
           ret                              ; DS:SI = bad character

sspn4:     loop    sspn1                    ; count text string characters
                                            ; and check next character

sspn5:     clc                              ; all characters were OK
           ret                              ; return CY flag false

strspn  endp

;
; STRBRK:        Character-set search routine
;
; Call with:     DS:SI = text string to search
;                BX    = length of text string
;                ES:DI = character list to search for
;                DX    = length of character list
;
; Returns:       CY    = false if no matching characters
;                          in text string
;                or
;                CY    = true if matching character found
;                          in text string, and
;                DS:SI = matched character within text string
;
; Destroys:      AX, BX, CX, SI, DI
;
        public  strbrk
strbrk  proc    near

           or      bx,bx                    ; check text length
           jz      sbrk3                    ; exit if no text string
```

(continued)

Figure 5-3. *continued*

```
        or      dx,dx                   ; check list length
        jz      sbrk3                   ; exit if no list

sbrk1:  lodsb                           ; get next text string char
        mov     cx,dx                   ; CX = list length
        repnz scasb                     ; scan character list
        jnz     sbrk2                   ; jump if no chars matched

        dec     si                      ; point to matching char
        stc                             ; return CY flag true
        ret                             ; and DS:SI = matched char

sbrk2:  sub     di,dx                   ; reset char list address
        dec     bx                      ; count list characters
        jnz     sbrk1                   ; loop, not end of list

sbrk3:  clc                             ; no matching characters
        ret                             ; return CY flag false

strbrk  endp

_TEXT   ends

        end
```

STRCMP is a general-purpose string comparison routine that uses the following parameters:

DS:SI = string1 address
BX   = string1 length
ES:DI = string2 address
DX   = string2 length

The result of the comparison is determined by the first nonequal character in the strings. If the first differing character in *string1* is less than the character in *string2*, then *string1* is less than *string2*. If the strings have different lengths but contain identical characters up to the end of the shorter string, then the shorter string is considered less than the longer string. For example:

"ABC" is less than "ABD"
"ABC" is less than "ABCD"

STRCMP returns the results of the string comparison in the CPU's zero and sign flags:

if string1 = string2, Z = true
if string1 < string2, Z = false and S = true
if string1 > string2, Z = false and S = false

Thus, you can call STRCMP and then follow it with a signed conditional branch, just as you could branch on the comparison of two registers. Here is an example of a call to STRCMP:

```
string1 db      'ABCDEF'
s1_len  equ     $-string1
string2 db      'ABCD'
s2_len  equ     $-string2
        .
        .
        .
        mov     si,offset string1 ; DS:SI = address string1
        mov     bx,s1_len         ; BX = length string1
        mov     di,offset string2 ; ES:DI = address string2
        mov     dx,s2_len         ; DX = length string2
        call    strcmp            ; compare strings
        jl      label1            ; jump if string1 is
                                  ; less than string2
```

STRNDX is a general-purpose string search routine with these arguments:

DS:SI = pattern string address
BX   = pattern string length
ES:DI = text string address
DX   = text string length

Both the pattern string and the text string can be any length (up to an entire segment). Because STRNDX searches the text string for the first occurrence of the complete pattern string, the pattern string should always be shorter than the text string.

If no match is found, STRNDX returns the carry flag true (1). If a match is found, STRNDX returns the carry flag false (0), and ES:DI points to the first character of the matching sequence within the string being searched. Thus, calls to STRNDX typically take the following form:

```
string1 db      'DEF'              ; pattern string (string
s1_len  equ     $-string1          ; to search for)
string2 db      'ABCDEFGHI'        ; text string (string to
s2_len  equ     $-string2          ; be searched within)
        .
        .
        .
        mov     si,offset string1 ; DS:SI = pattern address
        mov     bx,s1_len         ; BX = pattern length
        mov     di,offset string2 ; ES:DI = text address
        mov     dx,s2_len         ; DX = text length
        call    strndx            ; search string2
        jc      label1            ; jump if no match
```

STRSPN is a general-purpose string validation routine. It is called with the following arguments:

    DS:SI = text string address
    BX   = text string length
    ES:DI = validation string address
    DX   = validation string length

STRSPN tests each character of the text string against the validation string. If every character of the text string is a member of the validation string, STRSPN returns the carry flag false (0). If one or more characters in the text string are not found in the validation string, STRSPN returns the carry flag true (1), and DS:SI points to the in-valid character within the text string.

STRSPN is best used for screening keyboard input. For example, if the user enters a string representing a decimal integer, you can quickly check the entry by using the address and length of the keyboard input as the text string, along with the address and length of the following validation string:

```
valstr   db      '0123456789-+'   ; validation string
val_len equ      $-valstr         ; length of val string

buffer   db      80 dup (0)       ; input buffer
buf_len equ      $-buffer         ; buffer length
         .
         .
         .
                                  ; get input from user
         mov     dx,offset buffer ; input buffer address
         mov     cx,buf_len       ; input buffer length
         mov     bx,stdin         ; standard input handle
         mov     ah,3fh           ; fxn 3fh = read
         int     21h              ; transfer to MS-DOS
         sub     ax,2             ; any input?
         jz      error            ; no input, jump

                                  ; validate user's input
         mov     bx,ax            ; BX = text length
         mov     si,offset buffer ; DS:SI = text address
         mov     dx,val_len       ; DX = val str length
         mov     di,offset valstr ; ES:DI = val str addr
         call    strspn           ; call validation routine
         jc      error            ; input not valid, jump
```

If the input string passes the screening with STRSPN, you can then pass it to one of the conversion routines from the previous chapter (such as ATOI.ASM or ATOL.ASM) and turn it into a binary value.

STRBRK is a general-purpose routine for finding one of a set of characters within a text string. It has these parameters:

    DS:SI = text string address
    BX   = text string length
    ES:DI = character list address
    DX   = character list length

STRBRK compares in order each position of the text string against every member of the character list. If STRBRK finds a match in the character list, it returns the carry flag true (1), with DS:SI pointing to the character within the text string. If every character in the text string is not found in the character list, STRBRK returns the carry flag false (0).

The best application of STRBRK is in searching for delimiters. For instance, suppose that the user enters a string consisting of several fields and that the program's instructions allow fields to be separated with spaces, commas, or dashes (hyphens). You can find the end of the first field by passing STRBRK both the address and length of the keyboard input as the text string and the address and length of the following delimiter list:

```
delims  db      20h,',','-'         ; delimiter characters
del_len equ     $-delims            ; length of list

buffer  db      80 dup (0)          ; input buffer
buf_len equ     $-buffer            ; buffer length
        .
        .
        .
                                    ; get input from user
        mov     dx,offset buffer    ; input buffer address
        mov     cx,buf_len          ; input buffer length
        mov     bx,stdin            ; standard input handle
        mov     ah,3fh              ; fxn 3fh = read
        int     21h                 ; transfer to MS-DOS
        sub     ax,2                ; any input?
        jz      error               ; no input, jump

                                    ; look for delimiter
        mov     bx,ax               ; BX = text length
        mov     si,offset buffer    ; DS:SI = text address
        mov     dx,val_len          ; DX = delim list length
        mov     di,offset valstr    ; ES:DI = delim address
        call    strspn              ; call delimiter routine
        jnc     error               ; no delimiter, jump
```

Upon return from STRBRK, you can find the end of the following field simply by incrementing SI and calling STRBRK again. Of course, you must handle the last field as a special case and include the code for a carriage return (0DH) in the character list.

The ways in which STRSPN and STRBRK handle zero-length parameter strings differ subtly. If STRSPN is supplied a text string of zero length, it returns the carry flag false (0) to indicate that all members of the text string were valid. If it is given a text string containing at least one character and a zero-length validation string, STRSPN returns the carry flag true (1) to indicate that the text string was invalid. STRBRK, in contrast, returns the carry flag false (0) if either the text string or the character list has zero length.

MASM String Package #2

The listing STRINGS2.ASM (Figure 5-4) is the source code for our second package of string routines. This package addresses an altogether different category of string operations: concatenation, extraction, and translation. STRINGS2.ASM contains six public routines: STRCAT, STRDUP, STRXTR, STRXLT, STRLWR, and STRUPR. All of these procedures accept string pointers and lengths and return the address and length of a new string, leaving the original string(s) unchanged; in general, the registers used for parameters and results are symmetric with the STRINGS1 package. The names of some of the STRINGS2.ASM routines, like those in the first string package, were picked for symmetry with the C standard runtime library, but you should not assume that MASM and C routines that have the same name perform exactly the same way.

```
;
; STRINGS2.ASM -- MASM String Package #2 contains routines
;                 STRCAT, STRDUP, STRXTR, STRXLT, STRLWR, and STRUPR.
;
; Copyright (C) 1991 Ray Duncan

bufsize equ     1024                    ; size of buffer
                                        ; for temporary strings


_DATA   segment word public 'DATA'

lctab   dw      26                      ; strlwr translation table
        dw      'A'
        db      'abcdefghijklmnopqrstuvwxyz'

uctab   dw      26                      ; strupr translation table
        dw      'a'
        db      'ABCDEFGHIJKLMNOPQRSTUVWXYZ'

strbuf  db      bufsize dup (?)         ; temporary string buffer

strptr  dw      strbuf                  ; current buffer pointer

_DATA   ends

_TEXT   segment word public 'CODE'

        assume  cs:_TEXT

;
; STRCAT:        String concatenation routine
```

Figure 5-4.
STRINGS2.ASM, the source code for MASM string package #2.

(continued)

Figure 5-4. *continued*

```
;
; Call with:   DS:SI = address of string1
;              BX    = length of string1
;              ES:DI = address of string2
;              DX    = length of string2
;
; Returns:     DS:SI = address of result string
;                          in temporary storage
;              BX    = length of result string
;
; Destroys:    DI, ES

        public  strcat
strcat  proc    near

        push    cx                      ; save register

        push    di                      ; save string2 address
        push    es

        mov     cx,bx                   ; save string1 length

        add     bx,dx                   ; BX = result string length

        call    strmem                  ; get temporary storage
                                        ; for result string

        cld                             ; copy string1 to result
        rep movsb

        pop     ds                      ; get string2 address
        pop     si
        mov     cx,dx
        rep movsb                       ; copy string2 to result

        push    es                      ; let DS:SI = address of
        push    di                      ; result string
        pop     si
        pop     ds
        sub     si,bx                   ; correct for bytes moved

        pop     cx                      ; restore register
        ret                             ; back to caller

strcat  endp
```

(continued)

Figure 5-4. *continued*

```
;
; STRDUP:       String duplication routine
;
; Call with:    DS:SI = address of string
;               BX    = length of string
;
; Returns:      DS:SI = address of string copy
;                       in temporary storage
;               BX    = length of string copy
;
; Destroys:     Nothing

        public  strdup
strdup  proc    near

        push    cx                      ; save registers
        push    di
        push    es

        call    strmem                  ; get temporary storage
                                        ; to hold string copy

        mov     cx,bx                   ; make copy of string
        cld
        rep movsb

        push    es                      ; let DS:SI = address
        push    di                      ; of copy
        pop     si
        pop     ds
        sub     si,bx                   ; correct for bytes moved

        pop     es                      ; restore registers
        pop     di
        pop     cx
        ret                             ; back to caller

strdup  endp

;
; STRXTR:       String extraction routine
;
; Call with:    DS:SI = address of string
;               BX    = length of string
;               CX    = offset of substring
;               DX    = length of substring
;
; Returns:      DS:SI = address of substring
;                       in temporary storage
;               BX    = length of substring
```

(continued)

Figure 5-4. *continued*

```
;
;                   If BX = 0, then substring offset
;                   was invalid and DS:SI is unchanged
;
; Destroys:         Nothing

        public  strxtr
strxtr  proc    near

        push    cx                      ; save register

        add     si,cx                   ; point to substring
        sub     bx,cx                   ; adjust string length
        jnb     sxtr1                   ; length OK, proceed

        xor     bx,bx                   ; bad substring
        jmp     sxtr3                   ; return length = 0

sxtr1:  cmp     bx,dx                   ; clamp length?
        jb      sxtr2                   ; yes, jump
        mov     bx,dx                   ; no, set substring length

sxtr2:  call    strdup                  ; make copy of substring
                                        ; in temporary storage

sxtr3:  pop     cx                      ; restore register
        ret                             ; back to caller

strxtr  endp


;
; STRXLT:           String translation routine
;
; Call with:        DS:SI = address of text string
;                   BX    = length of text string
;                   ES:DI = address of translation table
;
;                   The translation table has the
;                   following format:
;
;                   dw  number of character codes in table (n)
;                   dw  character code of first position (m)
;                   db  translation value for character (m)
;                   db  translation value for character (m + 1)
;                       .
;                       .
;                       .
;                   db  translation value for character (m + n - 1)
;
```

(continued)

Figure 5-4. *continued*

```
;               In the table, any character positions
;               containing zero are ignored.  Any characters
;               in the text string falling outside the range
;               defined by the table are unchanged.
;
; Returns:      DS:SI = address of translated string
;                       in temporary storage
;               BX    = length of translated string
;               ES:DI = translation table address (unchanged)
;
; Destroys:     Nothing

        public  strxlt
strxlt  proc    near

        call    strdup                  ; make copy of string
                                        ; to be translated

        push    bx                      ; save registers
        push    cx
        push    si
        mov     cx,bx                   ; use CX for loop count
        jcxz    sxlt3                   ; exit if zero length

sxlt1:  mov     bl,[si]                 ; next character
        xor     bh,bh
        sub     bx,es:[di+2]            ; correct for table base
        js      sxlt2                   ; jump, outside table
        cmp     bx,es:[di]
        jae     sxlt2                   ; jump, outside table

        mov     bl,es:[bx+di+4]         ; get translation value
        or      bl,bl                   ; is it zero?
        jz      sxlt2                   ; yes, ignore it
        mov     [si],bl                 ; store translated value

sxlt2:  inc     si                      ; bump text string pointer
        loop    sxlt1                   ; process next character

sxlt3:  pop     si                      ; restore registers
        pop     cx
        pop     bx
        ret                             ; back to caller

strxlt  endp


;
; STRLWR:       Converts string to lowercase
;
```

(continued)

Figure 5-4. *continued*

```
; Call with:    DS:SI = address of string
;               BX    = length of string
;
; Returns:      DS:SI = address of lowercase
;                       string in temporary storage
;               BX    = length of lowercase string
;
; Destroys:     Nothing

        public  strlwr
strlwr  proc    near

        push    di                      ; save registers
        push    es

        mov     di,seg lctab            ; ES:DI = address of
        mov     es,di                   ; lowercase translation table
        mov     di,offset lctab

        call    strxlt                  ; translate string

        pop     es                      ; restore registers
        pop     di
        ret                             ; back to caller

strlwr  endp


;
; STRUPR:       Converts string to uppercase
;
; Call with:    DS:SI = address of string
;               BX    = length of string
;
; Returns:      DS:SI = address of uppercase
;                       string in temporary storage
;               BX    = length of uppercase string
;
; Destroys:     Nothing

        public  strupr
strupr  proc    near

        push    di                      ; save registers
        push    es

        mov     di,seg uctab            ; ES:DI = address of
        mov     es,di                   ; uppercase translation table
        mov     di,offset uctab

        call    strxlt                  ; translate string
```

(continued)

Figure 5-4. *continued*

```
            pop     es                      ; restore registers
            pop     di
            ret                             ; back to caller

strupr  endp

;
; STRMEM:     Allocates temporary storage for string
;
; Call with:  BX    = length needed
;
; Returns:    ES:DI = address of temporary storage
;             BX    = length (unchanged)
;
; Destroys:   Nothing

strmem  proc    near

            mov     di,seg strptr           ; ES:DI = address within
            mov     es,di                   ; temporary string buffer
            assume  es:_DATA
            mov     di,strptr
            add     strptr,bx               ; update buffer pointer

                                            ; check for buffer overflow
            cmp     strptr,offset (strbuf+bufsize)
            jb      smem1                   ; jump if no overflow

            mov     di,offset strbuf        ; reset buffer pointer
            mov     strptr,di
            add     strptr,bx
            assume  es:NOTHING

smem1:  ret                                 ; back to caller

strmem  endp

_TEXT   ends

        end
```

Most of the public routines contained in STRINGS2.ASM utilize a building-block routine, STRMEM, which is not public. STRMEM allocates temporary storage for a result string, using a simple ring buffer strategy. When STRMEM is asked for a certain amount of storage, it returns the current pointer into the ring buffer and then increments the pointer by the specified size, wrapping the pointer when necessary. Any storage address obtained from STRMEM is eventually overwritten, the intervening length of time depending on the number of subsequent calls to STRMEM, the size of the ring buffer, and the size of the strings being placed in the buffer.

The simpleminded memory-allocation strategy used by STRMEM (and thus by all the routines in STRINGS2.ASM) is usually not a problem, because strings are typically being concatenated, extracted, or translated in order to build other strings and are then discarded. If, however, you plan to perform other string operations between the time you obtain a result string and the time you use it, you should probably copy it to some other buffer for safekeeping.

STRCAT is a general-purpose string concatenation routine that uses the following parameters:

DS:SI = string1 address
BX   = string1 length
ES:DI = string2 address
DX   = string2 length

The address and length of the result string are returned in registers DS:SI and BX, with ES:DI destroyed and the other registers and the original strings unchanged. For safety, be sure that the ring buffer used by STRMEM (whose size is defined by the equate *bufsize*) is at least four times as long as the longest string that will be passed to STRCAT.

STRDUP duplicates a string. Its arguments are the following:

DS:SI = string address
BX   = string length

It returns the address of a copy of the original string in registers DS:SI, with all other registers unchanged. Most of the other routines in STRINGS2 use STRDUP to create a copy of an argument string before altering it.

STRXTR extracts a substring. It has these parameters:

DS:SI = string address
BX   = string length
CX   = offset of substring
DX   = length of substring

It returns the address and length of the substring (which has been copied to temporary storage) in registers DS:SI and BX, with other registers unchanged. If the requested substring overruns the end of the original string, the returned length is reduced appropriately to return a true substring. Similarly, if the beginning offset of the requested substring lies outside the original string, a length of zero is returned.

STRXLT translates a string using a supplied character translation table. Its parameters are the following:

DS:SI = address of string to be translated
BX   = length of string to be translated
ES:DI = address of translation table

The format of the translation table (shown in the STRXLT routine in Figure 5-4, page 82) allows you to abbreviate the table to include only those codes you want to translate. STRXLT ignores any zero translation values in the table.

Here is a sample translation table that can be used to change all uppercase vowels to question marks, leaving all uppercase consonants and all lowercase letters, numbers, and oddball characters unchanged:

```
dw      26
dw      'A'
db      '?BCD?FGH?JKLMN?PQRST?VWX?Z'
```

(For purposes of illustration, we'll consider Y a vowel; no outraged letters, please.) STRXLT returns, predictably, the address and length of the translated string in registers DS:SI and BX, leaving the original string and other registers unchanged.

STRLWR translates a string to lowercase, and STRUPR translates a string to uppercase. Their arguments are the following:

DS:SI = address of string
BX   = length of string

Both routines work by calling STRXLT with the address of an appropriate translation table, and both return the address and length of the translated string in registers DS:SI and BX, with other registers and the original string unchanged. STRLWR is especially useful when you are making a fully qualified pathname (drive, path, filename, and extension) "pretty" for output.

MASM String Package #3

The listing STRINGS3.ASM (Figure 5-5) is the source code for our third and last package of string routines. It contains two public routines for case-insensitive string comparison and searching, STRCMPI and STRNDXI, and one building-block routine, STRUPR2. STRUPR2 is intended only for internal use within the package and is not public; therefore, it cannot be referenced from other modules.

```
;
; STRINGS3.ASM -- MASM String Package #3
;               contains routines STRCMPI and STRNDXI.
;
; Copyright (C) 1991 Ray Duncan

_TEXT   segment word public 'CODE'
```

Figure 5-5.   (continued)
STRINGS3.ASM, the source code for MASM string package #3.

Figure 5-5. *continued*

```
        extrn   strcmp:near             ; from STRINGS1
        extrn   strndx:near             ; from STRINGS1
        extrn   strupr:near             ; from STRINGS2

        assume  cs:_TEXT


;
; STRCMPI:      Case-insensitive string comparison
;
; Call with:    DS:SI = address of string1
;               BX    = length of string1
;               ES:DI = address of string2
;               DX    = length of string2
;
; Returns:      Z     = true  if strings are equal
;               or
;               Z     = false if strings are not equal, and
;               S     = true  if string1 < string2
;               S     = false if string1 > string2
;
; Destroys:     Nothing
;
        public  strcmpi
strcmpi proc    near

        push    bx                      ; save registers
        push    cx
        push    dx
        push    si
        push    di
        push    ds
        push    es

        call    strupr2                 ; translate both strings
                                        ; to uppercase

        call    strcmp                  ; compare uppercase strings

        pop     es                      ; restore registers
        pop     ds
        pop     di
        pop     si
        pop     dx
        pop     cx
        pop     bx
        ret                             ; return S and Z flags

strcmpi endp
```

(continued)

Figure 5-5. *continued*

```
;
; STRNDXI:      Case-insensitive string search
;
; Call with:    DS:SI = pattern address
;               BX    = pattern length
;               ES:DI = address of string to be searched
;               DX    = length of string to be searched
;
; Returns:      CY    = true if no match
;               ES:DI = unchanged
;               or
;               CY    = false if match, and
;               ES:DI = pointer to match for pattern
;                       string within searched string
;
; Destroys:     Nothing
;
        public  strndxi
strndxi proc    near

        push    ax                      ; save registers
        push    bx
        push    cx
        push    dx
        push    si
        push    di
        push    bp
        push    ds
        push    es

        call    strupr2                 ; translate both strings
                                        ; to uppercase

        push    di                      ; save offset of duplicate
                                        ; string to be searched

        call    strndx                  ; search uppercase string

        jc      sndx3                   ; jump, no match found

        pop     bx                      ; match found, calculate neg
        sub     bx,di                   ; offset in duplicate string

        pop     es                      ; restore registers and
        pop     ds                      ; let ES:DI = offset of
        pop     bp                      ; match in original string
        pop     di
        sub     di,bx
        pop     si
        pop     dx
```

(continued)

Figure 5-5. *continued*

```
        pop     cx
        pop     bx
        pop     ax
        clc                             ; return carry = false
        ret

sndx3:  pop     di                      ; no match found, discard
                                        ; address of duplicate

        pop     es                      ; restore registers
        pop     ds
        pop     bp
        pop     di
        pop     si
        pop     dx
        pop     cx
        pop     bx
        pop     ax
        ret                             ; return carry = true

strndxi endp

;
; STRUPR2:      Duplicates two strings and translates
;               the duplicates to uppercase
;
; Call with:    DS:SI = string1 address
;               BX    = string1 length
;               ES:DI = string2 address
;               DX    = string2 length
;
; Returns:      DS:SI = address of uppercase string1
;                       in temporary storage
;               BX    = string1 length
;               ES:DI = address of uppercase string2
;                       in temporary storage
;               DX    = string2 length
;
; Destroys:     Nothing
;

strupr2 proc    near

        push    ds                      ; save address and length
        push    si                      ; of string1
        push    bx

        push    es                      ; get address and length
        push    di                      ; of string2 for strdup
        push    dx
        pop     bx
```

(continued)

Figure 5-5. *continued*

```
        pop     si
        pop     ds

        call    strupr                  ; duplicate string2 and
                                        ; translate to uppercase

        push    ds                      ; save address and length
        push    si                      ; of string2 copy
        push    bx
        pop     dx
        pop     di
        pop     es

        pop     bx                      ; restore address and
        pop     si                      ; length of string1
        pop     ds

        call    strupr                  ; duplicate string1 and
                                        ; translate to uppercase

        ret                             ; return to caller

strupr2 endp

_TEXT   ends

        end
```

STRCMPI is a case-insensitive string comparison routine with these parameters:

    DS:SI = string1 address
    BX   = string1 length
    ES:DI = string2 address
    DX   = string2 length

The result of the comparison is determined by the first nonequal character in the strings, ignoring case for the characters A–Z and a–z. If the first differing character in *string1* is less than the character in *string2*, then *string1* is less than *string2*. If the strings are of different lengths but contain identical characters up to the end of the shorter string, then the shorter string is less than the longer string. For example:

    "ABC" is less than "ABD"
    "ABC" is less than "ABCD"
    "abc" is equal to "ABC"
    "abc" is less than "ABCD"

The results of STRCMPI are returned in the CPU's zero and sign flags, the same way they are in the routine STRCMP:

> if string1 = string2, Z = true
> if string1 < string2, Z = false and S = true
> if string1 > string2, Z = false and S = false

Thus, after calling STRCMPI to compare two strings, a program can test the results by executing a conditional jump (such as JL, JE, or JG), exactly as it would after comparing two bytes or words. STRCMPI preserves all registers and the original strings.

STRNDXI is a case-insensitive string search routine with these arguments:

> DS:SI = pattern string address
> BX   = pattern string length
> ES:DI = text string address
> DX   = text string length

Because STRNDXI searches the text string for the first occurrence of the complete pattern string, the pattern string should be shorter than the text string. Case is ignored for the characters A–Z and a–z. All of the following cases would find a match:

> pattern = "def", text string = "ABCDEFGHI"
> pattern = "DEF", text string = "ABCDEFGHI"
> pattern = "DEF", text string = "abcdefghi"

If no match is found, STRNDXI returns the carry flag true (1). If a match is found, STRNDXI returns the carry flag false (0), with ES:DI pointing to the first character of the matching sequence within the string being searched. The other registers, as well as the original strings, are unchanged.

The building-block routine STRUPR2, which is called both by STRCMPI and by STRNDXI, duplicates the two argument strings and folds the lowercase characters in both strings to uppercase. STRCMPI and STRNDXI then simply call the original STRCMP and STRNDX routines (in STRINGS1.ASM) and pass the results back to the original caller. Of course, the overhead of character copying and translating causes STRCMPI and STRNDXI to be much slower than their case-sensitive counterparts STRCMP and STRNDX.

WARNING: In its present form, STRUPR2 calls STRDUP (from STRINGS2.ASM) to make the string duplicates. Thus, the length of the strings STRCMPI and STRNDXI can handle is governed by the size of the ring buffer in STRINGS2.ASM (unlike STRCMP and STRNDX, which search or compare strings in place). To compare or search strings longer than 255 bytes, you must modify the buffer size in STRINGS2.ASM or rewrite STRUPR2 to allocate its memory from a local heap (discussed in Chapter 11) or from the operating system's global heap (by calling MS-DOS Int 21H Function 48H).

Studying STRCMPI and STRNDXI should help to convince you of the benefits of modular, structured MASM programming. As you began this chapter, writing a case-insensitive string compare or string search routine that left the original strings un-altered might have seemed like a tiresome and messy assignment. But as you can see now, the job is almost trivial if the proper building blocks are in place. Once you have case-sensitive compare and search routines, string duplication, and string translation routines in hand (each of which is small enough to be easily compre-hended), you must simply put them together in the right order.

The dependency relationships that exist among the various string functions are sum-marized graphically in Figure 5-6.

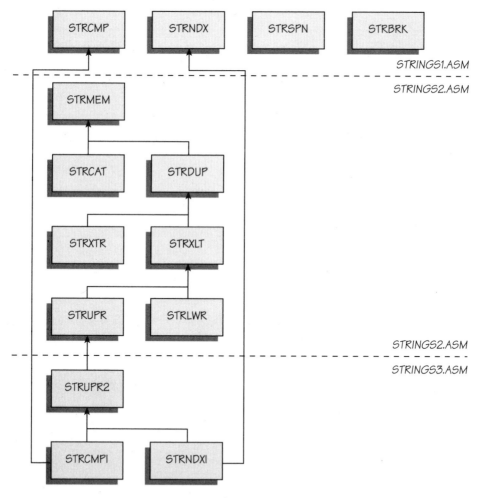

Figure 5-6.
Dependency relationships among the various string functions presented in this chapter.

PROCEDURES INTRODUCED IN THIS CHAPTER

Procedure Name	Action	Parameters	Results
STRBRK	Searches for first instance of character from list	DS:SI = segment:offset of string to be searched BX = length of string to be searched ES:DI = segment:offset of list of characters to be searched for DX = length of character search list	If matching character found: Carry flag = true DS:SI = segment:offset of matched character within searched string If no matching character found: Carry flag = false
STRCAT	Concatenates two strings	DS:SI = segment:offset of *string1* BX = length of *string1* ES:DI = segment:offset of *string2* DX = length of *string2*	DS:SI = segment:offset of result string BX = length of result string
STRCMP	Compares strings (case sensitive)	DS:SI = segment:offset of *string1* BX = length of *string1* ES:DI = segment:offset of *string2* DX = length of *string2*	If strings are equal: Zero flag = true If strings are not equal: Zero flag = false Sign flag = true if *string1* < *string2*, false if *string1* > *string2*
STRCMPI	Compares strings (case insensitive)	Same as STRCMP	Same as STRCMP
STRDUP	Duplicates string	DS:SI = segment:offset of original string BX = length of original string	DS:SI = segment:offset of duplicate string BX = length of duplicate string
STRLWR	Folds string to lowercase	DS:SI = segment:offset of original string BX = length of original string	DS:SI = segment:offset of lowercase string BX = length of lowercase string

(continued)

PROCEDURES INTRODUCED IN THIS CHAPTER *continued*

Procedure Name	Action	Parameters	Results
STRNDX	Searches string for pattern (case sensitive)	DS:SI = segment:offset of pattern BX = length of pattern ES:DI = segment:offset of string to be searched DX = length of string to be searched	If match found: Carry flag = false ES:DI = segment:offset of match within searched string If no match found: Carry flag = true
STRNDXI	Searches string for pattern (case insensitive)	Same as STRNDX	Same as STRNDX
STRSPN	Validates string	DS:SI = segment:offset of string to be validated BX = length of string to be validated ES:DI = segment:offset of validation character string DX = length of validation character string	If string is valid: Carry flag = false If string is not valid: Carry flag = true DS:SI = segment:offset of first invalid character within string being validated
STRUPR	Folds string to uppercase	DS:SI = segment:offset of original string BX = length of original string	DS:SI = segment:offset of uppercase string BX = length of uppercase string
STRXLT	Translates string	DS:SI = segment:offset of original string BX = length of original string ES:DI = segment:offset of translation table	DS:SI = segment:offset of translated result string BX = length of translated result string ES:DI = segment:offset of translation table
STRXTR	Extracts substring from string	DS:SI = segment:offset of original string BX = length of original string CX = offset of substring DX = length of substring	DS:SI = segment:offset of extracted string BX = length of extracted string

Companion Disk

The companion disk directory \CH05 contains the programs and modules that are listed below.

Routines Presented in This Chapter

STRINGS1.ASM   MASM string package #1

STRINGS2.ASM   MASM string package #2

STRINGS3.ASM   MASM string package #3

Routine Previously Discussed

ITOH.ASM   Converts a single-precision (16-bit) unsigned integer to a hexadecimal ASCII string

Demonstration Programs

TRYSTR1   MAKE file for TRYSTR1.EXE

TRYSTR1.ASM   Interactive demonstration program

TRYSTR2   MAKE file for TRYSTR2.EXE

TRYSTR2.ASM   Interactive demonstration program

TRYSTR3   MAKE file for TRYSTR3.EXE

TRYSTR3.ASM   Interactive demonstration program

TRYSTR4   MAKE file for TRYSTR4.EXE

TRYSTR4.ASM   Noninteractive demonstration program

The interactive program TRYSTR1.ASM demonstrates use of the routines STRNDX, STRCMP, STRSPN, and STRBRK in module STRINGS1.ASM. To build TRYSTR1.EXE, enter this command:

```
C>MAKE TRYSTR1   <Enter>
```

When you run TRYSTR1.EXE, it prompts you for two strings and then calls the string compare, search, validation, and delimiter routines. It displays the resulting state of the CPU flags for each routine, as well as the offset of the matched string for STRNDX and the offset of the first invalid character or delimiter for STRSPN and STRBRK, respectively.

Because the four string routines have different uses, you should concentrate on one string operation at a time when experimenting with TRYSTR1.EXE, ignoring the results returned by the other three. Remember that the displayed values for registers SI or DI might or might not be meaningful, depending on the value of the carry flag. To end the demo program, press the Enter key in response to the prompt.

The interactive program TRYSTR2.ASM demonstrates use of the routines STRCAT, STRLWR, and STRUPR in module STRINGS2.ASM. To build TRYSTR2.EXE, enter this command:

```
C>MAKE TRYSTR2  <Enter>
```

When you run TRYSTR2.EXE, it prompts you for two strings, concatenates them, and then displays the concatenated string as well as the uppercase and lowercase versions of the same string. To exit the demonstration program, press the Enter key at any prompt.

The interactive program TRYSTR3.ASM demonstrates use of the routines STRNDXI and STRCMPI in module STRINGS3.ASM. To build TRYSTR3.EXE, enter the following command:

```
C>MAKE TRYSTR3  <Enter>
```

When you run TRYSTR3.EXE, it first prompts you for two strings, then calls the case-insensitive string compare and search routines, and finally displays the resulting state of the carry and zero flags, as well as the offset of the matched string (if any) in the case of STRNDXI.

Because STRCMPI and STRNDXI have different uses, you should concentrate on one of them at a time when using the TRYSTR3.EXE demo program, ignoring the results returned for the other. It takes a fairly unusual pair of strings to get useful information from both functions at the same time!

The noninteractive program TRYSTR4.ASM demonstrates use of the STRXTR routine in module STRINGS2.ASM. To build TRYSTR4.EXE, enter this command:

```
C>MAKE TRYSTR4  <Enter>
```

When you run TRYSTR4.EXE, it performs five string extraction operations on a text string consisting of the entire alphabet and displays the results of each operation. Examining the source code of TRYSTR4 as well as the actual output of the program makes the use of STRXTR easier to understand.

6

Times and Dates

The previous two chapters covered the basic principles of numeric conversion and string handling. Now let's apply these principles to a somewhat more complex task: the conversion and formatting of times and dates. It's worth examining this programming problem in detail because times and dates, which consist of multiple fields separated by special delimiter characters, are typical of the special input and output needs you encounter in real-world applications. Time and date formatting also provides a convenient venue for a brief discussion of internationalization.

MS-DOS Binary Time and Date Formats

Application programs run under MS-DOS must be able to handle the two distinct representations of times and dates used by that operating system. We can refer to these representations as the 4-byte formats and the 2-byte formats. The 4-byte formats for time or date are used by the MS-DOS function calls that deal directly with the system's real-time clock driver:

Int 21H Function 2AH	Get System Date
Int 21H Function 2BH	Set System Date
Int 21H Function 2CH	Get System Time
Int 21H Function 2DH	Set System Time

The 4-byte formats are easy to work with because each element of the time or date is stored in 1 or 2 complete bytes, with no need for shifts or masking of bits. (See Figure 6-1 on the next page.) Although the 4-byte time format allows an accuracy of hundredths of seconds, the real-time clocks of most MS-DOS systems do not maintain time to this resolution. For example, on IBM PCs and compatibles, the clock frequency is 18.2 Hz—that is, the highest resolution to which you can measure elapsed time without a great deal of extra effort is approximately 0.055 seconds.

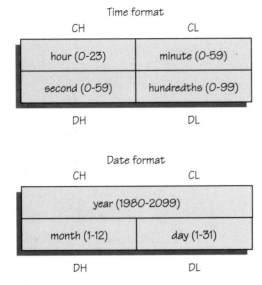

Figure 6-1.
The 4-byte time and date formats used by Int 21H Functions 2AH through 2DH. These system services accept arguments or return results in registers CX and DX.

The 2-byte formats for time or date are used by MS-DOS principally in disk directories and are provided to application programs in connection with certain directory-related file management functions:

Int 21H Function 0FH	Open File with FCB
Int 21H Function 11H	Search for First File
Int 21H Function 12H	Search for Next File
Int 21H Function 16H	Create File with FCB
Int 21H Function 4EH	Search for First File
Int 21H Function 4FH	Search for Next File
Int 21H Function 57H	Get/Set File Date and Time

The 2-byte formats pack the time and date into bit fields, which must be shifted and masked with AND operations to access the information. (See Figure 6-2.) In the case of the 2-byte format for time, some information is lost: Seconds are stored only in units of two, and information about hundredths of seconds is not maintained.

Time format

bits 0BH-0FH = hours (0-23)
bits 05H-0AH = minutes (0-59)
bits 00H-04H = two-second increments (0-29)

Date format

bits 09H-0FH = year (relative to 1980)
bits 05H-08H = month (1-12)
bits 00H-04H = day (1-31)

Figure 6-2.
*The 2-byte time and date formats found in directory entries and file control
blocks. They are used by various directory-related Int 21H functions.*

Other Time and Date Formats

Two other time and date formats are used internally by MS-DOS and the ROM
BIOS. The first format, which is 6 bytes long, is peculiar to the operating system's real-time clock driver (CLOCK$) and is encountered only when that
driver is opened by name and read or written directly. The second format,
which represents the time and date as the cumulative number of seconds
elapsed since an arbitrary time and date, is used only by the ROM BIOS's Int
1AH timer interface. Application programs do not ordinarily encounter either
of these special formats.

Internationalization Support

MS-DOS's internationalization support consists of Int 21H function calls that return
tables of formatting information specific to the country in which MS-DOS is being
used: Int 21H Function 38H (Get or Set Current Country) or Int 21H Function 65H
(Get Extended Country Information). The operation of these functions is controlled

by the COUNTRY= directive in the system's CONFIG.SYS file or, if the COUNTRY= directive is absent, by the OEM's selection of a default country. Although the binary 2-byte and 4-byte time and date formats are common to all versions of MS-DOS, a program can use the internationalization support functions to adapt its display of times and dates to the needs and language of the end user.

Int 21H Function 38H, Get or Set Current Country, is available in MS-DOS versions 2.0 and later. It returns a data structure that includes date and time format codes, a currency symbol, and separator characters for time, date, and decimal points. Unfortunately, this service was only partially implemented in PC-DOS versions 2.0 and 2.1, and the layout of the information provided to the program under PC-DOS 2.x is not the same as it is under MS-DOS versions 2.1 and later and PC-DOS versions 3.0 and later. (See Figures 6-3 and 6-4.) Int 21H Function 65H, Get Extended Country Information, was added to PC-DOS and MS-DOS in version 3.3; it returns a superset of the information provided by Int 21H Function 38H. In order to be executable on the widest possible range of MS-DOS systems, the programs in this chapter will use Int 21H Function 38H only.

Adding internationalization support to your programs is tedious, but it is well worth the effort, especially if you are developing a commercial product. The U.S. market is not infinitely large, and the competition in most niches is fierce and growing stronger. In contrast, many markets in other countries are still relatively open. A little time invested in internationalization support might increase your share of such markets considerably.

But it's also a matter of simple courtesy. Think of European users, for example, who are accustomed to typing dates with the day first and the month second. If those users need your product badly enough, they'll buy it even without internationalization support—but they'll be constantly annoyed by incorrectly entered dates that are rejected and require re-entry or that slip by validity checks but have the month and day interchanged.

Offset	Length	Description
0	2	date format
		0 = USA mdy
		1 = Europe dmy
		2 = Japan ymd
2	2	ASCIIZ currency symbol character
4	2	ASCIIZ thousands separator character
6	2	ASCIIZ decimal separator character
8	24	reserved

Figure 6-3.
The internationalization information returned by Int 21H Function 38H under PC-DOS 2.x.

Offset	Length	Description
0	2	date format *0 = USA mdy* *1 = Europe dmy* *2 = Japan ymd*
2	5	ASCIIZ currency symbol string
7	2	ASCIIZ thousands separator character
9	2	ASCIIZ decimal separator character
0BH	2	ASCIIZ date separator character
0DH	2	ASCIIZ time separator character
0FH	1	currency format *bit 0 = 0 if currency symbol precedes value* * = 1 if currency symbol follows value* *bit 1 = 0 if no space between value and currency symbol* * = 1 if one space between value and currency symbol*
10H	1	number of digits after decimal in currency
11H	1	time format *bit 0 = 0 if 12-hour clock* * = 1 if 24-hour clock*
12H	4	far pointer to case-map routine
16H	2	ASCIIZ data-list separator
18H	10	reserved

Figure 6-4.

The internationalization information returned by Int 21H Function 38H under PC-DOS 3.x and MS-DOS versions 2.1 and later. The "case-map call address" is the segment and offset of a procedure that performs country-specific lowercase-to-uppercase mapping on character values from 80H through 0FFH.

Converting Binary Times and Dates to ASCII

The module TD.ASM (Figure 6-5 on the following page) contains six time and date formatting routines that can be called from your program:

SYSDCVT	Converts current system date to ASCII string
SYSTCVT	Converts current system time to ASCII string
DIRDCVT	Converts date in 2-byte directory format to ASCII string
DIRTCVT	Converts time in 2-byte directory format to ASCII string
DCVT	Converts date in 4-byte binary format to ASCII string
TCVT	Converts time in 4-byte binary format to ASCII string

All of these routines accept the address and length of a buffer in registers DS:SI and the length of the buffer in register BX. Time or date information is supplied in registers CX and DX for the routines that use the 4-byte format or in register AX for the 2-byte data formats. The time or date is converted to an ASCII string in a format determined by the country designation and is left in the calling routine's buffer.

```
;
; TD.ASM -- Time and date output formatting functions.
;
; Copyright (C) 1991 Ray Duncan

DGROUP  group   _DATA

_DATA   segment word public 'DATA'

cbuff   db      34 dup (0)              ; current country info
dbuff   db      8  dup (' ')           ; date formatting buffer
tbuff   db      11 dup (' ')           ; time formatting buffer

                                       ; filled in by GETCTRY
doffs   dw      0                      ; offset of ASCII day
moffs   dw      0                      ; offset of ASCII month
yoffs   dw      0                      ; offset of ASCII year

                                       ; date format determined
                                       ; by int 21h fxn 38h
dtab    dw      mdy                    ; 0 = USA format
        dw      dmy                    ; 1 = Europe format
        dw      ymd                    ; 2 = Japan format

mdy     dw      dbuff+3                ; USA: month day year
        dw      dbuff
        dw      dbuff+6

dmy     dw      dbuff                  ; Europe: day month year
        dw      dbuff+3
        dw      dbuff+6

ymd     dw      dbuff+6                ; Japan: year month day
        dw      dbuff+3
        dw      dbuff

_DATA   ends

_TEXT   segment word public 'CODE'

        assume  cs:_TEXT,ds:DGROUP
```

Figure 6-5.   *(continued)*

TD.ASM, routines that convert binary times and dates to ASCII strings.

Figure 6-5. *continued*

```
;
; SYSDCVT:      Formats current system date
;
; Call with:    BX    = length of result string (max = 8)
;               DS:SI = address for result string
;
; Returns:      Nothing
;
; Destroys:     Nothing
;
        public  sysdcvt
sysdcvt proc    near

        push    ax                      ; save registers
        push    bx
        push    cx
        push    dx

        mov     ah,2ah                  ; fxn 2ah = get date
        int     21h                     ; transfer to MS-DOS

        call    dcvt                    ; convert date to ASCII

        pop     dx                      ; restore registers
        pop     cx
        pop     bx
        pop     ax
        ret                             ; back to caller

sysdcvt endp

;
; SYSTCVT:      Formats current system time
;
; Call with:    BX    = length of result string (max = 11)
;               DS:SI = address for result string
;
; Returns:      Nothing
;
; Destroys:     Nothing
;
        public  systcvt
systcvt proc    near

        push    ax                      ; save registers
        push    bx
        push    cx
        push    dx
```

(continued)

Figure 6-5. *continued*

```
        mov     ah,2ch                  ; fxn 2ch = get time
        int     21h                     ; transfer to MS-DOS

        call    tcvt                    ; convert time to ASCII

        pop     dx                      ; restore registers
        pop     cx
        pop     bx
        pop     ax
        ret                             ; back to caller

systcvt endp


;
; DIRDCVT:      Formats directory date
;
; Call with:    AX    = directory date
;               BX    = length of result string (max = 8)
;               DS:SI = address for result string
;
; Returns:      Nothing
;
; Destroys:     Nothing
;
        public  dirdcvt
dirdcvt proc    near

        push    ax                      ; save registers
        push    bx
        push    cx
        push    dx

        mov     dx,ax                   ; isolate months and days
        and     dx,01ffh
        mov     cl,3                    ; position month
        shl     dx,cl
        shr     dl,cl                   ; position day

        mov     cl,9                    ; position year
        shr     ax,cl
        add     ax,1980
        mov     cx,ax

        call    dcvt                    ; convert date to ASCII

        pop     dx                      ; restore registers
        pop     cx
        pop     bx
```

(continued)

Figure 6-5. *continued*

```
        pop     ax
        ret                             ; back to caller

dirdcvt endp

;
; DIRTCVT:      Formats directory time
;
; Call with:    AX   = directory time
;               BX   = length of result string (max = 11)
;               DS:SI = address for result string
;
; Returns:      Nothing
;
; Destroys:     Nothing
;
        public  dirtcvt
dirtcvt proc    near

        push    ax                      ; save registers
        push    bx
        push    cx
        push    dx

        mov     dx,ax                   ; isolate seconds field
        and     dx,1fh                  ; and position it
        mov     cl,9                    ; (includes seconds * 2)
        shl     dx,cl

        mov     cl,3                    ; position hours
        shr     ax,cl

        mov     cl,2                    ; position minutes
        shr     al,cl
        mov     cx,ax

        call    tcvt                    ; convert to ASCII

        pop     dx                      ; restore registers
        pop     cx
        pop     bx
        pop     ax
        ret                             ; back to caller

dirtcvt endp

;
; DCVT:         Formats ASCII date
;
```

(continued)

Figure 6-5. *continued*

```
; Call with:    BX    = length of result string (max = 8)
;               CX    = year (1980+)
;               DH    = month (1-12)
;               DL    = day (1-31)
;               DS:SI = address for result string
;
; Returns:      Nothing
;
; Destroys:     AX, BX, CX, DX
;
        public  dcvt
dcvt    proc    near

        cmp     bx,8                    ; be sure requested length
        jle     dcvt1                   ; is OK
        mov     bx,8                    ; too long, use 8 max

dcvt1:  push    es                      ; save registers
        push    di
        push    si
        push    bx

        call    getctry                 ; get country information

        mov     si,moffs                ; convert month to ASCII
        mov     al,dh
        call    b2dec

        mov     si,doffs                ; convert day to ASCII
        mov     al,dl
        call    b2dec

        mov     si,yoffs                ; convert year, corrected to
        sub     cx,1900                 ; range 80-99, to ASCII
        mov     al,cl
        call    b2dec

        mov     ax,ds                   ; transfer ASCII date string
        mov     es,ax                   ; to caller's buffer
        mov     si,offset DGROUP:dbuff
        pop     cx                      ; buffer length
        pop     di                      ; buffer address
        push    di
        rep movsb                       ; copy string

        pop     si                      ; restore registers
        pop     di
        pop     es
        ret                             ; return to caller
```

(continued)

Figure 6-5. *continued*

```
dcvt    endp

;
; TCVT:         Formats ASCII time
;
; Call with:    BX    = length of result string (max = 11)
;               CH    = hour
;               CL    = minute
;               DH    = second
;               DL    = hundredths of seconds
;               DS:SI = address for result string
;
; Returns:      Nothing
;
; Destroys:     AX, BX, CX, DX
;
        public  tcvt
tcvt    proc    near

        cmp     bx,11                   ; be sure requested length
        jle     tcvt1                   ; is OK
        mov     bx,11                   ; too long, use 11 max

tcvt1:  push    es                      ; save registers
        push    di
        push    si
        push    bx

        call    getctry                 ; get country information

        mov     al,ch                   ; convert hours to ASCII
        mov     si,offset DGROUP:tbuff
        call    b2dec

        mov     al,cl                   ; convert minutes to ASCII
        add     si,3
        call    b2dec

        mov     al,dh                   ; convert seconds to ASCII
        add     si,3
        call    b2dec

        mov     al,dl                   ; convert hundredths to ASCII
        add     si,3
        call    b2dec

        mov     ax,ds                   ; transfer ASCII time string
        mov     es,ax                   ; to caller's buffer
        mov     si,offset DGROUP:tbuff  ; source buffer address
        pop     cx                      ; buffer length
```

(continued)

Figure 6-5. *continued*

```
        pop     di                      ; destination buffer address
        push    di
        rep movsb                       ; copy string

        pop     si                      ; restore registers
        pop     di
        pop     es
        ret                             ; return to caller

tcvt    endp

;
; B2DEC:        Converts binary 0-99 to two ASCII digits
;
; Call with:    AL    = value
;               DS:SI = storage address
;
; Returns:      Nothing
;
; Destroys:     AX
;
b2dec   proc    near

        aam                             ; divide AL by 10 ->
                                        ; AH = quot, AL = rem
        add     ax,'00'                 ; convert to ASCII chars
        xchg    ah,al
        mov     [si],ax                 ; and store digits
        ret                             ; back to caller

b2dec   endp

;
; GETCTRY:      Gets country information from MS-DOS
;
; Call with:    Nothing
;
; Returns:      Nothing in registers, sets local variables
;
; Destroys:     Nothing
;
getctry proc    near

        test    doffs,-1                ; did we already get info?
        jnz     getc4                   ; if we did, just exit

        push    ax                      ; save registers
        push    bx                      ; (in case destroyed by
        push    cx                      ; int 21h fxn 38h)
        push    dx
```

(continued)

Figure 6-5. *continued*

```
        mov     ax,3000h                ; fxn 30h = get MS-DOS version
        int     21h                     ; transfer to MS-DOS

        or      al,al                   ; is this MS-DOS version 1.x?
        jz      getc1                   ; yes, jump
        push    ax                      ; no, save MS-DOS version

        mov     ax,3800h                ; get current country info
        mov     dx,offset DGROUP:cbuff
        int     21h                     ; transfer to MS-DOS

        pop     ax                      ; restore MS-DOS version
        jc      getc1                   ; jump if get country failed

        cmp     al,3                    ; is this MS-DOS version 3.x?
        jne     getc2                   ; jump if version 2

                                        ; no, it's MS-DOS version 3
        mov     al,cbuff+9              ; get decimal separator
        mov     bh,cbuff+11            ; get date separator
        mov     bl,cbuff+13            ; get time separator
        jmp     getc3

getc1:                                  ; MS-DOS version 1.x, or get
                                        ; country info function failed
        mov     word ptr cbuff,0       ; force date format = mdy

getc2:                                  ; versions 1.x and 2.x
        mov     al,'.'                  ; force decimal separator
        mov     bh,'/'                  ; force date separator
        mov     bl,':'                  ; force time separator

getc3:  mov     tbuff+8,al             ; store decimal separator
        mov     tbuff+2,bl             ; store time separator
        mov     tbuff+5,bl
        mov     dbuff+2,bh             ; store date separator
        mov     dbuff+5,bh

                                        ; set date field offsets
        mov     bx,word ptr cbuff      ; using country information
        shl     bx,1                    ; date code * 2 = table index
        mov     bx,[bx+dtab]
        mov     ax,[bx]                 ; offset for ASCII day
        mov     doffs,ax
        mov     ax,[bx+2]               ; offset for ASCII month
        mov     moffs,ax
        mov     ax,[bx+4]               ; offset for ASCII year
        mov     yoffs,ax

        pop     dx                      ; restore registers
```

(continued)

Figure 6-5. *continued*

```
        pop     cx
        pop     bx
        pop     ax

getc4:  ret                             ; back to caller

getctry endp

_TEXT   ends

        end
```

The formatted time string returned by the TCVT, SYSTCVT, and DIRTCVT functions takes this form (with *dd* as hundredths of seconds):

hh:mm:ss.dd

The maximum length of the returned string is always 11 characters, regardless of the length specified by the calling program. The calling program can, however, specify a shorter length if it doesn't need all of the time fields. (For example, a program can specify a length of 5 characters to display hours and minutes only.) If Int 21H Function 38H is available, the colons and the period in the format are replaced by the appropriate time and decimal delimiters for the current country.

The default format for the date strings created by DCVT, SYSDCVT, and DIRDCVT is the *mdy* (month-day-year) format:

mm-dd-yy

When internationalization information is available from Int 21H Function 38H, the country-specific delimiter is used instead of hyphens, and the date format is adapted to the current country. The date takes the form *dmy* (day-month-year) for European users or *ymd* (year-month-day) for Japanese users.

Here is an example of a call to the SYSDCVT function to format the current date, followed by a call to MS-DOS to display the current date on the console:

```
stdout  equ     1                       ; standard output handle
        .
        .
        .
msg1    db      'The date is: '         ; static part of message
msg2    db      '           '           ; receives formatted date
m2len   equ     $-msg2                  ; length of format buffer
m1len   equ     $-msg1                  ; length of entire message
        .
        .
        .
        mov     si,seg msg2             ; DS:SI = address of buffer
```

```
mov     ds,si
mov     si,offset msg2
mov     bx,m2len              ; BX = length of buffer
call    SYSDCVT              ; format current date

mov     dx,offset msg1       ; DS:DX = message address
mov     cx,m1len             ; CX = message length
mov     bx,stdout            ; BX = std output handle
mov     ah,40h               ; fxn 40h = write
int     21h                  ; transfer to MS-DOS
```

The other time and date formatting functions are invoked similarly. The parameters and results for each function are documented in the source code listing.

Inside the TD.ASM Module

The lowest-level routine in the TD.ASM module is GETCTRY, which is called by all the other routines to obtain internationalization information from MS-DOS. The GETCTRY routine pokes the time, date, and decimal delimiters into the buffers used to build the ASCII time and date strings. It also sets up a table of offsets determining where the ASCII representations of the day, month, and year will be stored. If Int 21H Function 38H is not available (MS-DOS versions 1.x) or is only partially implemented (MS-DOS versions 2.x), GETCTRY substitutes reasonable default values for the information the system does not supply.

The routines that do all the formatting work are DCVT (converts the date to an ASCII string) and TCVT (converts the time to an ASCII string). They both use a small helper routine called B2DEC to convert binary values in the range 0 through 99 into 2 ASCII bytes. The full time and date strings are built up in a local buffer, and then the length supplied in register BX—clamped to a maximum of 11 characters for times or 8 characters for dates—determines how much of the formatted string is copied back to the caller's buffer.

The routines SYSDCVT and SYSTCVT are simple. They first call the system function Get Date (Int 21H Function 2AH) or Get Time (Int 21H Function 2CH) and then use DCVT or TCVT to convert the results of these calls to ASCII. Similarly, the routines DIRDCVT and DIRTCVT—whose arguments are dates or times in the 2-byte directory format—merely use shifts and logical AND operations to convert the directory bit fields into the 4-byte date or time format before calling DCVT or TCVT.

Converting ASCII Times and Dates to Binary

Now that you have a battery of routines to convert binary times and dates to ASCII, you also need routines to perform the converse operations. Accordingly, the module SCANTD.ASM (Figure 6-6 on the following page) contains two procedures:

SCANTIME	Converts ASCII time to 4-byte binary format
SCANDATE	Converts ASCII date to 4-byte binary format

As you might expect, SCANTIME converts an ASCII string of the form

hh:mm:ss

to a binary time. (The seconds field shown here is optional.) SCANDATE converts an ASCII string of the form

mm/dd/yy

to a binary date. SCANTIME and SCANDATE perform a moderate amount of validation on the strings they process, ensuring that all necessary fields are present and separated by appropriate delimiters and that each field has a reasonable value.

```
;
; SCANTD.ASM -- Time and date input conversion functions.
;
; Copyright (C) 1991 Ray Duncan

DGROUP  group   _DATA

_DATA   segment word public 'DATA'

                                        ; working variables
n1          dw      0                   ; first converted field
n2          dw      0                   ; second converted field
n3          dw      0                   ; third converted field

dlmtab      db      '/-.'               ; valid date delimiters
dlmtab_len  equ $-dlmtab               ; length of table

tlmtab      db      ':.'               ; valid time delimiters
tlmtab_len  equ $-tlmtab               ; length of table

                                        ; date format table
dftab       dw      mdy                 ; code 0 = mon/day/year
            dw      dmy                 ; code 1 = day/mon/year
            dw      ymd                 ; code 2 = year/mon/day

dfptr       dw      0                   ; becomes address of
                                        ; mdy, dmy, or ymd

mdy         dw      n2                  ; day
            dw      n1                  ; month
            dw      n3                  ; year

dmy         dw      n1                  ; day
            dw      n2                  ; month
            dw      n3                  ; year
```

Figure 6-6.   *(continued)*

SCANTD.ASM, routines that convert ASCII time and date strings to 4-byte binary format.

Figure 6-6. *continued*

```
ymd     dw      n3                      ; day
        dw      n2                      ; month
        dw      n1                      ; year

daytab  dw      31,28,31                ; days in month
        dw      30,31,30
        dw      31,31,30
        dw      31,30,31

cbuff   db      34 dup (0)              ; current country info

_DATA   ends

_TEXT   segment word public 'CODE'

        assume  cs:_TEXT,ds:DGROUP
        extrn   atoi:near

;
; SCANTIME:     Converts ASCII time to 4-byte binary format
;
; Call with:    DS:SI = address of string
;
; Returns:      Carry = set if bad time
;               or
;               Carry = clear if good time
;               CH    = hour
;               CL    = minute
;               DH    = second
;               DL    = hundredths
;               DS:SI = address + 1 of terminator
;
; Destroys:     Nothing
;
        public  scantime
scantime proc   near

        push    ax                      ; save registers
        push    bx
        push    di
        push    es

        call    getctry                 ; get country information

        call    chknum                  ; convert first field
        jc      scant9                  ; jump, bad number
        mov     n1,ax                   ; save result
```

(continued)

Figure 6-6. *continued*

```
        mov     al,[si-1]                   ; check time delimiter
        call    chktlm
        jc      scant9                      ; jump if no good

        call    chknum                      ; convert second field
        jc      scant9                      ; jump, bad number
        mov     n2,ax                       ; save result

        mov     n3,0                        ; force seconds = 0

        mov     al,[si-1]                   ; another field present?
        call    chktlm                      ; if no delimiter
        jc      scant1                      ; assume seconds are absent

        call    chknum                      ; convert third field
        jc      scant9                      ; jump, bad number
        mov     n3,ax                       ; save value

scant1:                                     ; now validate entry
        cmp     word ptr n1,0               ; hours must be 0-23
        jc      scant9                      ; jump, bad hour
        cmp     word ptr n1,24
        cmc
        jc      scant9                      ; jump, bad hour

        cmp     word ptr n2,0               ; minutes must be 0-59
        jc      scant9                      ; jump, bad minute
        cmp     word ptr n2,60
        cmc
        jc      scant9                      ; jump, bad minute

        cmp     word ptr n3,0               ; seconds must be 0-59
        jc      scant9                      ; jump, bad second
        cmp     word ptr n3,60
        cmc
        jc      scant9                      ; jump, bad second

                                            ; load results
        mov     ch,byte ptr n1              ; hours
        mov     cl,byte ptr n2              ; minutes
        mov     dh,byte ptr n3              ; seconds
        mov     dl,0                        ; hundredths always = 0

scant9:                                     ; common exit point
        pop     es                          ; restore registers
        pop     di
        pop     bx
        pop     ax
        ret                                 ; return to caller
```

(continued)

Figure 6-6. *continued*

```
scantime endp

;
; SCANDATE:      Converts ASCII date to 4-byte binary format
;
; Call with:     DS:SI = address of string
;
; Returns:       Carry = set if bad date
;                or
;                Carry = clear if good date
;                CX    = year (1980+)
;                DH    = month (1-12)
;                DL    = day (1-31)
;                DS:SI = address + 1 of terminator
;
; Destroys:      Nothing
;
        public  scandate
scandate proc   near

        push    ax                      ; save registers
        push    bx
        push    di
        push    es

        call    getctry                 ; get country information

        call    chknum                  ; convert first field
        jc      scand9                  ; jump, bad number
        mov     n1,ax                   ; save result

        mov     al,[si-1]               ; get first date delimiter
        call    chkdlm                  ; and check it
        jc      scand9                  ; exit, bad delimiter

        call    chknum                  ; convert second field
        jc      scand9                  ; jump, bad number
        mov     n2,ax                   ; save result

        mov     al,[si-1]               ; get second date delimiter
        call    chkdlm                  ; and check it
        jc      scand9                  ; exit, bad delimiter

        call    chknum                  ; convert third field
        jc      scand9                  ; jump, bad number
        mov     n3,ax                   ; and save result

                                        ; validate entry, load results
        mov     bx,dfptr                ; point to year
```

(continued)

Figure 6-6. *continued*

```
        mov     bx,[bx+4]               ; year must be 80-99
        cmp     word ptr [bx],80
        jc      scand9                  ; jump, bad year
        cmp     word ptr [bx],100
        cmc
        jc      scand9                  ; jump, bad year
        mov     cx,[bx]                 ; load year and correct
        add     cx,1900                 ; to range 1980-1999

                                        ; adjust days/month table
        mov     daytab+2,28             ; assume not leap year
        test    word ptr [bx],3         ; is it a leap year?
        jnz     scand1                  ; jump, not multiple of 4
        mov     daytab+2,29             ; fix table for leap year

scand1: mov     bx,dfptr                ; point to month
        mov     bx,[bx+2]
        cmp     word ptr [bx],1         ; month must be 1-12
        jc      scand9                  ; jump, bad month
        cmp     word ptr [bx],13
        cmc
        jc      scand9                  ; jump, bad month
        mov     dh,byte ptr [bx]        ; load month result
        mov     di,[bx]                 ; also prepare to index
        dec     di                      ; into days/month table
        shl     di,1

        mov     bx,dfptr                ; point to day
        mov     bx,[bx]
        cmp     word ptr [bx],1         ; day must be >= 1
        jc      scand9                  ; jump, bad day
        mov     ax,[di+daytab]          ; get max day for this month
        cmp     ax,[bx]                 ; from table, compare it
        jc      scand9                  ; jump, bad day
        mov     dl,byte ptr [bx]        ; load day result

scand9:                                 ; common exit point
        pop     es                      ; restore registers
        pop     di
        pop     bx
        pop     ax
        ret                             ; return to caller

scandate endp

;
; CHKDLM:       Checks date delimiter
;
; Call with:    AL   = character to check
;
```

(continued)

Figure 6-6. *continued*

```
; Returns:      Carry = clear if delimiter OK
;                  or
;               Carry = set if bad delimiter
;
; Destroys:     ES, DI, CX
;
chkdlm  proc    near

        push    ds                      ; make delimiter table
        pop     es                      ; addressable
        mov     di,offset DGROUP:dlmtab ; address of base of table
        mov     cx,dlmtab_len           ; length of table
        repne scasb                     ; compare delimiter to table
        je      chkd9                   ; jump if match found
                                        ; (carry is clear)
        stc                             ; else force carry = set
chkd9:  ret                             ; back to caller

chkdlm  endp


;
; CHKTLM:       Checks time delimiter
;
; Call with:    AL   = character to check
;
; Returns:      Carry = clear if delimiter OK
;                  or
;               Carry = set if bad delimiter
;
; Destroys:     ES, DI, CX
;
chktlm  proc    near

        push    ds                      ; make delimiter table
        pop     es                      ; addressable
        mov     di,offset DGROUP:tlmtab ; address of base of table
        mov     cx,tlmtab_len           ; length of table
        repne scasb                     ; compare delimiter to table
        je      chkt9                   ; jump if match found
                                        ; (carry is clear)
        stc                             ; else force carry = set
chkt9:  ret                             ; back to caller

chktlm  endp


;
; CHKNUM:       Checks for valid ASCII numeric field
;               and converts it to binary
;
```

(continued)

Figure 6-6. *continued*

```
; Call with:    DS:SI = address of ASCII numeric field
;
; Returns:      Carry = clear if field OK and
;               AX    = binary value of field
;               or
;               Carry = set if bad delimiter
;
; Destroys:     SI
;
chknum  proc    near

        cmp     byte ptr [si],'0'       ; check if >= '0'
        jb      chkn1                   ; jump, bad digit
        cmp     byte ptr [si],'9'+1     ; check if <= '9'
        cmc                             ; invert carry flag
        jc      chkn1                   ; jump, bad digit
        call    atoi                    ; convert ASCII field and
        clc                             ; clear carry flag
chkn1:  ret                             ; back to caller

chknum  endp

; GETCTRY:      Gets country information from MS-DOS
;
; Call with:    Nothing
;
; Returns:      Nothing in registers, sets local variables
;
; Destroys:     Nothing
;
getctry proc    near

        test    dfptr,-1                ; did we already get info?
        jnz     getc3                   ; if we did, just exit

        push    ax                      ; save registers
        push    bx                      ; (in case destroyed by
        push    cx                      ; int 21h fxn 38h)
        push    dx

        mov     ax,3000h                ; fxn 30h = get MS-DOS version
        int     21h                     ; transfer to MS-DOS

        or      al,al                   ; is this MS-DOS version 1.x?
        jz      getc1                   ; yes, jump

        mov     ax,3800h                ; get current country info
        mov     dx,offset DGROUP:cbuff
        int     21h                     ; transfer to MS-DOS
```

(continued)

Figure 6-6. *continued*

```
getc1:  mov    bx,word ptr cbuff    ; get date code (default = 0)
        shl    bx,1                 ; extract pointer to
        mov    ax,[bx+dftab]        ; date format table
        mov    dfptr,ax

getc2:  pop    dx                   ; restore registers
        pop    cx
        pop    bx
        pop    ax

getc3:  ret                         ; back to caller

getctry endp

_TEXT   ends

        end
```

The calling sequences for SCANTIME and SCANDATE are almost identical. Both are called with the address of the ASCII string to be converted in registers DS:SI. Both use the carry flag as a general indicator of success or failure: If the carry flag is set on return, the date or time could not be converted; if the carry flag is clear on return, the date or time string was valid and successfully converted. In the latter case, the date or time is returned in the 4-byte binary format in registers CX and DX, and DS:SI points to the last byte plus 1 of the converted string.

A typical call to the SCANDATE function looks like this:

```
buffer  db     '08/22/90',0         ; ASCII date string
year    dw     0                    ; receives binary year
month   db     0                    ; receives binary month
day     db     0                    ; receives binary day
        .
        .
        .
        mov    si,seg buffer        ; DS:SI = address of string
        mov    ds,si
        mov    si,offset buffer
        call   SCANDATE             ; convert date to binary
        jc     error                ; jump if bad date
        mov    year,cx              ; save binary year
        mov    month,dh             ; save binary month
        mov    day,dl               ; save binary day
```

The SCANTIME function is invoked similarly. Of course, SCANDATE or SCANTIME is usually called with the address of a buffer containing a date or time string read from a file or the keyboard rather than with the address of a static string as in the example above.

Inside the SCANTD.ASM Module

The SCANTIME and SCANDATE routines build on a number of helper routines that are not exported for use by other modules. The most important is GETCTRY, which is similar to the GETCTRY procedure in TD.ASM: It checks the MS-DOS version and calls the Get or Set Current Country service (Int 21H Function 38H) if the operating system version is 2.0 or later. GETCTRY uses the date format code returned by MS-DOS to set up a pointer that assists SCANDATE in interpreting ASCII date strings. Code 0 is the *mdy* format used in the United States; code 1 is the *dmy* format used in many European countries; and code 2 is the *ymd* format preferred in Japan.

Two other simple helper routines are CHKTLM and CHKDLM, which test whether a character belongs to the valid set of time and date delimiters. The actual delimiters are stored in tables named TLMTAB and DLMTAB. You can alter or expand the tables freely for your own purposes; the CHKTLM and CHKDLM routines adjust their actions accordingly.

The helper routine CHKNUM is called by SCANTIME and SCANDATE to convert an ASCII numeric string to a binary integer. The routine ATOI (Chapter 4, Figure 4-1), which is called to do the conversion work, simply terminates on any nonnumeric character and does not return error codes. You must therefore wrap the call to ATOI inside the procedure CHKNUM, which first tests for the existence of at least one numeric character.

If these various helper routines are functioning properly, SCANTIME and SCANDATE operate in a similar and straightforward manner. They first convert all the ASCII numeric fields in the supplied string to binary by successive calls to CHKNUM, CHKTLM, and CHKDLM—terminating with an error flag if a required field is missing or an invalid delimiter is encountered. The results are stored in the working variables N1, N2, and N3.

At this point, SCANTIME and SCANDATE diverge somewhat. SCANTIME checks the converted fields (hours, minutes, and seconds) to ensure that each field has a legal value. Hundredths of seconds can be ignored in the SCANTIME routine (even if they are present in the input string) because their usefulness in an interactive program is questionable. Finally, the hour, minute, and second values are loaded into the appropriate registers, and the SCANTIME routine returns to its original caller.

In the case of SCANDATE, validation of the input is more complicated because the routine must adapt itself to the three date formats supported by MS-DOS and to the existence of leap years. SCANDATE uses the pointer DFPTR, set by the GETCTRY subroutine, to determine which of the three working variables N1, N2, and N3 contain the day, month, and year. SCANDATE tests the year first; if the year is legal, it is used to update the table DAYTAB (containing the number of days in each month) to allow for 29 days in February during a leap year. Next, the month is checked for validity; if it passes, it is used to extract the maximum legal day number for that month from DAYTAB. Finally, the day is checked to ensure that it is in the acceptable range. SCANDATE then loads up the registers with the results and exits.

PROCEDURES INTRODUCED IN THIS CHAPTER

Procedure Name	Action	Parameters	Results
DCVT	Converts date in 4-byte binary format to ASCII string	DS:SI = segment:offset of buffer to receive string BX = length of buffer CX = year (1980+) DH = month (1–12) DL = day (1–31)	Nothing (string in buffer)
DIRDCVT	Converts date in directory format to ASCII string	DS:SI = segment:offset of buffer to receive string BX = length of buffer AX = directory date	Nothing (string in buffer)
DIRTCVT	Converts time in directory format to ASCII string	DS:SI = segment:offset of buffer to receive string BX = length of buffer AX = directory time	Nothing (string in buffer)
SCANDATE	Converts ASCII date to 4-byte binary format	DS:SI = segment:offset of ASCII date string	If function successful: Carry = clear CX = year (1980+) DH = month (1–12) DL = day (1–31) DS:SI = segment:offset of terminator character + 1 If function unsuccessful: Carry = set
SCANTIME	Converts ASCII time to 4-byte binary format	DS:SI = segment:offset of ASCII time string	If function successful: Carry = clear CH = hour CL = minute DH = second DL = centiseconds DS:SI = segment:offset of terminator character + 1 If function unsuccessful: Carry = set

(continued)

PROCEDURES INTRODUCED IN THIS CHAPTER *continued*

Procedure Name	Action	Parameters	Results
SYSDCVT	Converts current system date to ASCII string	DS:SI = segment:offset of buffer to receive string BX = length of buffer	Nothing (string in buffer)
SYSTCVT	Converts current system time to ASCII string	DS:SI = segment:offset of buffer to receive string BX = length of buffer	Nothing (string in buffer)
TCVT	Converts time in 4-byte binary format to ASCII string	DS:SI = segment:offset of buffer to receive string BX = length of buffer CH = hour CL = minute DH = seconds DL = centiseconds	Nothing (string in buffer)

Companion Disk

The companion disk directory \CH06 contains the programs and modules that are listed below.

Routines Presented in This Chapter

SCANTD.ASM   Converts ASCII times and dates to binary format

TD.ASM   Converts binary times and dates to ASCII strings

Routine Previously Discussed

ATOI.ASM   Converts a decimal ASCII string to a single-precision (16-bit) signed integer

Demonstration Programs

TRYTD   MAKE file for TRYTD.EXE

TRYTD.ASM   Noninteractive demonstration program

TRYSCTD   MAKE file for TRYSCTD.EXE

TRYSCTD.ASM   Interactive demonstration program

The noninteractive program TRYTD.ASM demonstrates use of the conversion routines SYSTCVT, SYSDCVT, DIRTCVT, and DIRDCVT in module TD.ASM. To build TRYTD.EXE, enter this command:

```
C>MAKE TRYTD   <Enter>
```

When you run TRYTD.EXE, it obtains, formats, and displays the current time and date. It then obtains, formats, and displays the time and date associated with its own directory entry (that is, the time and date that the file TRYTD.EXE was created or last modified).

The interactive program TRYSCTD.ASM demonstrates use of the SCANTIME and SCANDATE routines in module SCANTD.ASM, the TCVT and DCVT routines in module TD.ASM, and the primitive ASCII-to-binary conversion routine ATOI.ASM. To build TRYSCTD.EXE, enter this command:

```
C>MAKE TRYSCTD   <Enter>
```

When you execute TRYSCTD.EXE, it prompts you for a date, which it validates, converts to binary, converts back to ASCII, and displays. It next prompts you for a time, which it converts in both directions and displays. This cycle then repeats. When the program detects an invalid date or time, it displays an error message. You can exit the program at any time by pressing the Enter key at a prompt.

You can experiment with MS-DOS's internationalization support by adding various COUNTRY= directives to your CONFIG.SYS file, restarting your system, and then running TRYTD or TRYSCTD again to observe the effect on their processing of times and dates.

7

Sorting Numbers and Strings

A glance into any algorithms textbook will soon have you shaking your head, as professors debate the pros and cons of sorting algorithms, the performance of various algorithms, and the types of data for which certain algorithms are best and worst suited. Although these issues are relevant to programmers—they translate into computing time, and that time costs money—sorting techniques do tend to be the province of mathematicians and computer scientists.

Many kinds of sorts are described in computing literature: selection sort, insertion sort, bubble sort, Shellsort, Quicksort, radix sort, Heapsort, Mergesort, and so on. The simpler and more obvious sorting methods, such as the infamous bubble sort, are the ones that self-trained programmers hit on intuitively. Unfortunately, these methods often perform poorly unless they are used on exactly the right data sets, because they involve the most comparisons or data movement.

The really powerful sorts, which perform well for all kinds of data, have been developed by people with an extraordinary understanding of information theory, mathematics, and digital computers. The work done by these people is fascinating because it is extremely abstract yet supremely practical—abstract because a new sort algorithm can come from a flash of pure insight, but practical because such an algorithm can be implemented, tested, and put to use immediately.

Quicksort is an interesting example. It was invented in 1960 by C. A. R. Hoare, one of the pioneers and legends in computer science. Since then, it has been analyzed in great detail in books, journals, and dissertations. Quicksort is an excellent general-purpose sorting technique to add to your bag of tricks: It works in place, it works well on all kinds of data, it is easy to implement, it is particularly suited to languages that support recursion—and it's very unlikely that you would have thought of it on your own.

How Quicksort Works

The Quicksort algorithm looks deceptively simple—so simple, in fact, that you might find it hard to see where anything "real" is happening, even though the algorithm can be easily translated into working code. Quicksort works by dividing a data set into two parts and then calling itself recursively to sort each part. Here is a C representation of the overall algorithm (adapted from the Pascal example in Robert Sedgewick's splendid book *Algorithms*):

```c
quicksort(int left, int right)
{
    int i;

    if (right > left)
    {
        i = partition(left, right);

        quicksort(left, i - 1);

        quicksort(i + 1, right);
    }
}
```

The parameters *left* and *right* define a subset of the data to be sorted. Let's assume that the data is in an array and that *left* and *right* are simply indexes to that array. Then the entire data set can be sorted with the function call

```c
quicksort(0, N - 1)
```

where *N* is the number of items in the array.

Sedgewick describes it in this fashion:

> The crux of the method is the *partition* procedure, which must rearrange the array to make the following conditions hold:
>
> 1. The element *array[i]* is in its final place in the array for some *i*.
> 2. All the elements in *array[left]*, ...,*array[i-1]* are less than or equal to *array[i]*.
> 3. All the elements in *array[i+1]*, ...,*array[right]* are greater than or equal to *array[i]*.

In other words, Quicksort is called (either by another procedure or by itself) with a couple of pointers that define the beginning and the end of a set of data. It then arbitrarily picks a member of that set around which the rest of the set will be partitioned. With simple comparisons and exchanges, Quicksort rearranges the data set so that all members less than the partitioning value lie to its left and all members greater than the partitioning value lie to its right. Finally, Quicksort calls itself twice to sort the data set to the left and the data set to the right of the partitioning item. With this divide-and-conquer approach, Quicksort eventually gets down to data sets in which it has nothing to do.

Sorting Integers with Quicksort

Let's look at a practical example of how the Quicksort algorithm works. Figure 7-1 contains the C source code for a function called *qsi()* that performs a Quicksort on integer arrays. Note that the C code is intrinsically recursive because it uses automatic variables, which are allocated on the stack when the routine is entered.

```c
/*
    This function "quicksorts" an array of integers declared as
        int items[n];
    recursing to sort subsets of the array.  Called with the index
    to the left and right members of the array to be sorted.
*/

void qsi(int left, int right)
{
    int i, j, t;                        // scratch variables

    if(right > left)                    // skip unnecessary calls
    {
        i = left - 1; j = right;        // initialize scan pointers

                                        // partition array on value
                                        // of rightmost item
        do {

                                        // scan right for item >=
                                        // partitioning value
            do i++;
                while(items[i] < items[right]);

                                        // scan left for item <=
                                        // partitioning value
            do j--;
                while(items[j] > items[right] && j > 0);

            t = items[i];               // interchange items
            items[i] = items[j];
            items[j] = t;

        } while(j > i);                 // do until pointers cross

        items[j] = items[i];            // undo last swap and
        items[i] = items[right];        // put partitioning
        items[right] = t;               // element into position

        qsi(left, i - 1);               // sort items to left of
                                        // partitioning element
```

Figure 7-1.

An integer Quicksort function in C.

(continued)

Figure 7-1. *continued*

```
        qsi(i + 1, right);              // sort items to right of
    }                                   // partitioning element
}
```

The QSI routine (Figure 7-2) is in turn a direct assembly-language rendering of the C code in Figure 7-1. It is called with the addresses of the first and last members of an array of 16-bit signed integers, and it returns after sorting the array with all registers unchanged. The comments in the MASM source code are analogous to statements from the C version, so you can use the C listing as a sort of high-level road map to the MASM routine.

```
;
; QSI.ASM -- Quicksort for 16-bit integers.
;
; Copyright (C) 1991 Ray Duncan
;
; Call with:    DS:SI = address of first item to sort
;               DS:DI = address of last item to sort
;               Assumes items are 2-byte integers
;
; Returns:      Nothing (data sorted in place)
;
; Destroys:     Nothing

itemsiz equ     2                       ; bytes per integer

_TEXT   segment word public 'CODE'

        assume  cs:_TEXT,ds:NOTHING,es:NOTHING

                                        ; stack variables
left    equ     [bp-8]                  ; first item to sort
right   equ     [bp-4]                  ; last item to sort

        public  qsi
qsi     proc    near

        cmp     di,si                   ; if right <= left
        jna     qsi5                    ; just exit

        push    bp                      ; set up stack frame
        mov     bp,sp                   ; and local variables
        push    es
```

Figure 7-2.   *(continued)*

QSI.ASM, an integer Quicksort procedure in assembly language. This routine is symmetric with the C-language integer Quicksort in Figure 7-1.

Figure 7-2. *continued*

```
        push    di                      ; offset last item
        push    ds
        push    si                      ; offset first item
        push    dx
        push    cx
        push    bx
        push    ax

        sub     si,itemsiz              ; SI = i = left - 1
                                        ; DI = j = right
        mov     bx,di                   ; BX = right

qsi1:                                   ; partition array on
                                        ; value of rightmost item

qsi2:                                   ; scan right for item
                                        ; >= partitioning value

        add     si,itemsiz              ; i++

        mov     ax,[si]                 ; while (items[i] < items[right])
        cmp     ax,[bx]                 ; (guaranteed to terminate
        jl      qsi2                    ;   when i = right)

qsi3:                                   ; scan left for item
                                        ; <= partitioning value

        sub     di,itemsiz              ; j--

        cmp     di,left                 ; while (items[j] > items[right])
        jna     qsi4                    ; && (j > left)
        mov     ax,[di]
        cmp     ax,[bx]
        jg      qsi3

qsi4:   mov     ax,[di]                 ; exchange items
        xchg    ax,[si]
        mov     [di],ax

        cmp     di,si                   ; while (j > i)
        ja      qsi1                    ; (do until pointers cross)

        mov     ax,[di]                 ; undo last exchange
        xchg    ax,[si]
        mov     [di],ax

        mov     ax,[bx]                 ; put partitioning
        xchg    ax,[si]                 ; element into position
        mov     [bx],ax
```

(continued)

Figure 7-2. *continued*

```
        push    si                      ; save i

        mov     di,si                   ; qsi (left, i - 1)
        sub     di,itemsiz
        mov     si,left
        call    qsi

        pop     si                      ; qsi (i + 1, right)
        add     si,itemsiz
        mov     di,right
        call    qsi

        pop     ax                      ; restore registers
        pop     bx                      ; discard stack frame
        pop     cx
        pop     dx
        pop     si
        pop     ds
        pop     di
        pop     es
        pop     bp

qsi5:   ret                             ; return to caller

qsi     endp

_TEXT   ends

        end
```

To keep the code readable, and to allow us to generalize this routine later in the chapter to sort items of any size and type, some obvious coding shortcuts are omitted from the QSI routine—for example, the CMPSW instructions are not used to scan forward and backward in the array. QSI also saves all registers and sets up a stack frame to provide the underpinnings for the later, more general version of the procedure, although neither operation is strictly necessary in this version.

When you study or change the code in QSI.ASM, pay attention to comparisons followed by conditional branches. You must be sure to use the unsigned conditional jumps such as JA and JB when comparing addresses and to use the signed conditional jumps such as JG and JL when comparing values. Using the wrong type of jump in the wrong place can result in some nasty and elusive bugs—the kind that depend on address sizes and thus on the order of statements in your source code or even on the order in which modules are linked.

Optimizing Quicksort

How could the Quicksort implementation in *qsi()* or QSI.ASM be improved? The fundamental algorithm is efficient as it stands because the inner loops are simple increments and comparisons. It's hard to see how you could shorten these loops, and even the simplest compiler can generate good code for them.

One obvious target for optimization is the strategy for picking a partitioning value. Our example simply used the rightmost element, a reasonable course when the data is very disordered, because on average it comes up with a partitioning value "in the middle." When the data starts out nearly sorted, however, using the rightmost element is a bad strategy because each time the data is partitioned, most of it ends up in one subset.

Other possible optimizations include use of a *goto* in *qsi()* or a branch in QSI.ASM when the pointers cross, to eliminate the final unnecessary exchange (which must be restored). You could also eliminate recursion from the algorithm. (Read more about these topics in Chapter 9 of Sedgewick's *Algorithms,* and try out some of the optimizations for yourself.)

Another candidate for optimization in QSI.ASM is this sequence of six instructions:

```
mov     ax,[di]
xchg    ax,[si]
mov     [di],ax
mov     ax,[bx]
xchg    ax,[si]
mov     [bx],ax
```

Your immediate instinct might be to replace it with the following:

```
mov     ax,[si]
xchg    ax,[di]
xchg    ax,[bx]
mov     [si],ax
```

Try it—and you'll find that the Quicksort immediately stops working. When QSI recurses and calls itself with pointers to an array that contains only two elements, two of the three index registers are pointing to the same element, and the three-way swap of values does not work as expected.

A Generalized Quicksort Routine

Although Quicksort isn't difficult to implement, you don't want to reimplement it with custom coding every time you have something to sort. It would be ideal to have a general-purpose Quicksort routine that could somehow handle any kind of data sent its way. If you look to the high-level languages for guidance, you quickly find that creating such a general-purpose routine is not impractical.

Standard C runtime libraries, for example, include a function called *qsort()*, which has four parameters: the base address of an array of data, the number of items in the array, the length (in bytes) of each item, and the address of a function that can compare two data items of the type contained in the array and return a signed value as follows:

<0	if item 1 < item 2
0	if item 1 = item 2
>0	if item 1 > item 2

Thus, *qsort()* can be seen as a kind of sorting "engine." If you are using one of C's native data types, you can usually construct an appropriate comparison function for use with *qsort()* in a few lines of code. (See Figure 7-3.) In the case of strings, the standard library function *strcmp()* is perfectly suited to use with *qsort()*. Even if you are not using a native C data type, *qsort()* assumes that you know enough about the data representation to tell it whether one item is "smaller" than another.

```
int compare(int *n1, int *n2)
{
        if(*n1 < *n2) return -1;        /* if n1 < n2 return -1 */
                                        /* if n1 = n2 return  0 */
        return(*n1 > *n2);              /* if n1 > n2 return  1 */

}
```

Figure 7-3.
A routine that compares two integers (suitable for use with qsort()*, a C runtime library function).*

QSORT.ASM (Figure 7-4) is a similar generalized sorting engine that can be used in assembly-language programs. It sorts arrays of any kind of data in place if you provide an appropriate comparison routine. QSORT is called with the following parameters:

DS:SI = address of first array element
DS:DI = address of last array element
AX   = length of each array element in bytes
ES:BX = address of comparison routine

It returns all registers unchanged.

```
;
; QSORT.ASM -- General-purpose Quicksort.
;
; Copyright (C) 1991 Ray Duncan
;
; Call with:     DS:SI = address of first item to sort
;                DS:DI = address of last item to sort
;                ES:BX = address of compare routine
;                AX    = length of each item
;
; Returns:       Nothing (data sorted in place)
;
; Destroys:      Nothing
;
; The external compare routine must be declared as 'proc far'
; and must accept the following parameters:
;                DS:SI = address of first item to compare
;                ES:DI = address of second item to compare
;                CX    = length to compare
; The compare routine must return DS:SI and ES:DI unchanged and
; the result of the comparison in the CPU flags as follows:
;                Z = T          if item 1 = item 2
;                Z = F, S = T if item 1 < item 2
;                Z = F, S = F if item 1 > item 2

_TEXT   segment word public 'CODE'

        assume  cs:_TEXT,ds:NOTHING,es:NOTHING

                                        ; stack variables
compare equ     dword ptr [bp-4]        ; address of compare routine
itemsiz equ     [bp-6]                  ; bytes per item
left    equ     [bp-8]                  ; first item to sort
right   equ     [bp-10]                 ; last item to sort

        public  qsort
qsort   proc    near

        cmp     di,si                   ; if right <= left
        jna     qsort5                  ; just exit

        push    bp                      ; set up stack frame
        mov     bp,sp                   ; and local variables

        push    es                      ; save address of
        push    bx                      ; compare routine
        push    ax                      ; save bytes per item
```

Figure 7-4. *(continued)*

QSORT.ASM, a generalized Quicksort "engine" for assembly-language programs (comparable to the qsort() *function in the standard C runtime library).*

Figure 7-4. *continued*

```
        push    si                      ; offset first item
        push    di                      ; offset last item

        push    cx                      ; save remaining registers
        push    dx

        push    ds                      ; make data addressable by
        pop     es                      ; ES for exchange routine

        sub     si,itemsiz              ; SI = i = left - 1
                                        ; DI = right
        mov     bx,di                   ; BX = j = right

qsort1:                                 ; partition array on
                                        ; value of rightmost item

qsort2:                                 ; scan right for item
                                        ; >= partitioning value

        add     si,itemsiz              ; i++

        mov     cx,itemsiz
        call    compare                 ; while (items[i] < items[right])
        jl      qsort2

        xchg    bx,si                   ; SI = j, BX = i, DI = right

qsort3:                                 ; scan left for item
                                        ; <= partitioning value

        sub     si,itemsiz              ; j--

        cmp     si,left                 ; while (items[j] > items[right])
        jna     qsort4                  ; && (j > left)
        mov     cx,itemsiz
        call    compare
        jg      qsort3

qsort4: xchg    bx,di                   ; SI = j, DI = i, BX = right

        mov     cx,itemsiz
        call    exch                    ; exchange items

        xchg    si,di                   ; SI = i, DI = j, BX = right
        xchg    di,bx                   ; SI = i, DI = right, BX = j

        cmp     bx,si                   ; while (j > i)
        ja      qsort1                  ; (do until pointers cross)
```

(continued)

Figure 7-4. *continued*

```
        xchg    bx,di                   ; SI = i, DI = j, BX = right
        mov     cx,itemsiz
        call    exch                    ; undo last exchange

        xchg    bx,di                   ; SI = i, DI = right, BX = j
        mov     cx,itemsiz
        call    exch                    ; put partitioning element
                                        ; into position

        push    si                      ; save i

        mov     di,si                   ; qsort (left, i - 1)
        sub     di,itemsiz
        mov     si,left
        les     bx,compare
        mov     ax,itemsiz
        call    qsort

        pop     si                      ; qsort (i + 1, right)
        add     si,itemsiz
        mov     di,right
        les     bx,compare
        mov     ax,itemsiz
        call    qsort

        pop     dx                      ; restore registers
        pop     cx
        pop     di
        pop     si
        pop     ax
        pop     bx
        pop     es
        pop     bp

qsort5: ret                             ; return to caller

qsort   endp

;
; EXCH:       Exchanges two data items
;
; Call with:  DS:SI = address of first item
;             DS:DI = address of second item
;             CX    = item length
;
; Returns:    Nothing
;
; Destroys:   AX, CX
;
```

(continued)

Figure 7-4. *continued*

```
exch      proc      near

          cmp       cx,2               ; are items words?
          jne       exch1              ; no, jump

          mov       ax,[di]            ; items are words
          xchg      ax,[si]            ; exchange them quickly
          mov       [di],ax
          ret

exch1:    push      si                 ; save addresses
          push      di

exch2:    mov       al,[di]            ; exchange items
          xchg      al,[si]            ; byte by byte
          mov       [di],al
          inc       si
          inc       di
          loop      exch2

          pop       di                 ; restore addresses
          pop       si
          ret

exch      endp

_TEXT     ends

          end
```

Because the comparison routine is entered by a far call from QSORT, it must be declared in your application program with *proc far*. QSORT passes it the following parameters:

DS:SI = address of first item to compare

ES:DI = address of second item to compare

CX   = length to compare

The comparison routine must return registers DS:SI and ES:DI unchanged, although it can destroy registers AX and CX without causing problems for QSORT. The result of the compare operation must be returned to QSORT in the CPU's zero and sign flags as follows:

if item 1 = item 2, Z = true

if item 1 < item 2, Z = false and S = true

if item 1 > item 2, Z = false and S = false

Figures 7-5 and 7-6 contain sample source code for comparison routines that work with 16-bit integers or with strings.

```
;
; COMPI -- Compares two integers (for use with QSORT.ASM).
;
; Call with:    DS:SI = address of integer 1
;               ES:DI = address of integer 2
;               CX    = length of data (not used here)
;
; Returns:      Result in CPU flags
;
; Destroys:     AX
;
compi   proc    far
        mov     ax,[si]
        cmp     ax,[di]
        ret
compi   endp
```

Figure 7-5.

COMPI, a subroutine to compare two integers (suitable for use with QSORT.ASM).

```
;
; COMPS -- Compares two strings (for use with QSORT.ASM).
;
; Call with:    DS:SI = address of string 1
;               ES:DI = address of string 2
;               CX    = length of data
;
; Returns:      Result in CPU flags
;
; Destroys:     CX
;
comps   proc    far
        push    si
        push    di
        repz    cmpsb
        pop     di
        pop     si
        ret
comps   endp
```

Figure 7-6.

COMPS, a subroutine to compare two strings (suitable for use with QSORT.ASM).

QSORT is recursive and makes heavy use of the stack. It requires at least 24 bytes for each invocation (possibly more, depending on the compare routine supplied by the caller) and can easily recurse to a depth of 8 or 10 calls when sorting large arrays. Consequently, any application program that uses QSORT should have a stack of at least 4 KB to allow a margin of safety.

PROCEDURES INTRODUCED IN THIS CHAPTER

Procedure Name	Action	Parameters	Results
QSI	Integer Quicksort	DS:SI = segment:offset of first item to sort DS:DI = segment:offset of last item to sort	Nothing (data sorted in place)
QSORT	General-purpose Quicksort "engine"	DS:SI = segment:offset of first item to sort DS:DI = segment:offset of last item to sort ES:BX = segment:offset of comparison routine AX = length of each item	Nothing (data sorted in place)

Companion Disk

The companion disk directory \CH07 contains the programs and modules that are listed below.

Routines Presented in This Chapter

QSI.ASM	A Quicksort routine for single-precision integers
QSORT.ASM	A generalized Quicksort "engine"

Routines Previously Discussed

ATOI.ASM	Converts a decimal ASCII string to a single-precision (16-bit) signed integer
ITOA.ASM	Converts a single-precision (16-bit) signed integer to an ASCII string in any radix

Demonstration Programs

TRYQSI	MAKE file for TRYQSI.EXE
TRYQSI.ASM	Interactive demonstration program

TRYQSORT	MAKE file for TRYQSORT.EXE
TRYQSORT.ASM	Interactive demonstration program

The interactive program TRYQSI demonstrates use of the routines QSI, ATOI, and ITOA. To build TRYQSI.EXE, enter this command:

```
C>MAKE TRYQSI  <Enter>
```

When you run TRYQSI.EXE, it prompts you to enter from 1 to 25 numbers, converts the ASCII numbers to binary, and puts the values into an array. When you press the Enter key after entering some numbers, TRYQSI sorts the array and prints the sorted values. Press the Enter key at the *Item 01:* prompt to exit the demo program, or press Ctrl-C or Ctrl-Break at any time to terminate the demo.

The interactive program TRYQSORT demonstrates use of the routines QSORT, ATOI, and ITOA. TRYQSORT, which is actually two demo programs in one, can process either strings or integers; you determine which by setting the equates STRINGS and SINGLES to true or false near the beginning of the source file. (Of course, both equates should not be set to true at the same time.) Conditional assembly statements throughout the remainder of the source file cause appropriate code to be generated for the type of data you want to enter, sort, and display.

To build TRYQSORT.EXE, enter this command:

```
C>MAKE TRYQSORT  <Enter>
```

TRYQSORT prompts you for as many as 25 items (either integers or strings, depending on how the program was built). When you press the Enter key, TRYQSORT calls QSORT to put the list in order and finally displays the sorted list. The program can be terminated by pressing the Enter key at the first prompt or by pressing Ctrl-C or Ctrl-Break at any time.

You can examine the operation of Quicksort and gain a deeper understanding of the algorithm by running TRYQSI.EXE or TRYQSORT.EXE under the control of the CodeView debugger. This will let you see each line of the source code as it is executed and monitor the contents of the registers and the depth of recursion. You can even set a watchpoint on the array being sorted and see the data moving around.

8

Using the MS-DOS File System

File system is one of those overloaded computer terms that can have two completely different meanings. When used to refer to a volume of storage, such as a floppy disk, *file system* means the interdependent tables, control areas, and storage areas written on the disk—taken together, the various elements of a file system define the location of all files, the contents of the files, and the disk's free space. When used in connection with an operating system, the term *file system* refers to those internal routines that translate an application program's requests to manipulate files into directives to the system's disk device driver, which in turn issues hardware-dependent commands to the disk.

On an MS-DOS disk, a file system consists of the boot sector; the root directory; the file storage area, which also contains any directories other than the root directory; and the File Allocation Table (FAT), which describes the use of each allocation unit (cluster) in the file storage area. (See Figure 8-1 on the following page.) These various areas are initialized by the FORMAT program. The boot sector in particular contains a table called the BIOS Parameter Block (BPB), which completely describes the disk's characteristics (heads, tracks, sectors per track, sectors in the root directory, and so on). By convention, floppy disks are occupied by only one file system; a hard disk, however, can be divided ("partitioned") so that it contains many file systems—not all of which are necessarily compatible with MS-DOS.

Let's turn now to the software part of the file system. MS-DOS has a file system module for FAT disks embedded in its kernel. This file system cannot be replaced, but you can use the "network redirector interface" to install file system modules that support disks in other formats. When an application program makes a file request via the Int 21H interface, the MS-DOS kernel determines which file system module should receive the request, performs certain preliminary processing on the request, and then passes the request along. The FAT file system module converts the application program's file function calls into requests for the transfer of logical disk sectors,

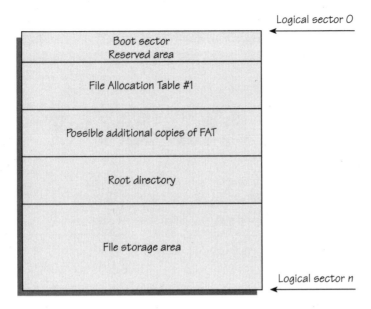

Figure 8-1.
An MS-DOS FAT file system. When used to refer to physical storage media, the term
file system *means all the files on a disk or a logical volume and all the control*
structures and directories necessary to access those files.

using the information it finds on the disk in the boot sector, the FAT, and the directories. The driver in turn converts logical sector numbers into physical unit, head, cylinder, and track addresses and calls the ROM BIOS to perform the actual data transfer. (See Figure 8-2.)

Basic MS-DOS File Operations

Most operating systems offer these fundamental file management capabilities:

- Opening an existing file or creating a new file
- Reading and writing data within a file after the file has been opened or created
- Seeking to a specific position within a file (setting the file pointer)
- Closing a file when access to its contents is no longer needed
- Renaming or deleting a file

MS-DOS is no exception; in fact, MS-DOS supports two distinct sets of function calls that work in different ways but provide somewhat parallel functionality. These sets are commonly referred to as the FCB-based file functions and the handle-based file functions (Figure 8-3 on page 146). The FCB (File Control Block) functions were originally designed for compatibility with Digital Research's CP/M operating system. They do not support the hierarchical (tree-like) disk structure of MS-DOS versions

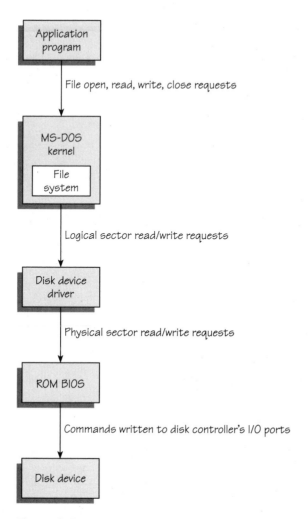

Figure 8-2.
The relationship of application programs, the MS-DOS kernel (with its embedded FAT file system module), the disk driver, the ROM BIOS, and the physical disk device.

2.0 and later and are now a historical curiosity. The handle functions support the hierarchical directory structure and have direct counterparts in UNIX, OS/2, and the C runtime library. The routines contained in this book use only the handle-based file functions that are available in all MS-DOS versions 2.0 and later; the parameters and results for the most commonly used of these functions are listed in Figure 8-4 on page 147.

Operation	FCB-Based Functions	Handle-Based Functions
Open file	Int 21H Function 0FH	Int 21H Function 3DH
		Int 21H Function 6CH
Create file	Int 21H Function 16H	Int 21H Function 3CH
		Int 21H Function 5AH
		Int 21H Function 5BH
		Int 21H Function 6CH
Read file	Int 21H Function 14H	Int 21H Function 3FH
	Int 21H Function 21H	
	Int 21H Function 27H	
Write file	Int 21H Function 15H	Int 21H Function 40H
	Int 21H Function 22H	
	Int 21H Function 28H	
Set file pointer		Int 21H Function 42H
Lock/unlock file region		Int 21H Function 5CH
Close file	Int 21H Function 10H	Int 21H Function 3EH
Commit file		Int 21H Function 68H
Set disk transfer address	Int 21H Function 1AH	
Get/set file date and time		Int 21H Function 57H
Get file size	Int 21H Function 23H	Int 21H Function 42H
Get/set file attributes		Int 21H Function 43H
Delete file	Int 21H Function 13H	Int 21H Function 42H
Rename file	Int 21H Function 17H	Int 21H Function 56H
Find first file	Int 21H Function 11H	Int 21H Function 4EH
Find next file	Int 21H Function 12H	Int 21H Function 4FH

Figure 8-3.
*The basic MS-DOS file management functions fall into two distinct but parallel
groups: the FCB-based file functions and the handle-based file functions.*

To *open* a file, a program identifies the file to MS-DOS by name, using an ASCIIZ
(null-terminated) string. It also specifies the access rights it needs (read-only, write-
only, or read-write) and whether it is willing to share simultaneous access to the file
with other programs. If the file exists, and if no conflict exists between the requested access rights and another program's sharing mode, MS-DOS returns an identifier—called a *handle*—that the program can use for subsequent access to the file.
The handle is actually an indirect index into a data structure called the System File
Table (SFT). MS-DOS uses the SFT to keep track of all open files in the system, but
an application program uses a handle simply as a "magic number" or "token" that
symbolizes the corresponding file.

Function	Parameters	Results
Int 21H Function 3CH Create file	AH = 3CH CX = file attribute DS:DX = address of ASCIIZ filename	If function successful: Carry = clear AX = handle If function unsuccessful: Carry = set AX = error code
Int 21H Function 3DH Open file	AH = 3CH AL = access mode DS:DX = address of ASCIIZ filename	If function successful: Carry = clear AX = handle If function unsuccessful: Carry = set AX = error code
Int 21H Function 3FH Read file	AH = 3FH BX = handle CX = number of bytes DS:DX = buffer address	If function successful: Carry = clear AX = bytes transferred If function unsuccessful: Carry = set AX = error code
Int 21H Function 40H Write file	AH = 40H BX = handle CX = number of bytes DS:DX = buffer address	If function successful: Carry = clear AX = bytes transferred If function unsuccessful: Carry = set AX = error code
Int 21H Function 42H Set file pointer	AH = 42H AL = method (0 = relative to start of file, 1 = relative to current file position, 2 = relative to end of file) BX = handle CX:DX = method-based file offset	If function successful: Carry = clear DX:AX = actual file offset If function unsuccessful: Carry = set AX = error code
Int 21H Function 3EH Close file	AH = 3EH BX = handle	If function successful: Carry = clear If function unsuccessful: Carry = set AX = error code
Int 21H Function 41H Delete file	AH = 41H DS:DX = address of ASCIIZ filename	If function successful: Carry = clear If function unsuccessful: Carry = set AX = error code
Int 21H Function 56H Rename file	AH = 56H DS:DX = address of ASCIIZ current filename ES:DI = address of ASCIIZ new filename	If function successful: Carry = clear If function unsuccessful: Carry = set AX = error code

Figure 8-4.

The basic MS-DOS handle-based file functions used by almost all application programs.

When a file is *created,* the program supplies an ASCIIZ filename and an attribute parameter that characterizes the file as, for example, hidden or read-only. If the operation is successful, the system adds an entry to the disk directory and, again, returns a handle that the program uses for subsequent access to the file. (An additional open operation is not needed and would needlessly expend another handle.) The create function available in MS-DOS versions 2.x (Int 21H Function 3CH) must be used with care because if the file already exists, it is simply replaced (truncated to zero length), and any existing data in the file is lost. Later versions of MS-DOS offer additional file creation functions, including one that fails if the file already exists and another that generates a name for a temporary file as a function of the current time.

After a file is opened or created, a program is ready to work on the file's contents. To *read* data from the disk into RAM, the program supplies the operating system with a buffer address, the number of bytes to read, and a handle; the data on the disk is unchanged, and the previous contents of the buffer are lost. To *write* data from RAM onto the disk, the program supplies the same three parameters used in a read operation. In this case, however, the contents of RAM are unchanged, and the previous contents of the disk area are lost. Data need not be physically transferred between the disk and RAM when a program's read or write request logically completes; MS-DOS buffers disk data internally for extended periods to improve performance.

MS-DOS maintains a *file pointer* in the SFT for each open file handle. When a program issues a read or write request, the current value of the file pointer for that handle determines the byte offset from the start of the file where the data transfer will begin. When the operation completes, the system updates the file pointer to point 1 byte past the last byte read or written. MS-DOS also allows a program to set the file pointer to an arbitrary value—often referred to as a *seek* operation. The seek function accepts a 32-bit, byte offset and a method code specifying whether the offset is relative to the start of the file (method 0), to the current file pointer position (method 1), or to the end of the file (method 2). (This kind of logical seek should not be confused with the physical seek performed by a disk drive, which involves moving the read-write head to a specific cylinder.)

Although the seek function accepts an offset relative to the start of the file, to the current file pointer position, or to the end of the file as a parameter, it always *returns* the resulting absolute file pointer relative to the start of the file. This allows two special uses of the function, which you might find handy: To obtain the current position of the file pointer without modifying it, you can request a seek relative to the current file pointer position (method 1) with an offset of zero. To find the size of a file, you can call for a seek relative to the end of the file (method 2) with an offset of zero.

A program *closes* a file to notify MS-DOS that it no longer needs to use the file. MS-DOS then flushes any unwritten data associated with the file to disk, updates the disk directory (if necessary) to reflect any changes made to the file, and releases the handle and the corresponding entry in the SFT for reuse.

Handles are not involved when a program *deletes* or *renames* a file; the file is identified by an ASCIIZ string, as it is for the open and create operations. When a file is deleted, the first character of its entry in the disk directory is changed to a reserved value, and the disk sectors previously assigned to the file are freed. However, the remainder of the directory entry and the contents of the sectors are not altered until they are assigned to a new file. This gaping hole in system security has given rise to an entire category of utility software and to at least one personal fortune.

Sequential and Random File Access

Three more terms that come up continually in discussions of file management are *records, sequential access,* and *random access.* Although MS-DOS sees a file as simply a named collection of bytes, programmers usually think of a file as composed of records. Typically, each record describes a particular person or object, can be compounded of many fields of different types, and is an integral number of bytes in length. The key features of a record—for our purposes—are that it has a predictable structure and that its length either is a constant (for a given file) or is somehow encoded in the record itself.

Sequential access refers to reading or writing consecutive records in a file. Sequential access techniques are rooted in the magnetic tape drives of yesteryear. The most common example of sequential access is the processing of a text file, in which each line can be considered a record delimited by a newline character. A program that processes files sequentially need not concern itself with the file pointer and never needs to perform a seek operation, because MS-DOS maintains the file pointer automatically.

Random access refers to reading and writing nonsequential records—in other words, the physical ordering of the records in the file does not determine the order in which they are processed. (The processing, of course, is not at all random.) In simple programs, random access is typically used with files that contain fixed-length records, allowing the program to calculate the location of a specific record by multiplying the record number by the record size. The indexed file access methods used by more sophisticated applications are much more versatile.

MS-DOS draws little distinction between sequential and random file access. When a file is opened or created, its file pointer is initially set to zero. If a program simply issues read or write requests without ever setting the file pointer position, its access to the file is sequential. If a process requires random access, it need only position the file pointer appropriately before each read or write request. Naturally, these techniques can be used together and even interleaved; for example, a program can seek to a specific record and then process sequential records by consecutive read or write operations.

Chapters 9 and 10 discuss sequential and random access files in more detail. In the meantime, let's look at a simple routine that performs sequential file access to provide a service almost every application program needs.

The FCOPY Routine and How It Works

The procedure FCOPY, whose source code is found in Figure 8-5, provides a convenient way to create a backup file or a temporary working file. The routine accepts a flag in AX and far pointers to two ASCIIZ filenames in DS:SI and ES:DI. The first name must refer to a file that already exists. The contents of that file are copied into a newly created file with the second name. The flag is 0 if an existing file with the same name as the destination file can be overwritten; the flag is 1 if an existing file with the same name should be preserved. The routine returns the carry flag clear if the operation was successful or the carry flag set if the operation failed.

```
;
; FCOPY.ASM -- Copies an existing file to a new file with
;              the specified name.  Provides control of
;              overwrite for existing files.  Uses all
;              available memory to buffer file data.
;
; Copyright (C) 1991 Ray Duncan
;
; Call with:    DS:SI = segment:offset of input filename
;               BX    = length of input filename
;               ES:DI = segment:offset of output filename
;               DX    = length of output filename
;               AX    = 0 if existing file can be overwritten,
;                       1 if existing file should preserved
;
; Returns:      Carry = clear if copy succeeded
;               or
;               Carry = set if copy failed
;
; Destroys:     Nothing
;
; Warning:      Routine needs at least 256 bytes of stack space.

xfrsize equ     0fff0h                  ; bytes per I/O request
                                        ; (must be multiple of 16)

bufsize equ     80                      ; local filename buffer size

jmpc    macro   p1                      ; this macro builds a
        local   p2                      ; "long" conditional jump
        jnc     p2                      ; on carry flag = set and
        jmp     p1                      ; avoids "out-of-range" errors
p2:
        endm
```

Figure 8-5. *(continued)*

FCOPY.ASM, a routine that copies an existing file to a new file with the specified name and location. All available memory is used to speed up the copy and minimize disk head movement.

Figure 8-5. *continued*

```
_TEXT    segment byte public 'CODE'

         assume  cs:_TEXT

         public  fcopy
fcopy    proc    near                    ; copy file

                                         ; local variables
ifname   equ     [bp]-bufsize            ; input filename
ofname   equ     ifname-bufsize          ; output filename
copyseg  equ     word ptr ofname-2       ; copy buffer segment
copysiz  equ     copyseg-4               ; copy buffer size (bytes)
ihandle  equ     copysiz-2               ; input file handle
ohandle  equ     ihandle-2               ; output file handle

                                         ; parameters from caller
ofnpar   equ     [bp]+2                  ; input filename
ifnpar   equ     [bp]+6                  ; output filename
copyflg  equ     [bp]+16                 ; copy operation type

         push    ax                      ; save registers
         push    bx
         push    cx
         push    dx
         push    ds
         push    si
         push    es
         push    di
         push    bp
         mov     bp,sp
         lea     sp,ohandle              ; allocate stack frame

         mov     copyseg,-1              ; assume no memory allocated
         mov     ihandle,-1              ; assume no input file
         mov     ohandle,-1              ; assume no output file

         push    ss                      ; copy name of input file
         pop     es                      ; to buffer in stack frame
         lea     di,ifname
         mov     cx,bx
         cld
         rep movsb
         mov     byte ptr es:[di],0      ; make filename ASCIIZ

         lds     si,ofnpar               ; copy name of output file
         lea     di,ofname               ; to buffer in stack frame
         mov     cx,dx
         cld
         rep movsb
```

(continued)

Figure 8-5. *continued*

```
        mov     byte ptr es:[di],0       ; make filename ASCIIZ

        mov     ax,3d20h                 ; open input file as
        push    ss                       ; read-only, deny-write
        pop     ds
        lea     dx,ifname
        int     21h                      ; transfer to MS-DOS
        jmpc    fcopy4                   ; jump if open failed
        mov     ihandle,ax               ; save handle for input file

        cmp     word ptr copyflg,0       ; is overwrite allowed?
        je      fcopy1                   ; yes, jump
        mov     ax,3d40h                 ; no, try to open output file
        push    ss                       ; as read-only, deny-none
        pop     ds
        lea     dx,ofname
        int     21h                      ; transfer to MS-DOS
        jc      fcopy1                   ; proceed, file doesn't exist

        mov     bx,ax                    ; file exists, close it again
        mov     ah,3eh
        int     21h                      ; transfer to MS-DOS
        jmp     fcopy4                   ; exit, overwrite not allowed

fcopy1: mov     ah,3ch                   ; create output file with
        mov     cx,0                     ; normal file attributes
        lea     dx,ofname
        int     21h                      ; transfer to MS-DOS
        jmpc    fcopy4                   ; exit, create failed
        mov     ohandle,ax               ; save handle for output file

        mov     bx,0ffffh                ; find amount of memory available
        mov     ah,48h                   ; by asking for impossible amount
        int     21h                      ; transfer to MS-DOS
        or      bx,bx
        jz      fcopy4                   ; jump if nothing to allocate

        mov     ax,bx                    ; now BX = largest block size
        xor     cx,cx                    ; in paragraphs
        shl     ax,1                     ; let CX:AX = largest block
        rcl     cx,1                     ; size in bytes
        shl     ax,1
        rcl     cx,1
        shl     ax,1
        rcl     cx,1
        shl     ax,1
        rcl     cx,1
        mov     word ptr copysiz,ax      ; save block size in bytes
        mov     word ptr copysiz+2,cx
```

(continued)

Figure 8-5. *continued*

```
                mov     ah,48h              ; allocate copy buffer
                int     21h                 ; transfer to MS-DOS
                jmpc    fcopy4              ; jump if allocation failed
                mov     copyseg,ax          ; save segment of copy buffer

fcopy2:                                     ; fill copy buffer
                mov     di,word ptr copysiz ; SI:DI = size of buffer
                mov     si,word ptr copysiz+2
                mov     bx,ihandle          ; BX = input file handle
                mov     ds,copyseg          ; DS:DX = buffer base address
                xor     dx,dx
                mov     ax,3f00h            ; MS-DOS read function number
                call    xfer                ; now read input file
                mov     bx,si               ; SI:DI = length actually read
                or      bx,di               ; did we get any data?
                jz      fcopy5              ; no, we're at end of file

                push    si                  ; write copy buffer
                push    di                  ; SI:DI = length to write
                mov     bx,ohandle          ; BX = output file handle
                mov     ds,copyseg          ; DS:DX = buffer base address
                xor     dx,dx
                mov     ax,4000h            ; MS-DOS write function number
                call    xfer                ; now write output file
                pop     ax                  ; DX:AX = length requested
                pop     dx                  ; SI:DI = length written
                cmp     si,dx               ; compare requested to actual
                jne     fcopy3              ; jump, disk is full
                cmp     di,ax
                je      fcopy2              ; loop to fill buffer again

fcopy3:         mov     bx,ohandle          ; disk is full
                mov     ah,3eh              ; close output file
                int     21h                 ; transfer to MS-DOS
                push    ss
                pop     ds                  ; now delete output file
                lea     dx,ofname           ; DS:DX = output filename
                mov     ah,41h
                int     21h                 ; transfer to MS-DOS
                mov     ohandle,-1          ; zap output handle

fcopy4:         stc                         ; copy failed, set carry flag

fcopy5:         pushf                       ; save success/failure flag
                cmp     copyseg,-1          ; was buffer allocated?
                je      fcopy6              ; no, jump
                mov     es,copyseg          ; yes, release copy buffer
                mov     ah,49h
                int     21h                 ; transfer to MS-DOS
```

(continued)

Figure 8-5. *continued*

```
fcopy6: cmp     ihandle,-1              ; input file open?
        je      fcopy7                 ; no, jump
        mov     bx,ihandle             ; close input file
        mov     ah,3eh
        int     21h                    ; transfer to MS-DOS

fcopy7: cmp     ohandle,-1             ; output file open?
        je      fcopy8                 ; no, jump
        mov     bx,ohandle             ; close output file
        mov     ah,3eh
        int     21h                    ; transfer to MS-DOS

fcopy8: popf                           ; get success/failure flag
        mov     sp,bp                  ; discard stack frame
        pop     bp                     ; restore registers
        pop     di
        pop     es
        pop     si
        pop     ds
        pop     dx
        pop     cx
        pop     bx
        pop     ax
        ret                            ; back to caller

fcopy   endp


;
; XFER:         Fills copy buffer from input file
;               or writes copy buffer to output file
;
; Call with:    SI:DI = length to transfer
;               DS:DX = buffer address
;               BX    = file handle
;               AX    = MS-DOS function (3F00H = read, 4000H = write)
;
; Returns:      SI:DI = length actually read or written
;
xfer    proc    near
                                       ; local variables
bavail  equ     word ptr [bp-4]        ; buffer bytes available
bused   equ     bavail-4               ; buffer bytes expended
baddr   equ     bused-4                ; current buffer address
dosfxn  equ     baddr-2                ; MS-DOS function number

        push    bp                     ; set up stack frame
        mov     bp,sp
        lea     sp,dosfxn
```

(continued)

Figure 8-5. *continued*

```
        mov     dosfxn,ax              ; save MS-DOS function number
        mov     bavail,di              ; save size of I/O buffer
        mov     bavail+2,si
        mov     baddr,dx               ; save buffer base address
        mov     baddr+2,ds
        mov     bused,0                ; reset total bytes transferred
        mov     bused+2,0

xfer1:          .                      ; prepare to read or write
        mov     cx,xfrsize             ; assume maximum I/O size
        cmp     bavail+2,0             ; near end of buffer?
        jne     xfer2                  ; no, jump
        cmp     bavail,cx              ; can we transfer maximum?
        ja      xfer2                  ; yes, jump
        mov     cx,bavail              ; no, clamp transfer size

xfer2:  push    cx                     ; save requested size
        mov     ds,baddr+2             ; DS:DX = buffer address
        mov     dx,baddr               ; BX already = handle
        mov     ax,dosfxn              ; MS-DOS function number
        int     21h                    ; call MS-DOS function

        add     bused,ax               ; accumulate bytes transferred
        adc     bused+2,0
        sub     bavail,ax              ; decrement bytes available
        sbb     bavail+2,0
        add     baddr+2,xfrsize/16     ; update transfer address
        pop     cx                     ; bytes transferred = requested?
        cmp     cx,ax
        jne     xfer3                  ; no, done with transfer
        cmp     cx,xfrsize             ; was requested = maximum?
        je      xfer1                  ; yes, loop to transfer again

xfer3:  mov     di,word ptr bused      ; total number of bytes
        mov     si,word ptr bused+2    ; transferred to/from file
        mov     sp,bp                  ; discard stack frame
        pop     bp
        ret                            ; return to caller

xfer    endp

_TEXT   ends

        end
```

Here is an example of FCOPY in action:

```
oldfile        db       'MYFILE.DAT',0 ; existing file
oldfile_len equ      $-oldfile
newfile        db       'MYFILE.BAK',0 ; file to be created
newfile_len equ      $-newfile
        .
        .
        .
        mov      si,seg oldfile      ; DS:SI = addr of old filename
        mov      ds,si
        mov      si,offset oldfile
        mov      bx,oldfile_len      ; BX = length of old filename
        mov      di,seg newfile      ; ES:DI = addr of new filename
        mov      es,di
        mov      di,offset newfile
        mov      dx,newfile_len      ; DX = length of new filename
        xor      ax,ax               ; flag = create or overwrite
        call     fcopy               ; make backup file
        jc       error               ; jump if function failed
```

FCOPY has several interesting aspects. First, the flag parameter allows the calling program to specify an action to take if the new file already exists (similar to the OpenFlag argument in OS/2's DosOpen function). Second, the routine is network-friendly in its use of access and sharing modes. Third, the routine utilizes all available memory to minimize movement of the disk head. Fourth, the routine cleans up gracefully by deleting the destination file if the copy operation fails at any point. Accordingly, let's inspect the logic of FCOPY in a bit more detail.

FCOPY first saves all of the affected registers and builds a stack frame to contain the various addresses and other parameters that were passed to the routine. Next, FCOPY tries to allocate some memory. Actually, FCOPY allocates *all* the available contiguous memory, in a two-step process: First, the routine asks MS-DOS for an impossibly large amount of memory. MS-DOS predictably "fails" this request but returns information about the largest free memory block. Second, the routine in turn immediately requests that same free block. If no free memory is available, FCOPY gives up and returns with an error flag.

Assuming that some memory could be allocated, FCOPY tries to open the source file with an access mode of read-only and a sharing mode of deny-write. This ensures that the file won't change while FCOPY is using it, but it doesn't prevent other programs that also want to use the file in read-only mode from gaining access to the file. If the source file can be located, FCOPY tries to create the destination file. This attempt might require more than one step, depending on the flags parameter that was supplied to the routine. If the flag's value is 1, the calling program does not want to overwrite another file with the same name. In this case, FCOPY tries to open the destination file with an access mode of read-only and a sharing mode of deny-none (which gives FCOPY the best shot at determining whether such a file already exists). Then, if the open succeeds, FCOPY immediately closes the handle again and exits with an error code.

If the FCOPY flag is 1 but the open of the destination file fails, or if the FCOPY flag is 0, FCOPY tries to create the destination file. The operation can fail at this point for several reasons: A file with the same name exists but is being used by another program with an incompatible sharing mode; the destination file is to be placed in the root directory, and the root is full; the destination file is not in the root directory, but the subdirectory it would reside in must be expanded to hold the file, and the disk is full; and so on. In most cases, however, the creation of the destination file succeeds, and FCOPY is then ready to perform the actual file copy.

FCOPY reads as much data as it can from the source file, using chunks of 65,520 bytes (64 KB − 16), until its buffer is full or the end of the file is reached. FCOPY then writes data out to the destination file, watching for a "disk-full" condition. If a disk-full error occurs, FCOPY aborts the operation, deletes the destination file, and exits with an error flag. When the entire file has been transferred, FCOPY closes the source and destination files, releases its memory buffer, and returns a success flag.

Could the close operation ever fail in a way that wasn't the result of a hardware error? Actually, it could—if the destination file is on a removable disk—but the circumstances of such an error would be rather bizarre and unlikely.

Working with Filenames

Let's examine another fundamental file system issue: filenames. An MS-DOS system can contain many files with the same name and extension as long as the files are in different locations. MS-DOS requires only that each file be uniquely specified by the combination of a drive, path, name, and extension, in the following form:

x:\path\name.ext

The *path* can consist of one or more directory names, starting with the disk's root directory, separated by a backslash (\). A file specification of this sort, which unambiguously identifies one single file out of all the files in the system, is called a *fully qualified filename.*

If you had to enter fully qualified names every time you wanted to work with a file, your patience would be exhausted in about five minutes—especially if you organize your files in a tree directory structure with several levels. Fortunately, whenever you use a filename that omits the drive specifier or does not include a full path, MS-DOS fills in the missing information by supplying your current drive or current directory.

This ability to use locality as an implicit part of a filename is a tremendous convenience for the user, but it can be a nasty trap for the programmer. Suppose, for example, that you prompt the user for a filename. The user enters the following:

```
myfile.dat
```

Opening the file is no problem: MS-DOS knows that you mean MYFILE.DAT in the current directory of the current drive. Filenames with relative paths such as

```
d:subdir\myfile.dat
```

or even

```
d:..\subdir\myfile.dat
```

are no trouble either; MS-DOS can readily find the files.

Imagine, however, that within the program you also provide the user with a way of *changing* the current directory or the current drive. If you store an incomplete filename for later use and the user then selects a new drive or directory, your program might be unable to open the file again—or, worse yet, might open the wrong file.

Obviously, you need a subroutine that converts an incomplete file specification to a fully qualified filename that can be safely used at any time during a program's execution. QFN.ASM (Figure 8-6) is such a routine.

```
;
; QFN.ASM -- Qualifies filename.
;
; Copyright (C) 1991 Ray Duncan
;
; Call with:    DS:SI = filename address
;               AX    = length
;
; Returns:      Carry = clear if filename OK
;               DS:SI = qualified filename
;               AX    = length
;               or
;               Carry = set if bad filename
;
; Destroys:     DS:SI and AX if error returned

DGROUP   group   _DATA

_DATA    segment word public 'DATA'

cdrive   db      0                     ; current drive
cpath    db      '\',64 dup (0)        ; current directory

tbuff    db      64 dup (0)            ; target directory

qbuff    db      'X:\'                 ; qualified filename
         db      80 dup (0)

fname    dw      ?                     ; original filename address
flen     dw      ?                     ; original filename length

_DATA    ends
```

Figure 8-6.   *(continued)*

QFN.ASM, a routine that accepts a filename or directory name with a partial or implied path and returns the fully qualified form of the same name. The helper routine MAKELC translates a string to lowercase for a more attractive display.

Figure 8-6. *continued*

```
_TEXT    segment word public 'CODE'

         assume  cs:_TEXT,ds:DGROUP

         public  qfn
qfn      proc    near                    ; qualify filename

         push    bx                      ; save registers
         push    cx
         push    dx
         push    di
         push    es

         mov     flen,ax                 ; save length and
         mov     fname,si                ; address of filename

         mov     ax,ds                   ; make DGROUP addressable
         mov     es,ax                   ; with ES register

         mov     ah,19h                  ; fxn 19h = get drive
         int     21h                     ; transfer to MS-DOS
         mov     cdrive,al               ; save current drive

                                         ; save current directory
         mov     si,offset DGROUP:cpath+1 ; DS:SI = buffer
         mov     ah,47h                  ; fxn 47h = get directory
         mov     dl,0                    ; for current drive
         int     21h                     ; transfer to MS-DOS

                                         ; did caller specify drive?
         mov     di,fname                ; get address of name
         mov     cx,flen                 ; get length of name

         cmp     cx,2                    ; if drive, length must
                                         ; be >= two characters
         jl      qfn2                    ; too short, no drive
         cmp     byte ptr [di+1],':'     ; check for drive delimiter
         jne     qfn2                    ; no delimiter, jump

         mov     dl,[di]                 ; get ASCII drive code
         or      dl,20h                  ; fold to lowercase
         sub     dl,'a'                  ; convert it to binary
         mov     ah,0eh                  ; fxn 0eh = select drive
         int     21h                     ; transfer to MS-DOS

                                         ; be sure drive was selected
         mov     ah,19h                  ; fxn 19h = get current drive
         int     21h                     ; transfer to MS-DOS
         cmp     dl,al                   ; current = requested?
```

(continued)

Figure 8-6. *continued*

```
        je      qfn1                    ; jump if select succeeded
        jmp     qfn8                    ; exit, select failed

qfn1:   add     di,2                    ; bump pointer past drive
        sub     cx,2                    ; and decrement length

qfn2:                                   ; save current directory
                                        ; again for new drive
        mov     si,offset DGROUP:cpath+1 ; DS:SI = buffer address
        mov     ah,47h                  ; fxn 47h = get directory
        mov     dl,0                    ; use current drive
        int     21h                     ; transfer to MS-DOS

                                        ; scan off path, if any
        push    di                      ; save start of path
        mov     al,'\'                  ; AL = path delimiter
qfn3:   mov     fname,di                ; save path pointer
        mov     flen,cx                 ; save path length
        jcxz    qfn4                    ; jump if end of filename
        repne scasb                     ; any \ left in path?
        je      qfn3                    ; loop if \ found

qfn4:   pop     si                      ; recover path start address
        mov     di,offset DGROUP:tbuff  ; ES:DI = local buffer
        mov     cx,fname                ; calculate path length
        sub     cx,si
        jz      qfn6                    ; jump, no path at all
        cmp     cx,1                    ; is it root directory?
        je      qfn5                    ; jump if root
        dec     cx                      ; else discard last \

qfn5:   rep movsb                       ; transfer path and
        xor     al,al                   ; append null byte
        stosb

                                        ; now make target directory
        mov     dx,offset DGROUP:tbuff  ; the current directory
        mov     ah,3bh                  ; fxn 3bh = select directory
        int     21h                     ; transfer to MS-DOS
        jc      qfn8                    ; jump, no such directory

qfn6:                                   ; build up full pathname
        mov     ah,19h                  ; get current drive
        int     21h                     ; transfer to MS-DOS
        add     al,'A'                  ; convert binary to ASCII
        mov     qbuff,al                ; store ASCII drive code

                                        ; get current directory
        mov     dl,0                    ; DL = 0 for default drive
        mov     si,offset DGROUP:qbuff+3 ; DS:SI = buffer address
```

(continued)

Figure 8-6. *continued*

```
        mov     ah,47h              ; fxn 47h = get current dir
        int     21h                 ; transfer to MS-DOS
        jc      qfn8                ; jump if error

        mov     di,offset DGROUP:qbuff+3 ; point to path component
        cmp     byte ptr [di],0     ; is current dir = root?
        je      qfn7                ; yes, jump

        xor     al,al               ; scan for null byte at
        mov     cx,-1               ; end of pathname
        repne scasb
        mov     byte ptr [di-1],'\' ; and append backslash

qfn7:                               ; append filename to drive+path
        mov     si,fname            ; filename address
        cmp     byte ptr [si],'.'
        je      qfn8                ; exit if directory alias
        mov     cx,flen             ; filename length
        rep movsb                   ; copy filename

        mov     si,offset DGROUP:qbuff ; DS:SI = address
        mov     ax,di               ; and AX = length of
        sub     ax,si               ; fully qualified filename
        call    makelc              ; fold filename to lowercase
        clc                         ; carry = false for success
        jmp     qfn9                ; jump to common exit

qfn8:                               ; come here if any error detected
        stc                         ; carry = true to indicate error

qfn9:   pushf                       ; save carry flag
        push    ax                  ; save final length

        mov     dx,offset DGROUP:cpath ; restore original directory
        mov     ah,3bh              ; fxn 3bh = select directory
        int     21h                 ; transfer to MS-DOS

        mov     dl,cdrive           ; restore original drive
        mov     ah,0eh              ; fxn 0eh = set drive
        int     21h                 ; transfer to MS-DOS

        pop     ax                  ; get back AX = length
        popf                        ; also restore carry flag
        pop     es                  ; restore other registers
        pop     di
        pop     dx
        pop     cx
        pop     bx
        ret                         ; back to caller
```

(continued)

Figure 8-6. *continued*

```
qfn        endp

;
; MAKELC:         Folds string to lowercase
;
; Call with:      DS:SI = address of string
;                 AX    = length of string
;
; Returns:        Nothing
;
; Destroys:       Nothing
;
makelc  proc    near

        push    bx                      ; save BX contents
        xor     bx,bx                   ; BX will be string index

mlc1:   cmp     byte ptr [bx+si],'A'    ; change A-Z to a-z
        jb      mlc2
        cmp     byte ptr [bx+si],'Z'
        ja      mlc2
        or      byte ptr [bx+si],20h

mlc2:   inc     bx                      ; advance through string
        cmp     bx,ax                   ; done with string yet?
        jne     mlc1                    ; no, check next char

        pop     bx                      ; restore BX and
        ret                             ; return to caller

makelc  endp

_TEXT   ends

        end
```

Using the QFN Routine

QFN is called with the address of a file specification in registers DS:SI and the length in register AX. If the file specification includes a drive code, QFN checks to be sure that the drive exists. If no drive code is present, QFN adds the identifier for the current drive. Similarly, if a full path is included, QFN checks to be sure that the path exists. If the path is incompletely specified or missing altogether, QFN expands the path using the current directory of the current or specified drive.

If the drive and path components can be successfully resolved to a valid disk and directory in the system, QFN returns the carry flag clear (0). The address and length of the fully qualified filename are returned in registers DS:SI and AX, respectively. If the drive or path does not exist, QFN returns the carry flag set (1). The contents of registers other than DS, SI, and AX are always preserved. Here is an example of a call to QFN:

```
fname      db    'MYFILE.DAT'      ; filename to be qualified
fname_len  equ   $-fname           ; length of filename
           .
           .
           .
           mov   si,seg fname      ; DS:SI = addr of filename
           mov   ds,si
           mov   si,offset fname
           mov   ax,fname_len      ; length of filename
           call  qfn               ; qualify filename
           jc    error             ; jump if function failed
```

QFN does not try to determine whether a particular file exists—only whether the specified or implicit location for the file is feasible. Thus, you can use the routine to generate fully qualified names of files that are yet to be created or to evaluate drive and path combinations without a filename. If you supply QFN with a drive identifier only, it returns the drive and the current path for that drive. If you provide QFN with a partial or relative path terminated by a backslash, it returns a fully qualified drive and path combination.

How QFN Works

QFN's overall strategy is to let the operating system do the hard work, rather than having the routine try to inspect the directory structure to evaluate such horrid possibilities as the following:

```
z:dir1\..\dir2\..\myfile.dat
```

After saving the various registers and putting away the address and the length of the supplied filename, QFN obtains and saves the current drive and directory with Int 21H Functions 19H and 47H. QFN then picks off the drive code (if any) in the argument filename and calls Int 21H Function 0EH to select that drive as the current drive. Unfortunately, MS-DOS Function 0EH does not return an error code. The only way to tell whether Function 0EH succeeded is to follow it with a call to Function 19H and see whether the drive you asked for became the current drive.

Next, QFN extracts the path component from the supplied filename by scanning for the last backslash character, copies the path into a local buffer, adds a terminating null byte, and calls Int 21H Function 3BH to make the path the current directory. The operating system has the fun of figuring out relative paths (which do not begin with a backslash) and the meaning of any dot (.) or double-dot (..) aliases the path contains. If the call fails, you know that the path is invalid—some directory named in the path does not exist.

Once you get this far, the rest is easy. QFN simply calls Int 21H Functions 19H and 47H to get the current drive and directory, formats them together in an ASCII buffer, and appends the original filename. Then, it folds the drive code, path, and filename

163

to lowercase characters for visual consistency. Last, QFN restores the original path and drive and returns the address and length of the fully qualified filename to the calling program.

By asking the operating system to figure out any complexities in the original path and then retrieving the cleaned-up path, you can avoid a lengthy, messy coding problem. Of course, some MASM connoisseurs might say that the QFN code itself is lengthy and messy. At first glance, portions of it do appear redundant or unnecessary. But three principal reasons justify its complicated structure:

- The routine is able to handle drives and partial paths without a filename.

- A common clean-up and exit point contributes to code integrity and ease of maintenance.

- A backslash in an MS-DOS path has different meanings, depending on its position. If the backslash occurs at the start of the path, it represents the root directory and is followed immediately by the name of another directory with no intervening delimiter. If it occurs in any other position, it is simply a delimiter separating two directory names and has no intrinsic significance.

PROCEDURES INTRODUCED IN THIS CHAPTER

Procedure Name	Action	Parameters	Results
FCOPY	Copies existing file to create backup or temporary working file	DS:SI = segment:offset of name for existing file BX = length of existing filename ES:DI = segment:offset of name for new file DX = length of new filename AX = flags (0 = overwrite, 1 = do not overwrite)	If function successful: Carry = clear If function unsuccessful: Carry = set
QFN	Qualifies filename (converts partial or relative path and filename to completely specified drive, path, and filename)	DS:SI = segment:offset of filename AX = length of filename	If function successful: Carry = clear DS:SI = segment:offset of qualified filename AX = length of qualified filename If function unsuccessful: Carry = set

Companion Disk

The companion disk directory \CH08 contains the programs and modules that are listed below.

Routines Presented in This Chapter

FCOPY.ASM   Copies an existing file to create a backup or a temporary working file

QFN.ASM   Qualifies a filename (converts a filename with a relative or partial path to a filename with a drive specifier and a full and absolute path from the root directory)

Routines Previously Discussed

ARGC.ASM   Returns the number of command-tail arguments

ARGV.ASM   Returns the address and length of a specific command-tail argument

Demonstration Programs

QCOPY   MAKE file for QCOPY.EXE

QCOPY.ASM   Noninteractive demonstration of the FCOPY routine

TRYQFN   MAKE file for TRYQFN.EXE

TRYQFN.ASM   Interactive demonstration of the QFN routine

The noninteractive program QCOPY.ASM demonstrates use of the routine FCOPY. To build QCOPY.EXE, enter this command:

```
C>MAKE QCOPY  <Enter>
```

QCOPY efficiently copies a single file, utilizing all available memory to minimize the amount of head movement. The command format for QCOPY is the following:

```
QCOPY sourcefile destinationfile
```

The source and destination filenames can include a drive and path specifier and need not be on the same drive, as shown in this example:

```
C>QCOPY C:\MYDIR\MYFILE.DAT D:\BACKUP\MYFILE.BAK  <Enter>
```

The interactive program TRYQFN.ASM demonstrates use of the routine QFN. To build TRYQFN.EXE, enter this command:

```
C>MAKE TRYQFN  <Enter>
```

When you run TRYQFN.EXE, it prompts you to enter a filename, calls QFN to qualify the filename, and then displays the fully qualified filename. Press the Enter key at the prompt to exit the demo program, or press Ctrl-C or Ctrl-Break at any time.

9

Sequential Files

A sequential file is a collection of records that are accessed in order of their occurrence in the file. Sequential files are most useful under the following circumstances:

- When each record is strongly dependent on the records surrounding it (that is, the record out of context is meaningless)

- When you have a great deal of data to store and you want to use disk space as efficiently as possible

- When your data is relatively stable, can be updated in a batch mode, and does not need to be accessed interactively and randomly

In the old days when magnetic tape drives predominated, the efficient management of sequential files was developed into a fine art. Computer science textbooks from the 1960s devote an amazing amount of space to the topics of sorting, updating, and merging sequential files—you'll even find elaborate techniques for processing them backward (to avoid wasting time rewinding tapes). For instance, Donald Knuth's opus on sorting and searching, volume 3 of *The Art of Computer Programming*, contains more than a hundred pages on managing sequential files, complete with romantic subheadings such as "The Polyphase Merge" and "The Oscillating Sort."

In our own era of fast and cheap hard disks, B-trees, relational databases, SQL, and the like, the topic of sequential file processing is no longer stylish; indeed, it has a definite musty aura about it. For that matter, the fundamental model of file I/O in MS-DOS (a model derived from UNIX) drastically downgrades the usefulness of the classical sequential file algorithms because MS-DOS presents all files to applications as a randomly accessible array of bytes, leaving the applications free to use sequential access, random access, or any mixture of the two. Nevertheless, basic techniques for sequential file processing should be in every programmer's mental attic for retrieval when needed.

Sequential File Fundamentals

Implementing sequential file access in an application that runs under MS-DOS is relatively simple. When a file is opened or created, its file pointer is initially set to zero. If a program merely issues read or write requests one after another without explicitly setting the file pointer position, the program's access to the file is automatically sequential. After each operation, MS-DOS returns the count of the bytes transferred and updates the file pointer to point to the next byte to be read or written. The application detects an end-of-file condition (when reading) or a disk-full condition (when writing) by comparing the count of bytes requested to the count of bytes transferred. Neither event is flagged by the operating system as an error.

Typically, a program opens the input file, creates an output file, and copies records one at a time from the input to the output, making any necessary changes to the data on a record-by-record basis. (Chapter 8's FCOPY subroutine, which uses sequential access to duplicate an existing file, demonstrates the prototype of this strategy.) If the program has new records to add to the file, it sorts them into the same order as the input file and inserts them one by one into the record stream at the appropriate points. When the entire input file is processed, the program closes both files, renames the input file with the extension BAK, and assigns the original name of the input file to the output file.

The simplest type of sequential file consists of records that have the same internal structure and are the same size. This file design has certain advantages: If you later need random access to the file, you can quickly build up a compact index that associates a key for each record with its record number—that is, its sequential position, or "slot," in the main file. You can then access any record directly by looking up its key value in the index, multiplying the record number by the record size, setting the file pointer, and issuing a read or write operation. Alternatively, if a sequential file of fixed-length records is kept in sorted order, you can rapidly find a record by using a binary search, which is yet another example of a "divide-and-conquer" strategy. (Chapter 10, which focuses on random access files, examines indexes and binary searches in more detail.)

Sequential files containing records with a fixed length and structure are relatively rare, though, because they forfeit one of the main advantages offered by sequential file design: economical use of disk space. More commonly, sequential files will contain variable-length records whose length or contents are encoded in the record itself in one of the following ways:

- The end of the record is indicated by a reserved delimiter.

- The record begins with a record type code that implicitly specifies the record length.

- The record starts with a record length code that implicitly specifies the record type (rarely used).

- The record begins with explicit record length and record type codes.

You probably use the first encoding method every day: A text file is the prototypical sequential file of ordered, delimited, variable-length records. In text files, the end of each line (record) is indicated by a logical newline character. (A newline character actually can consist of more than one character and can also vary from system to system. In MS-DOS systems, each line is terminated by a carriage return/linefeed pair. Lines are usually terminated in UNIX by a linefeed alone and in Apple systems by a carriage return alone.)

The processing of delimited records can be slow and messy, however. First, because the delimiter characters cannot (by definition) occur within the body of a record, they must be represented in a special way when they occur as data rather than as delimiters. Second, the program cannot predict how much memory it should allocate to hold a specific record, or even what the maximum size of a record might be. Third, the program must inspect every byte of every record to find out where the next record starts.

Consequently, the other three encoding methods are better suited to efficient sequential processing, especially when the files contain a relatively small number of record types that must be searched and updated by many programs. For example, when a record's type is encoded in a record header, programs can quickly select the records they need and just as quickly bypass those they can ignore. It isn't necessary to scan each record for a delimiter to find the next record, because the program knows the length of each record type. Further, the contents of each record are not restricted in any way because delimiter characters need not be reserved.

The technique of explicitly encoding both a type and a length at the head of each record adds more bulk to a file than the other methods do, but it is also by far the most powerful and flexible method. Because record lengths are not "hard-wired" into programs, they can be changed at any time without altering programs that do not process that particular record type, and a record type is not forced to occupy a specific number of bytes even if all the bytes are not needed. New record types can also be added at any time without changing existing programs, because the programs can use the length information in the record header to skip a record type they don't recognize. The only record type that every program must recognize is the end-of-file marker. Reserving a special record type for this purpose helps to provide a simple cross-check of whether the file is intact—if the program reaches the physical end of the file without encountering an end-of-file record, it knows that a record header has been damaged or that part of the file has been lost.

Processing Nondelimited Sequential Records

Although the mainstream logic of a program that processes sequential files might be complicated, the drudgery components of the file access can be encapsulated into short, simple routines. The module SEQREC.ASM, which we'll examine here, contains a complete set of subroutines for reading and writing files containing typed, variable-length records. Each record is assumed to begin with a two-word header: The first word contains the record type, which is understood by the program that calls the routine; the second word contains the record length (including the header itself). Figure 9-1 on the following page illustrates the generalized record layout assumed by the routines in this module. Although nothing in the routines demands this, it's a good idea to reserve the record type 0 as an end-of-file marker. The structure of such a record is shown in Figure 9-2.

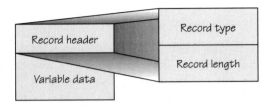

Figure 9-1.
The layout for records processed by SEQREC.ASM. The first two words of the record are a header.

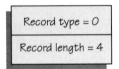

Figure 9-2.
An end-of-file marker for programs using the routines in SEQREC.ASM. The record header contains a record type of 0 and a length of 4.

The SEQREC.ASM module (Figure 9-3) contains four general-purpose routines: NEXTSREC, READSREC, SKIPSREC, and WRITESREC. All four take essentially the same parameters, which are intended to be symmetric with the parameters used by the MS-DOS Read File function (Int 21H Function 3FH) so that they will be easy to remember: a file handle in BX, a length in CX, and a buffer address in DS:DX. All four routines return the carry flag clear if the function is successful or the carry flag set if the function fails; other results are returned in registers or the caller's buffer as appropriate.

```
;
; SEQREC.ASM -- Sequential file record I/O routines.
;
; Copyright (C) 1991 Ray Duncan

hdrsize equ     4                       ; size of file header
typeofs equ     0                       ; header offset, record type
sizeofs equ     2                       ; header offset, record size


_TEXT   segment word public 'CODE'

        assume  cs:_TEXT
;
```

Figure 9-3.   *(continued)*
SEQREC.ASM, a suite of general-purpose routines for processing typed, variable-length records in sequential files.

Figure 9-3. *continued*

```
; NEXTSREC: Returns type of next record
;
; Call with:     BX    = file handle
;
; Returns:       If function successful:
;                Carry = clear
;                AX    = record type
;                CX    = record length
;
;                If function unsuccessful:
;                Carry = set
;
; Destroys:      Nothing (but CX and AX are meaningless
;                if function was unsuccessful)
;
        public  nextsrec
nextsrec proc   near

        push    dx                      ; save registers
        push    ds
        push    bp
        mov     bp,sp                   ; set up stack frame and
        sub     sp,hdrsize              ; allocate buffer for header
        lea     dx,[bp-hdrsize]         ; DS:DX = buffer address
        push    ss
        pop     ds                      ; BX already = file handle
        mov     cx,hdrsize              ; CX = record header size
        mov     ah,3fh                  ; fxn 3fh = read
        int     21h                     ; transfer to MS-DOS
        jc      nexts1                  ; jump if read error
        cmp     ax,hdrsize              ; be sure we got data
        stc                             ; set carry just in case
        jne     nexts1                  ; jump, end of file
        mov     ax,4201h                ; now back up file pointer
        mov     cx,-1                   ; CX:DX = negative offset
        mov     dx,-(hdrsize)           ; BX still = file handle
        int     21h                     ; transfer to MS-DOS
        jc      nexts1                  ; jump if seek error
        mov     cx,[bp-hdrsize+sizeofs] ; retrieve record length
        mov     ax,[bp-hdrsize+typeofs] ; and record type

nexts1: mov     sp,bp                   ; discard stack buffer
        pop     bp                      ; restore registers
        pop     ds
        pop     dx
        ret                             ; return to caller

nextsrec endp
```

(continued)

Figure 9-3. *continued*

```
;
; READSREC: Returns next sequential record
;
; Call with:    BX    = file handle
;               CX    = length of buffer
;               DS:DX = segment:offset of buffer
;
; Returns:      If function successful:
;               Carry = clear
;               AX    = record type
;               CX    = record length
;
;               If function unsuccessful:
;               Carry = set
;
; Destroys:     Nothing (but CX and AX are meaningless
;               if function was unsuccessful)
;
        public  readsrec
readsrec proc   near

        push    cx                      ; save buffer length
        call    nextsrec                ; get type, size next record
        pop     ax                      ; restore buffer length
        jc      reads1                  ; jump if error in NEXTSREC
        cmp     ax,cx                   ; does record fit in buffer?
        jb      reads1                  ; record too big, exit
        mov     ah,3fh                  ; fxn 3fh = read record
        int     21h                     ; transfer to MS-DOS
        jc      reads1                  ; jump, read error
        cmp     ax,cx                   ; was entire record read?
        jne     reads1                  ; no, read error
        push    bx
        mov     bx,dx                   ; point to record header
        mov     ax,[bx+typeofs]         ; fetch record type
        pop     bx
        jmp     reads2                  ; return with carry clear

reads1: stc                             ; error, set carry flag

reads2: ret                             ; return to caller

readsrec endp

;
; SKIPSREC: Skips next sequential record
;
; Call with:    BX    = file handle
;
```

(continued)

Figure 9-3. *continued*

```
; Returns:        If function successful:
;                 Carry = clear
;
;                 If function unsuccessful:
;                 Carry = set
;
; Destroys:       Nothing
;
        public  skipsrec
skipsrec proc   near

        push    ax                      ; save registers
        push    cx
        push    dx
        call    nextsrec                ; get type, size next record
        jc      skips1                  ; jump if error in NEXTSREC
        mov     dx,cx                   ; now bump file pointer
        mov     cx,0                    ; CX:DX = incrementing amount
        mov     ax,4201h                ; fxn 4201h = seek relative
        int     21h                     ; transfer to MS-DOS

skips1: pop     dx                      ; restore registers
        pop     cx
        pop     ax
        ret                             ; return to caller

skipsrec endp

;
; WRITESREC: Writes sequential record to file
;
; Call with:      BX    = file handle
;                 DS:DX = segment:offset of record
;                 Note: record length taken from record itself
;
; Returns:        If function successful:
;                 Carry = clear
;
;                 If function unsuccessful:
;                 Carry = set
;
; Destroys:       Nothing
;
        public  writesrec
writesrec proc  near

        push    ax                      ; save registers
        push    cx
        push    bx                      ; save file handle
```

(continued)

Figure 9-3. *continued*

```
        mov     bx,dx               ; get record length
        mov     cx,[bx+sizeofs]     ; from record header
        pop     bx                  ; restore file handle
        mov     ah,40h              ; fxn 40h = write
        int     21h                 ; transfer to MS-DOS
        jc      write1              ; jump, write error
        cmp     ax,cx               ; entire record written?
        je      write1              ; yes, return carry clear
        stc                         ; disk full, set carry flag

write1: pop     cx                  ; restore registers
        pop     ax
        ret                         ; return to caller

writesrec endp

_TEXT   ends

        end
```

Let's look at each routine contained in SEQREC.ASM in a little more detail. The routine NEXTSREC inspects the record header of the next record in the file, returning the record type in AX and the record length in CX. No net change in the file pointer position results; in other words, a program typically follows a call to NEXTSREC with a call to either SKIPSREC or READSREC, depending on the record type and on whether the program has a buffer large enough to handle the record. Here is a typical call to NEXTSREC:

```
handle  dw      0               ; valid handle for file
        .
        .
        .
        mov     bx,handle       ; BX = valid file handle
        call    nextsrec        ; get record type and length
        jc      error           ; jump if function failed
                                ; now AX = record type
                                ; CX = length
```

Note that the caller does not need to provide a buffer; NEXTSREC temporarily allocates space on the stack to read the record header.

READSREC reads the next record from the file, returning the record in the caller's buffer, the record type in AX, and the record length in CX. The file pointer is incremented appropriately. The call to READSREC fails if the buffer is not large enough to hold the record, leaving the file pointer unchanged. The call also fails if the physical end of the file has been reached. A call to READSREC resembles a call to NEXTSREC, except that the caller must provide a buffer large enough for any record that might be read (though not necessarily big enough for the largest record in the file, because such a record could be ignored by calling NEXTSREC and then SKIPSREC):

```
buffer  db      512                     ; buffer must be big enough
buf_len equ     $-buffer                ; for largest record read
handle  dw      0                       ; valid handle for file
         .
         .
         .
        mov     bx,handle               ; BX = valid file handle
        mov     cx,buf_len              ; CX = length of buffer
        mov     dx,seg buffer           ; DS:DX = buffer address
        mov     ds,dx
        mov     dx,offset buffer
        call    readsrec                ; read record into buffer
        jc      error                   ; jump if read failed
                                        ; now AX = record type
                                        ; CX = length
```

SKIPSREC skips the next record in the file by calling NEXTSREC to get the record type and length and then incrementing the file pointer appropriately. The routine does not return any values other than the success or failure indicator in the carry flag. A call to SKIPSREC is simple:

```
handle  dw      0                       ; valid handle for file
         .
         .
         .
        mov     bx,handle               ; BX = valid file handle
        call    skipsrec                ; skip next record in file
        jc      error                   ; jump if function failed
```

WRITESREC writes a record to a file from the caller's buffer. The record is assumed to have a valid header, and the length of the record is taken from the header rather than from CX. After the transfer, the file pointer is incremented appropriately. Here is an example:

```
buffer  db      512                     ; buffer contains header and data
buf_len equ     $-buffer                ; length of buffer
handle  dw      0                       ; valid handle for file
         .
         .
         .
        mov     bx,handle               ; BX = valid file handle
        mov     dx,seg buffer           ; DS:DX = buffer address
        mov     ds,dx
        mov     dx,offset buffer
        call    writesrec               ; write record to disk
        jc      error                   ; jump if write failed
```

Additional detailed information about the use of READSREC, NEXTSREC, SKIPSREC, and WRITESREC can be found in the source code. These routines should be viewed

175

primarily as prototypes; in production versions, you would want to add the ability to return error codes that would let the calling program distinguish, say, the physical end of the file from a buffer-too-small condition on a failed call to READSREC.

Processing Delimited Sequential Records

The subroutine RLINE.ASM (Figure 9-4) illustrates a basic approach to processing delimited, variable-length records. RLINE assumes that it is reading from an ASCII text file and that each line is terminated by a logical newline, which is a constant sequence of delimiter characters. (As already noted, the standard for MS-DOS is a carriage return followed by a linefeed.)

```
;
; RLINE.ASM -- Reads line from text file.
;
; Copyright (C) 1991 Ray Duncan
;
; Call with:     DS:DX = segment:offset of buffer
;                CX    = buffer size
;                BX    = text file handle
;                Note: The buffer should be larger than any line
;                that will be encountered in the text file.
;
;
; Returns:       If function successful:
;                Carry = clear
;                AX    = length of line including newline
;                           delimiter character(s), or 0 if
;                           end of file
;                DS:DX = segment:offset of text
;
;                If function unsuccessful:
;                Carry = set
;
; Destroys:      Nothing

DGROUP   group    _DATA

_DATA    segment word public 'DATA'

newline db       0dh,0ah                   ; logical newline char sequence
nl_len  equ      $-newline                 ; length of logical newline

_DATA    ends
```

Figure 9-4.   *(continued)*

RLINE.ASM, a subroutine that demonstrates processing delimited records in sequential files. RLINE reads a text file one line at a time. This routine can be generalized to handle any type of delimited record by passing the delimiter string's address and length as a parameter instead of hard-coding the delimiter string in the data segment.

Figure 9-4. *continued*

```
_TEXT    segment word public 'CODE'

         extrn    strndx:near               ; string search routine

         assume   cs:_TEXT

         public   rline
rline    proc     near

         push     bx                        ; save registers
         push     cx
         push     dx
         push     si
         push     di
         push     es

                                            ; read chunk from file
         mov      ah,3fh                    ; fxn 3fh = read
         int      21h                       ; transfer to MS-DOS
         jc       rline1                    ; return if read error
         or       ax,ax                     ; end of file?
         jz       rline1                    ; yes, return with carry clear

         push     ax                        ; save actual data length
         push     bx                        ; save input file handle
         push     dx                        ; save buffer base address
         push     ds

         push     ds                        ; set up for delimiter search
         pop      es                        ; ES:DI = string to search
         push     dx
         pop      di
         mov      dx,ax                     ; DX = string length
         mov      si,DGROUP                 ; DS:SI = address of logical
         mov      ds,si                     ; newline character sequence
         mov      si,offset DGROUP:newline
         mov      bx,nl_len                 ; BX = logical newline length
         call     strndx                    ; search for delimiter

         pop      ds                        ; restore buffer base address
         pop      dx
         pop      bx                        ; restore input file handle
         pop      ax                        ; restore original read length
         jc       rline1                    ; return if no delimiter found

         add      di,nl_len                 ; calculate actual line length
         sub      di,dx                     ; and save it
         push     di
```

(continued)

Figure 9-4. *continued*

```
            sub     ax,di               ; calculate amount of excess
            neg     ax                  ; data that was read
            cwd
            mov     cx,ax               ; CX:DX = amount to
            xchg    dx,cx               ; back up file pointer
            mov     ax,4201h            ; fxn 42h = seek
            int     21h                 ; transfer to MS-DOS

            pop     ax                  ; get back line length
            clc                         ; and return it to caller

rline1:     pop     es                  ; restore registers
            pop     di
            pop     si
            pop     dx
            pop     cx
            pop     bx
            ret                         ; return to caller

rline       endp

_TEXT       ends

            end
```

Like the procedures in the module SEQREC.ASM, the parameters for RLINE are symmetric with the MS-DOS Read File function (Int 21H Function 3FH): a file handle in BX, a buffer size in CX, and a buffer address in DS:DX. If a complete line can be read, RLINE clears the carry flag, leaves the text in the buffer, and returns the actual length of the line (including the delimiter characters) in AX; end-of-file is signified by carry clear with AX containing 0. The routine returns the carry flag set to indicate that a newline delimiter was not found or that some other error occurred. Here is an example of a call to RLINE:

```
buffer  db      512             ; buffer must be big enough
buf_len equ     $-buffer        ; for longest line in file
handle  dw      0               ; valid handle for file
            .
            .
            .
        mov     bx,handle       ; BX = valid file handle
        mov     cx,buf_len      ; CX = length of buffer
        mov     dx,seg buffer   ; DS:DX = buffer address
        mov     ds,dx
        mov     dx,offset buffer
        call    rline           ; read text line into buffer
        jc      error           ; jump if read failed
        or      ax,ax           ; was there any data?
        jz      done            ; jump if end of file
```

RLINE uses an often-ignored capability of the MS-DOS seek function (Int 21H Function 42H) to avoid the need for double-buffering. The routine first reads enough data to completely fill the buffer. (The calling program needs to make the buffer large enough for any line that might occur in the file but not so large that processing becomes inefficient.) RLINE then calls STRNDX (discussed in Chapter 5) to scan through the buffer, looking for the logical newline delimiter string. As shown here, the logical newline is hard-coded in RLINE's data segment, but you could easily generalize the procedure to handle any type of delimited sequential file by passing the address and length of the delimiter string to the routine as additional parameters. When the delimiter is found, RLINE calculates the amount of excess data in the buffer and backs up the file pointer so that the next read operation will begin at the start of the subsequent line.

Writing a counterpart routine to RLINE for writing text lines to files is left as an exercise for the reader. (Hint: Under ordinary conditions, no such special routine is needed.)

PROCEDURES INTRODUCED IN THIS CHAPTER

Procedure Name	Action	Parameters	Results
NEXTSREC	Returns record type of next record in sequential file	BX = handle	If function successful: Carry = clear AX = record type CX = record length If function unsuccessful: Carry = set
READSREC	Reads record from sequential file	BX = handle CX = buffer length DS:DX = segment:offset of buffer	If function successful: Carry = clear AX = record type CX = record length If function unsuccessful: Carry = set
RLINE	Reads line from text file	BX = handle CX = buffer length DS:DX = segment:offset of buffer	If function successful: Carry = clear AX = line length (including logical newline delimiter characters) If at end of file: Carry = clear AX = 0 If function unsuccessful: Carry = set

(continued)

PROCEDURES INTRODUCED IN THIS CHAPTER *continued*

Procedure Name	Action	Parameters	Results
SKIPSREC	Skips next record in sequential file	BX = handle	If function successful: Carry = clear If function unsuccessful: Carry = set
WRITESREC	Writes record to sequential file	BX = handle DS:DX = segment:offset of record header	If function successful: Carry = clear If function unsuccessful: Carry = set

Companion Disk

The companion disk directory \CH09 contains the programs and modules that are listed below.

Routines Presented in This Chapter

RLINE.ASM   Module that reads delimited lines from a text file

SEQREC.ASM   Module containing the procedures NEXTSREC, READSREC, SKIPSREC, and WRITESREC, which process typed, variable-length records

Routines Previously Discussed

ARGC.ASM   Returns the number of command-tail arguments

ARGV.ASM   Returns the address and length of a specific command-tail argument

ITOA.ASM   Converts a single-precision (16-bit) signed integer to an ASCII string in any radix

STRNDX.ASM   Scans through a string, looking for the specified pattern of bytes (contained in STRINGS1.ASM)

Demonstration Programs

TYPEFILE   MAKE file for TYPEFILE.EXE

TYPEFILE.ASM   Noninteractive demonstration of the RLINE routine

COPYSREC   MAKE file for COPYSREC.EXE

COPYSREC.ASM   Noninteractive demonstration of routines in SEQREC.ASM

SEQREC.DAT   Example file of sequential records for use with COPYSREC

The noninteractive program TYPEFILE.ASM demonstrates use of the routine RLINE. To build TYPEFILE.EXE, enter this command:

```
C>MAKE TYPEFILE  <Enter>
```

TYPEFILE displays the contents of a text file on the standard output device. The command format for TYPEFILE is the following:

```
TYPEFILE filename <Enter>
```

The filename can include a drive and path specifier.

The noninteractive program COPYSREC.ASM demonstrates use of the routines in SEQREC.ASM. To build COPYSREC.EXE, enter this command:

```
C>MAKE COPYSREC  <Enter>
```

COPYSREC makes a copy of an existing file that contains typed, variable-length records in the format discussed in this chapter, renaming the original file with the BAK extension. As it processes each record, it displays the record's type and length. The command format for COPYSREC is the following:

```
COPYSREC filename <Enter>
```

The filename can include a drive and path specifier. You can use the sample data file SEQREC.DAT, which is supplied on the companion disk, to observe the operation of the various routines in SEQREC.ASM under the control of CodeView or another debugger:

```
COPYSREC SEQREC.DAT <Enter>
```

10

Random Access Files

Although sequential files can be useful, most programs that manage data other than simple ASCII text use random access files instead. A random access file is structured, organized, or indexed in a way that lets you read or write a specific record within the file without inspecting all the records that physically precede it in the file. A typical random access file is the familiar dBASE data file. But random access files are also found in less obvious places. For example, a Microsoft Word document file is a random access file: You can jump directly to a specific page without scrolling through the document from the beginning.

Random access files can be divided into two general types: nonindexed and indexed. In a nonindexed random access file, the records are usually all the same size, and each record's position in the file is determined by the value in one of the record's fields (usually called the *record key*). In an indexed file, the records are stored in a main file and can be either ordered or disordered within that file. The index, which is usually stored in a separate file, consists of a copy of the record's key, associated with the record's number or relative position within the main file. When a program needs to find a record, it first locates the key within the index file, extracts the record pointer, and then fetches the record of interest from the main file.

The management of random access files—creating, updating, indexing, sorting, searching, and merging—touches on many key programming issues. Some of these topics have been studied and discussed intensely from the earliest days of computing: A peek into the textbooks written by Knuth, Sedgewick, Wirth, and others turns up an algorithm for every conceivable need, often accompanied by a careful cost-benefit analysis of its performance. We can't survey all that accumulated wisdom here, but this chapter will try to demonstrate some of the trade-offs and provide you with a few useful routines in the bargain.

Nonindexed File Fundamentals

An obvious—but somewhat dim-witted—way to find a record in a nonindexed random access file is to search the file sequentially, while taking advantage of your knowledge that the file is ordered. In other words, when looking for a record, you simply start at the beginning of the file and inspect records one after another until you find the record you want, find a record whose key tells you that the desired record does not exist, or reach the end of the file. If your file contains n records, you will process, on the average, $n/2$ records to find a particular record or to learn that it isn't there.

This brute-force technique isn't so bad for quick and dirty applications that use relatively small files. But its performance is dreadful on large files—and bad even on small files when the key values and the search targets are not evenly distributed. Of course, you could cheat a little and write your program so that it adapts to the data: If the program notices over time that the average number of records inspected is considerably more than half the number of records in the file, it could alter its behavior to start with the last record in the file and read toward the front of the file instead. But the effort this would take could be used more fruitfully in implementing a better search method.

A far superior search strategy when you are dealing with a nonindexed but ordered file of fixed-length records is the binary search (illustrated in Figure 10-1), another of the so-called divide-and-conquer algorithms.

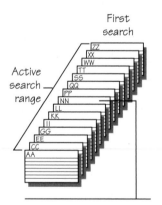

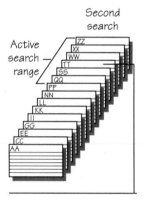

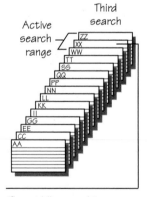

The middle record is examined. Because key XX comes after key NN, the second half of the file will be searched next.

Again, the middle record is examined. Key XX comes after key TT, so again the latter half of the search range will be inspected.

The middle record is examined and found to be the desired record.

Figure 10-1.

A simple binary search. The file contains 15 records, whose keys are two-character sequences. A search for the key XX requires the inspection of 3 records.

To begin a binary search, the program finds the size of the file, calculates the number of records in the file, and inspects the middle record. If that record matches the desired record, you're done. Otherwise, depending on whether the middle record's key was "before" or "after" the key of the record you want, the program next examines the middle record of the first or the last half of the file. It continues successively bisecting the file until it finds the desired record or establishes that the record isn't there.

Although the binary search algorithm is simple, it is surprisingly efficient. If a file contains n records, a maximum of $log_2(n) + 1$ and an average of $log_2(n) - 1$ comparisons are required to find a particular record. As you can see by the closeness of those two numbers, the binary search is also relatively insensitive to nonrandom distributions of keys in the data file or the search target. The algorithm, like the Quicksort algorithm discussed in Chapter 7, is especially well suited to languages that support recursion gracefully, such as C or Forth.

To illustrate the binary search algorithm, Figure 10-2 on the next page contains the source code for BSEARCH.ASM, a general-purpose binary search engine for assembly-language programs. BSEARCH is called with a file handle, the address of a structure containing the key to be matched, the record size, the address of a buffer to receive records, and the numbers of the first and last records to search. For example, this code searches a file containing one hundred 256-byte records, assuming 10-byte keys at offset 0 within the records, to find the record with the key CALIFORNIA:

```
recsize equ     256                 ; record length
keysize equ     10                  ; length of key field
keyoffs equ     0                   ; offset of key in record
        .
        .
        .
handle  dw      0                   ; valid handle for file
buffer  db      recsize dup (?)     ; buffer for record I/O
key     dw      keysize             ; length of key field
        dw      keyoffs             ; offset of key in record
        db      'CALIFORNIA'        ; key value to search for
        .
        .
        .
        mov     bx,handle           ; BX = valid file handle
        mov     cx,recsize          ; CX = record length
        mov     dx,seg buffer       ; DS:DX = address
                                    ; of record buffer
        mov     ds,dx
        mov     dx,offset buffer
        mov     bp,seg key          ; ES:BP = address
                                    ; of key structure
        mov     es,bp
        mov     bp,offset key
        mov     si,0                ; first record = 0
        mov     di,99               ; last record  = 99
```

(continued)

```
        call    bsearch         ; search for record
                                ; matching key
        jc      error           ; jump if record was
                                ; not found
                                ; now AX = record number
```

BSEARCH invokes itself recursively to successively bisect the file until the record is discovered or shown to be absent, and it then returns the status of the search in the carry flag and register AX. Note specifically that BSEARCH assumes the record numbers are zero-based and that it uses the STRCMP routine (introduced in Chapter 5) to compare keys.

```
;
; BSEARCH.ASM -- Binary search engine for MASM programs.
;
; Copyright (C) 1991 Ray Duncan
;
; Call with:    BX    = file handle
;               CX    = record length
;               DS:DX = record buffer address
;               SI    = first (left) record number
;               DI    = last (right) record number
;               ES:BP = key structure address
;
;               where the key structure is:
;               dw    n           length of key
;               dw    m           offset of key in record
;               db    n dup (?)  key value
;
; Returns:      If record found:
;               Carry = clear
;               AX    = record number
;
;               If record not found:
;               Carry = set
;               AX    = undefined
;
; Destroys:     Nothing

_TEXT   segment word public 'CODE'

        extrn   strcmp:near

        assume  cs:_TEXT

kbuff   equ     dword ptr [bp]          ; key address
right   equ     word ptr [bp+4]        ; last record number
left    equ     word ptr [bp+6]        ; first record number
```

Figure 10-2.   *(continued)*

BSEARCH.ASM, a general-purpose binary search engine for MASM programs.

Figure 10-2. *continued*

```
fbuff    equ      dword ptr [bp+8]      ; file buffer address
flen     equ      word ptr  [bp+12]     ; file record size
fhandle  equ      word ptr  [bp+14]     ; file handle


         public   bsearch
bsearch  proc     near

         cmp      si,di                 ; first > last record?
         jng      bsch1                 ; no, jump
         stc                            ; record absent, set carry
         ret                            ; flag and end search

bsch1:   push     bx                    ; save registers
         push     cx
         push     ds
         push     dx
         push     si
         push     di
         push     es
         push     bp
         mov      bp,sp                 ; point to stack frame

         mov      ax,si                 ; calculate record number
         add      ax,di                 ; at middle of file segment
         shr      ax,1                  ; (left + right) / 2
         push     ax                    ; save record number

                                        ; set file pointer
         mul      cx                    ; set CX:DX = file offset
         mov      cx,ax                 ; (BX already = handle)
         xchg     dx,cx
         mov      ax,4200h              ; fxn 42 subf 00h = seek
         int      21h                   ; transfer to MS-DOS

                                        ; now read record
         mov      cx,flen               ; CX = record length
         lds      dx,fbuff              ; DS:DX = record buffer
         mov      ah,3fh                ; fxn 3fh = read
         int      21h                   ; transfer to MS-DOS

         les      di,kbuff              ; ES:DI = key structure
         mov      si,dx                 ; DS:SI = record buffer
         add      si,es:[di+2]          ; DS:SI = key within record
         mov      bx,es:[di]            ; BX = length of key
         mov      dx,bx                 ; DX = length of key
         add      di,4                  ; ES:DI = address of key
         call     strcmp                ; now compare keys

         pop      ax                    ; matched, get record number
```

(continued)

Figure 10-2. *continued*

```
        jz      bsch4                   ; and exit with carry clear

        mov     bx,fhandle              ; set up to bisect file and
        mov     cx,flen                 ; perform recursive search
        mov     si,left
        mov     di,right
        lds     dx,fbuff
        les     bp,kbuff
        jl      bsch2                   ; branch on key comparison

        mov     di,ax                   ; record < search key
        dec     di                      ; set right = current - 1
        jmp     bsch3

bsch2:  mov     si,ax                   ; record > search key
        inc     si                      ; set left = current + 1

bsch3:  call    bsearch                 ; inspect next middle record

bsch4:  pop     bp                      ; restore registers
        pop     es                      ; leaving carry flag undisturbed
        pop     di
        pop     si
        pop     dx
        pop     ds
        pop     cx
        pop     bx

        ret                             ; and return to caller

bsearch endp

_TEXT   ends

        end
```

Knowing that binary searches are relatively quick and that nonindexed files are simpler to implement and maintain than indexed files, you might wonder why these files aren't used more often. The main reason is that updating nonindexed files is very costly in terms of both time and disk space. To add a record safely, you must copy the old file to a new file, insert the new record at the appropriate point, and then delete the old file (or save it as a backup). In other words, before you start you must have enough free disk space to hold the resulting file, and the program must read and write every record in the original file to create the updated file. But at least the original file is unaltered if the update isn't completed successfully.

A less secure approach to adding a record is to update the original file in place. The program first moves down one position all existing records located after the insertion point and then writes the new record into the slot that was opened up. In this scenario, before you start you need only enough free disk space to hold the new record. However, if the program updating the file crashes or if someone turns off the machine before the program completes, the file will most likely be left with a spurious duplicate of one of the old records, and the new record will be lost.

Deleting a record from a nonindexed file is also slow and messy. You can copy the old file to a new file, removing the record in the process; or you can delete the record in place, either by moving all subsequent records forward one position ("closing up" the file) or by marking the record as deleted with a special reserved key value. In the latter case, you must "pack" the file at some future point to physically remove the deleted records and reclaim the wasted space before those records start to affect search performance.

Altering the key field of an existing record incurs the problems of both adding a record in one place and deleting it in another. Of course, most alterations to records don't involve the key field—because the key tends to be a stable piece of data, such as someone's name or account number—and thus don't require a record movement.

Indexed File Fundamentals

As already mentioned, when information is stored in an indexed data file, the body of each data record is stored in a main file, and an abbreviated form of the data—a copy of the record's key—is stored in a separate index file. (It's fairly common for a data set to be indexed on several different key fields, creating several index files associated with the main data file.) The key field is the element of a record that identifies it for search purposes later—a customer name or account number, for example. When a program needs to inspect or alter a record, it first inspects the appropriate index file to locate the key for the record. If it finds a matching index entry, it extracts the record number or position from the index and uses this information to fetch the correct record from the main data file.

The fundamental premise of using an indexed data file is simple. Because the index is only a subset of the entire data set, it is much smaller and can be searched much more rapidly. In fact, it is often feasible to hold the entire index resident in memory at once, even if the main data file contains many megabytes. Special structures and techniques that would be impractical within the main data file can be used within the index file to further speed up the process of determining whether a certain key is present.

In some databases, both the index file and the main file are kept sorted in the same order. (See Figure 10-3 on the following page.) This approach has some minor advantages. The index file is compact because record numbers need not be kept in the index file; the position of a key in the index file corresponds directly to the position of the corresponding record in the main data file. You can also use the index file to find a particular starting record and then process records sequentially in the main file without further resort to the index.

Record	Main data file	Index file Key
0	AARDVARK	AARDVARK
1	CAMEL	CAMEL
2	DINGO	DINGO
3	PARROT	PARROT
4	YAK	YAK
5	ZEBRA	ZEBRA

Figure 10-3.
A data file in the same order as its index file. Although conceptually simple, this approach is very inefficient if the data is not static, because a great deal of data must be moved when records are added, deleted, or changed.

But the ordered-main-file approach also has some severe disadvantages. First, the main file can be sorted only one way at a time. If you have several indexes, you must designate one as the primary index and the others as subsidiaries with a less compact structure that includes record numbers. Second, the records must have a fixed size, which wastes disk space in many cases. Most important, this strategy entails all the inconveniences discussed earlier for nonindexed ordered files. Each time you add or delete a record or update the key field in a record, you must move many other records in the main file as well as updating the index file(s). Carrying out an update safely thus costs a great deal of execution time and free disk space.

A more common, and more efficient, approach is to completely decouple the order of the records in the main file from the order of the entries in the index files. (See Figure 10-4.) This allows records to be added, deleted, or updated in the main file with a minimum of data movement. When a record is deleted, it is simply given a special key value marking that position in the file as "available." When a record is added to the file, it can be stuck into the first free position in the file or added to the

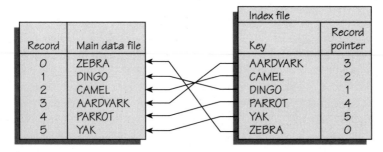

Record	Main data file	Index file Key	Record pointer
0	ZEBRA	AARDVARK	3
1	DINGO	CAMEL	2
2	CAMEL	DINGO	1
3	AARDVARK	PARROT	4
4	PARROT	YAK	5
5	YAK	ZEBRA	0

Figure 10-4.
An unordered data file with its index file. Because data in the main file never needs to be moved, this approach is more efficient than the scheme shown in Figure 10-3. The index file shown here is the simplest kind: Each entry has a uniform length, the entries are organized sequentially in order of key value, and each index key is associated with a record number or position in the main file.

end of the file if no empty slots are found. The program managing the database can update the indexes each time it adds or changes a record, or it can process an entire batch of records and then rebuild all the indexes simultaneously.

Now let's peek into the index file. Assuming that the main data file is unsorted, the simplest form of an index is a sorted list of keys associated with record numbers or file offsets (Figure 10-4), the latter depending on whether the records in the main data file are of fixed or variable sizes. If the index entries have a constant length, you can search such an index file exactly as you search a nonindexed random access data file: either with a binary search or sequentially until the desired key is matched or excluded.

Although an index file of this type is easily implemented, it has a number of important drawbacks, especially when the index grows so large that it cannot be held completely in memory while the main data file is in use. In real life, keys are seldom uniformly distributed; customer names tend to begin with A, B, C, D, H, M, S, and W rather than Q or V, for instance, and active account numbers are heavily weighted toward the most recently assigned number. This can lead to significant variations in index access times. Additionally, linearly sorted index files don't handle multiple index entries with the same key value very well. For example, with a binary search of the index, the program must scan the index file for a mismatch in *both* directions from the original match to identify all the candidate records. Another weakness is the amount of data movement involved in adding or deleting an index entry.

What we'd like to have is a design for index files that would drastically reduce— or, better yet, eliminate—the need for data movement when keys are added or changed. Computer science has come up with multiple answers to this dilemma over the years. One of the most common solutions is to structure the index as a "binary tree." (We'll return to the subject of binary trees and their variants in Chapter 11.)

Finding Records with Hashing

I'd be remiss if I let you escape this topic without taking a look at another fundamental technique for addressing information: *hashing*. Hashing is based on a concept quite different from the straight comparisons of keys we've been using. When you look up a record using hashing, you apply a transformation to the key to obtain a *hash code* that tells you where to find the record. In other words, you apply a *hashing function* to the key that maps all possible key values onto a (usually much smaller) set of possible record numbers.

Imagine a file containing five records with the keys APPLE, BANANA, GRAPEFRUIT, KIWI, and LEMON, arranged as shown in Figure 10-5 on the following page. Assume that the hashing method you've chosen is to sum the ASCII codes for the letters in the key and then find the remainder of that sum divided by the number of records in the file:

record number = *hash code* MOD *number of records in file*

Record	Main data file
0	APPLE
1	GRAPEFRUIT
2	BANANA
3	KIWI
4	LEMON

Figure 10-5.
A data file in which each record's position corresponds to its key's hash code.

Let's see how this would work if you were trying to fetch the record whose key is KIWI. You'd first sum the ASCII codes for the letters in the key (K = 4BH, I = 49H taken twice, and W = 57H), yielding the value 134H (308). You'd next divide by the number of records in the file (5) and obtain the remainder 3. Finally, you'd multiply the record size by 3 to obtain the byte offset of the record within the file, issue the appropriate MS-DOS function call to position the file pointer, and then read the record into memory. No laborious comparisons, no flip-flopping back and forth in the file, no traversing of trees—instead, a simple computation on the key yields the record position directly.

Of course, if the real world were that uncomplicated, no one would need programmers. The straightforward hashing scheme outlined above breaks down immediately for almost any noncontrived collection of records and keys. When you add a new record to the file, for instance, the hash code of each record changes immediately, because the code is a function of both the characters in the key and the number of records in the file. You also might need to move some records around to insert the new record, which is always undesirable. Worse yet, this scheme contains no provision for handling records with different keys that produce the same hash code, although such records are likely to occur, given that the selection and order of letters in English words (especially proper nouns) is far from random. This primitive hashing technique doesn't even differentiate between keys that have the same letters in a different order.

These potential problems can be approached on many levels. The most important step is to decouple the number of records in the file and their physical order from their hash codes. This is done by creating a separate *hash table,* whose size is fixed at the time the data file is created and whose positions correspond to hash codes. Each slot in the hash table contains either a record number or a magic value indicating that no record matching the hash code exists in the file (Figure 10-6). The hash table can be stored in a separate file (like an index file), located at the head or tail of the data file, or it can even (if the file is not too large) be built up on the fly by scanning the entire file each time it is opened. It turns out that lightly loaded hash tables give the best results, so the hash table typically has several times more slots than the maximum number of records that the file is ever expected to contain.

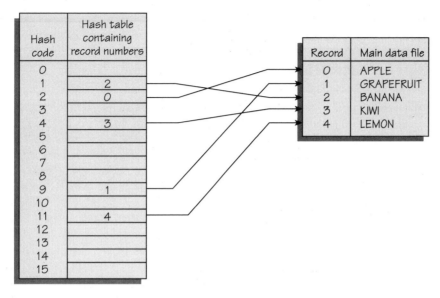

Figure 10-6.
A data file in which each record's position is decoupled from its key's hash code with a separate table.

Collisions—that is, records whose keys generate the same hash code (whether the keys are the same or different)—can be handled in two ways. The first method is to explicitly chain together all records with the same hash code. In this case, when you probe the hash table and find a record number, you then read the record and examine the key to ensure that it matches the key you are looking for. If the keys match, you have finished. If they do not, you must inspect the linkage field to see whether other records with the same hash code exist. You then chase down the chain and inspect each additional record until you either find the one you need or establish that it is not present. Explicit chaining is quite efficient for searching, especially if collisions are not numerous and only a few short chains of records are needed. It does, however, require the allocation of a link field in each record. With few collisions, most of the link fields are empty, resulting in lots of wasted space.

Open addressing, an alternative strategy for handling collisions, systematically generates additional hash codes from the same key and reprobes the hash table until either an empty hash table position or the desired record is found. The simplest implementation of open addressing—called *linear probing*—is to merely add a constant value to the hash code each time, "wrapping" the hash code when it exceeds the number of entries in the hash table. When you use open addressing to resolve collisions, you want to guarantee that the program visits all the positions in the hash table before it gives up. You can ensure this by making the number of entries in the hash table even and the incrementing value odd (preferably a prime). In a variation of open addressing called *double hashing,* the incrementing value is not a constant but is a function of the initially calculated hash code for the record key. Double hashing is widely used because it reduces clustering in the hash table.

Getting the Best Results with Hashing

The key to using hashing successfully is knowing when to use it and when to avoid it. Hashing is appropriate when the number of items in a file can be predicted fairly accurately, allowing you to ensure that the hash table will not fill up. In such situations, the very fast and near-constant search times that hashing can provide are nearly ideal. If you aren't confident that the hash table will not become heavily loaded, you should consider using a binary tree index, a balanced tree index, or other such approach. The biggest disadvantage of hashing is that it does not offer any ordered view of your data. If you need to fetch records from the file in the order of their keys (not their hash codes), you must either sort and rewrite the file (and then regenerate the hash table) or build a separate sorted index.

The hashing procedure—which converts a key into a hash code—becomes the heart of your program when you use a hashing access method. Because your program will call the hashing procedure frequently, it's important to shave every possible CPU cycle out of this procedure. Stick to shifts, adds, ANDs, ORs, and XORs within the hashing calculation; conserve hardware multiplies, and shun hardware divides at all costs. The latter are extremely expensive on the 8086/8088 and can increase the execution time of your hashing procedure by an order of magnitude. If you make the size of the hash table a power of 2, you can use the value that is 1 less than the size as an AND mask to find the modulus of the hash code and avoid the most obvious divide operation.

Optimally, a hashing scheme should scatter the possible keys across your hash table as evenly as possible and should distinguish between permutations of the same key elements (such as the two keys DOG and GOD). If the data in your file is static, you might be able to tune the hashing algorithm to produce the least number of collisions for your data set. Otherwise, when you cannot know the contents of the file in advance, you might as well settle for a reasonable hashing algorithm and turn your attention to efficient handling of collisions. You can never be certain that the user won't hand you a bizarre data set in which all the keys hash to the same value; just be sure that you can find all the records, even if the performance becomes dismal.

Figure 10-7 contains the source code for a simple hashing routine called HASH that you can use in assembly-language programs. HASH accepts the address and length of a string in DS:SI and CX, respectively, and the size of the hash table in slots in AX; and it returns an offset into the hash table in register BX (assuming that each slot occupies 2 bytes and that the maximum size of the hash table is 64 KB). To keep the code general and easily understood, this routine hasn't been fine-tuned for speed; you can try optimizing it later.

```
;
; HASH.ASM -- Calculates hash code for string.
;
; Copyright (C) 1991 Ray Duncan
;
; Call with:    DS:SI = segment:offset of string
;               CX    = length of string
;               AX    = number of slots in hash table
;                       (MUST be power of 2)
;
; Returns:      BX    = offset in hash table
;
; Destroys:     AX, CX, SI

_TEXT   segment word public 'CODE'

        assume  cs:_TEXT

        public  hash
hash    proc    near

        push    ax                      ; save number of slots
        xor     bx,bx                   ; initialize hash code
        jcxz    hash2                   ; jump if empty string
        xor     ax,ax                   ; initialize scratch register

hash1:  shl     bx,1                    ; rotate hash code 1 bit
        lodsb                           ; fetch next character
        add     bx,ax                   ; accumulate hash code
        loop    hash1                   ; get another character

hash2:  pop     ax                      ; retrieve slots in hash table
        dec     ax                      ; mask off hash code to
        and     bx,ax                   ; force it inside bounds
        shl     bx,1                    ; convert to word pointer
        ret                             ; back to caller

hash    endp

_TEXT   ends

        end
```

Figure 10-7.
*HASH.ASM, the source code for a simple procedure that calculates a 16-bit hash
code for the supplied string.*

A typical use of the HASH routine to find the hash code for the key CALIFORNIA and then to extract the record pointer from the hash table might look like this:

```
htsize   equ     256                  ; slots in hash table
           .
           .
           .
hashtab  dw      htsize dup (?)       ; hash table
key      db      'CALIFORNIA'         ; key string to hash
keysize  equ     $-key                ; length of key string
           .
           .
           .
         mov     si,seg key           ; DS:SI = address of key
         mov     ds,si
         mov     si,offset key
         mov     cx,keysize           ; CX = length of key
         mov     ax,htsize            ; AX = slots in hash table
         call    hash                 ; now hash key
         mov     ax,[bx]              ; probe hash table
```

PROCEDURES INTRODUCED IN THIS CHAPTER

Procedure Name	Action	Parameters		Results
BSEARCH	Binary search engine for random access files with fixed-length records	BX = CX = SI = DI = DS:DX = ES:BP =	handle record size first record number last record number segment:offset of buffer segment:offset of key structure	If search successful: Carry = clear AX = record number If search unsuccessful: Carry = set
HASH	Computes hash code	AX = CX = DS:SI =	slots in hash table (must be power of 2) key length segment:offset of key	BX = index to hash table

Companion Disk

The companion disk directory \CH10 contains the programs and modules that are listed below.

Routines Presented in This Chapter

BSEARCH.ASM	Binary search engine for ordered files with a constant record size
HASH.ASM	Computes a 16-bit hash code for a string

Routines Previously Discussed

QSORT.ASM	A generalized Quicksort "engine"
STRCMP.ASM	Compares two strings (in STRINGS1.ASM)

Demonstration Programs

TRYBSCH	MAKE file for TRYBSCH.EXE
TRYBSCH.ASM	Interactive demonstration of the BSEARCH routine
TRYHASH	MAKE file for TRYHASH.EXE
TRYHASH.ASM	Interactive demonstration of the HASH routine

The interactive program TRYBSCH.ASM demonstrates use of the routine BSEARCH. To build TRYBSCH.EXE, enter this command:

```
C>MAKE TRYBSCH  <Enter>
```

TRYBSCH has two functions: First, you can use it to build TRYBSCH.DAT, a sample data file. Second, you can use it to perform binary searches for the records in TRYBSCH.DAT; the program prompts you for a key, calls BSEARCH, and displays the result of the search. You can exit from TRYBSCH at any time by pressing the Enter key in response to a prompt.

The interactive program TRYHASH.ASM is similar to the TRYBSCH.ASM program, but it illustrates use of the routine in HASH.ASM. To build TRYHASH.EXE, enter this command:

```
C>MAKE TRYHASH  <Enter>
```

TRYHASH constructs a data file named TRYHASH.DAT and then performs searches on that file using a hashed access method. Again, you can exit the demonstration program at any time by pressing the Enter key in response to a prompt.

11

Heaps, Lists, and Binary Trees

Whenever we needed storage for some value or string in the MASM routines in earlier chapters, we used statically defined variables in the program's data segment, temporary variables in the stack frame, or, in the case of the string routines, a simple ring buffer maintained by the routine STRMEM (Chapter 5). These solutions work, but all three have significant disadvantages: Static variables expend memory even when they are not needed, stack frames can't be used to store data across successive calls to the same routine, and the data in a ring buffer is stable only for an unpredictable (but short) length of time. What we really need for efficient use of memory in these programs is a heap, as well as the more sophisticated data structures, such as lists and binary trees, that a heap makes possible.

Heaps are near and dear to the heart of C programmers, especially those who work with a machine such as a Macintosh, Amiga, or Atari, where sophisticated memory management routines are present in ROM and taken for granted. A MASM programmer working with IBM PCs and compatibles, however, is likely to exhibit a classic "fight-or-flight" reaction when confronted with a heap. When you start talking about heaps, the MASM programmer senses instinctively that data will be floating around in memory in some frivolous way and that the programmer's total power over the placement of every bit is in jeopardy.

Actually, heaps are neither as mysterious nor as dangerous as the gurus of high-level languages (HLLs) would have you believe. A *heap,* as the term is commonly used today, is simply an area or pool of memory that can be subdivided on demand into smaller blocks. The procedures that allocate, resize, and release chunks of memory from a heap are collectively called the *heap manager.*

Among computer scientists, the word *heap* has a more specific, specialized meaning. It refers to a tree-like data structure in which the key in each node is larger than (or the same as) the keys of all its child nodes. Simple, elegant algorithms have been worked out for inserting, deleting, replacing, and sorting the contents of such heaps.

(See, for example, Sedgewick's *Algorithms,* 2d ed., Chapter 11.) For the purposes of this chapter, however, we'll ignore these classic heaps and focus on the weaker, vulgar meaning of the word.

Local and Global Heaps

If you are programming in C or another HLL under MS-DOS, you have two heaps to worry about: the global heap and the local heap. The *global heap* is the entire area of dynamically allocatable memory, which is administered by the operating system. The program's code, data, and stack reside in blocks of memory allocated from the global heap by the system loader. The program can allocate additional memory from the global heap with appropriate operating-system function calls (Figure 11-1).

The *local heap* is an area of memory located in the program's near data segment (DGROUP). It is administered by procedures linked into the program from the HLL's

Int 21H Function	Action	Parameters	Results
Function 48H	Allocates global memory block	AH = 48H BX = requested size in paragraphs	If function successful: Carry = clear AX = initial segment address of allocated block If function unsuccessful: Carry = set AX = error code BX = size of largest available block in paragraphs
Function 49H	Releases global memory block	AH = 49H ES = segment address of block to be released	If function successful: Carry = clear If function unsuccessful: Carry = set AX = error code
Function 4AH	Resizes global memory block	AH = 4AH ES = segment address of block to be resized BX = new size of block in paragraphs	If function successful: Carry = clear If function unsuccessful: Carry = set AX = error code BX = size of largest available block in paragraphs

Figure 11-1.
MS-DOS function calls for control of the global heap. Global memory blocks are requested in units of paragraphs (16 bytes per paragraph) and return paragraph or segment addresses (physical memory addresses divided by 16).

runtime library. The local heap is conventionally located above the program's variable data, static data, and stack (Figure 11-2). It can grow until the total size of the data segment is 65,536 bytes. Objects within the local heap can be addressed with near pointers; allocating or releasing such objects does not require a call to the operating system. Consequently, access to the local heap is relatively fast.

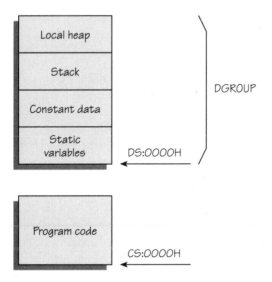

Figure 11-2.
The memory layout of a typical program written in a high-level language. The stack and the local heap are located at the top of the program's near data segment (DGROUP). The stack grows downward toward the constants and variables, whereas the heap grows upward toward the end of the segment.

A local heap serves three important purposes: to minimize the need for statically allocated variables, arrays, and other structures; to defeat the language's scoping rules for data; and to avoid stack overflows from the allocation of automatic data objects. (*Scoping rules* control whether a data item declared in one routine can be referenced by name in another procedure. *Automatic variables and structures* are created on the stack as a procedure executes, and they disappear when the procedure exits.)

Consider, for example, a program that needs to read a 4-KB configuration file into memory when executing its initialization procedure. Declaring a 4-KB static buffer for this purpose is wasteful because the 4 KB would simply be dead space in the data segment after the program initialization was completed (unless special pains were taken to map buffers required by other procedures onto the same memory addresses). Nor is it a good idea to allocate a 4-KB buffer as an automatic array on the stack—again, a 4-KB stack is much larger than most programs need, and the stack space would be wasted for the remainder of the program's execution.

A sensible solution is to allocate a 4-KB buffer from the program's local heap for as long as it is needed and then release the buffer back to the heap's free space before the end of the initialization procedure. The 4 KB of memory is then available for reuse throughout the program's execution and can be reallocated in chunks of any size required by the program's other procedures. The 1-KB or 2-KB overhead of the heap manager routines is more than repaid by the ability to efficiently use and reuse the free memory in the near data segment.

MASM Heap Management

Although most MASM programmers are in the habit of statically allocating all their data items, the arguments against this practice in C programs are equally valid for assembly language. You can make your programs considerably more elegant, flexible, and compact by adding a simple heap manager to your MASM repertoire. The routines in HEAP.ASM (Figure 11-3) are an example of the techniques and issues involved.

The procedures in HEAP.ASM work on the near data segment (the segment addressed by register DS), accepting and returning pointers that are offsets from DS. HEAP.ASM contains four public routines: HINIT, HALLOC, HREALLOC, and HFREE. (Other procedures in the file are local subroutines and should not be called directly by an application.) All four routines indicate an error by returning with the carry flag set or success by clearing the carry flag.

```
;
; HEAP.ASM -- Simple heap manager for MASM programs.
;
; Copyright (C) 1991 Ray Duncan
;
; To trade safety for speed, change the CHKPTRS equate
;
; !!!  The routines in this module all assume  !!!
; !!!  that the CPU direction flag is clear     !!!

true      equ     -1
false     equ     0

chkptrs   equ     true                    ; if true, HREALLOC and
                                          ; HFREE check all pointers


DGROUP    group   _DATA

_DATA     segment word public 'DATA'

hbase     dw      0                       ; base address of heap
hsize     dw      0                       ; size of heap
```

Figure 11-3. *(continued)*
HEAP.ASM, a simple heap manager for MASM programs.

Figure 11-3. *continued*

```
    _DATA   ends


    _TEXT   segment word public 'CODE'

            assume  cs:_TEXT,ds:DGROUP

    ;
    ; HINIT:        Initializes local heap
    ;
    ; Call with:    AX    = size in bytes
    ;               DS:SI = address of heap base
    ;
    ; Returns:      If function successful:
    ;               Carry = clear
    ;
    ;               If function unsuccessful:
    ;               Carry = set
    ;
    ; Destroys:     Nothing
    ;
            public  hinit
    hinit   proc    near

            push    ax                      ; save registers
            push    si

            and     ax,-2                   ; round down to even size
            cmp     ax,4                    ; check heap size
            jb      hinit1                  ; too small, return error

            mov     hsize,ax                ; save heap size
            mov     hbase,si                ; save heap base address
            sub     ax,2                    ; create header for block
            mov     [si],ax                 ; containing all free space
            inc     ax
            add     si,ax

    hinit1: pop     si                      ; return status in carry flag
            pop     ax
            ret

    hinit   endp


    ;
    ; HALLOC:       Allocates block from local heap
    ;
    ; Call with:    AX    = requested block size
    ;
```

(continued)

Figure 11-3. *continued*

```
; Returns:      If function successful:
;               Carry = clear
;               DS:SI = address of allocated block
;
;               If function unsuccessful:
;               Carry = set
;
; Destroys:     SI if function unsuccessful
;
        public  halloc
halloc  proc    near

        inc     ax                      ; round up to even
        and     ax,-2                   ; number of bytes
        call    hfind                   ; try to allocate block
        ret                             ; return HFIND status

halloc  endp


;
; HREALLOC:     Resizes previously allocated block
;
; Call with:    AX    = new requested block size
;               DS:SI = address of existing block
;
; Returns:      If function successful:
;               Carry = clear
;               DS:SI = address of resized block
;
;               If function unsuccessful:
;               Carry = set
;
; Destroys:     SI if function unsuccessful
;
        public  hrealloc
hrealloc proc   near

        push    ax                      ; save registers
        push    bx
        push    cx
        push    di
        push    es

        inc     ax                      ; round new size up to
        and     ax,-2                   ; even number of bytes

        if      chkptrs
        call    hvalid                  ; check if valid pointer
        jnc     hreal1                  ; pointer is OK
        jmp     hreal5                  ; bad pointer, exit
        endif
```

(continued)

Figure 11-3. *continued*

```
hreal1: mov     cx,ax             ; save new requested size
        mov     bx,si             ; save block base address
        mov     di,hbase          ; get address of heap end
        add     di,hsize

        mov     ax,[bx-2]         ; get current block size
        and     ax,-2             ; remove in-use bit
        cmp     cx,ax             ; is block growing?
        ja      hreal2            ; yes, jump
        je      hreal4            ; no size change, exit

        sub     ax,cx             ; block shrinking, find excess
        cmp     ax,2              ; enough for another header?
        jb      hreal4            ; no, leave block alone

        mov     [bx-2],cx         ; shrink existing block
        or      word ptr [bx-2],1 ; and set in-use bit
        add     bx,cx             ; create new block to hold
        sub     ax,2              ; excess memory
        mov     [bx],ax
        jmp     hreal4            ; now exit

hreal2: add     bx,ax             ; get addr of next block
        cmp     bx,di             ; reached end of heap?
        je      hreal3            ; yes, jump

        test    word ptr [bx],1   ; next block free?
        jnz     hreal3            ; no, must try elsewhere
        add     ax,[bx]           ; yes, are combined blocks
        add     ax,2              ; large enough?
        cmp     cx,ax
        ja      hreal3            ; no, jump

        mov     [si-2],cx         ; update block header and
        or      word ptr [si-2],1 ; set in-use flag

        sub     ax,cx             ; find excess memory
        jz      hreal4            ; no excess, jump

        mov     bx,si             ; create header for block
        add     bx,cx             ; containing excess memory
        sub     ax,2
        mov     [bx],ax
        jmp     hreal4            ; now exit

hreal3: mov     ax,cx             ; look elsewhere for
        mov     bx,si             ; sufficiently large block
        call    hfind
        jc      hreal5            ; none available, exit
```

(continued)

Figure 11-3. *continued*

```
        push    si                      ; save address of new block
        and     word ptr [bx-2],-2      ; mark old block available
        mov     cx,[bx-2]               ; get its length for move
        mov     di,si                   ; copy old block to new
        mov     si,bx
        push    ds
        pop     es
        rep movsb
        pop     si                      ; retrieve addr of new block

hreal4: call    hcoal                   ; coalesce any free blocks
        clc                             ; successful reallocation
                                        ; return carry = clear

hreal5: pop     es                      ; restore registers
        pop     di
        pop     cx
        pop     bx
        pop     ax
        ret                             ; return to caller

hrealloc endp

;
; HFREE:        Releases heap block
;
; Call with:    DS:SI = block pointer
;
; Returns:      If CHKPTRS is false:
;               Nothing
;
;               If CHKPTRS is true and pointer valid:
;               Carry = clear
;
;               If CHKPTRS is true and pointer invalid:
;               Carry = set
;
; Destroys:     Nothing
;
        public  hfree
hfree   proc    near

        if      chkptrs
        call    hvalid                  ; check if valid pointer
        jc      hfree1                  ; jump if bad pointer
        endif

        and     word ptr [si-2],-2      ; turn off in-use flag
        call    hcoal                   ; coalesce free blocks
```

(continued)

Figure 11-3. *continued*

```
hfree1: ret                             ; back to caller

hfree   endp

;
; HFIND:        Private subroutine for HALLOC and HREALLOC;
;               finds a free block in heap
;
; Call with:    AX    = requested block size
;
; Returns:      If function successful:
;               Carry = clear
;               DS:SI = address of allocated block
;
;               If function unsuccessful:
;               Carry = set
;
; Destroys:     SI if function unsuccessful
;
hfind   proc    near

        push    ax                      ; save registers
        push    bx
        push    cx
        push    di

        mov     cx,ax                   ; save requested block size
        mov     bx,hbase                ; get heap base address
        mov     di,bx
        add     di,hsize                ; get address of heap end

hfind1: mov     ax,[bx]                 ; pick up next block header
        add     bx,2
        test    ax,1                    ; this block free?
        jnz     hfind2                  ; not free if bit 0 set, jump
        cmp     ax,cx                   ; block free, large enough?
        jae     hfind4                  ; size is adequate, jump

hfind2: and     ax,-2                   ; go to next block
        add     bx,ax
        cmp     bx,di                   ; end of heap reached?
        jne     hfind1                  ; not yet, try next block

hfind3: stc                             ; couldn't allocate block
        jmp     hfind7                  ; return carry = set

hfind4: mov     si,bx                   ; save block base in SI
        je      hfind6                  ; jump if exactly right size
```

(continued)

Figure 11-3. *continued*

```
        sub     ax,cx                   ; find excess amount
        cmp     ax,2                    ; enough for another header?
        jae     hfind5                  ; yes, jump

        add     ax,cx                   ; no, skip this block
        jmp     hfind2

hfind5: add     bx,cx                   ; subdivide existing block
        sub     ax,2                    ; create header for free block
        mov     [bx],ax                 ; containing excess memory

hfind6: or      cx,1                    ; set block size and in-use
        mov     [si-2],cx               ; flag, also clear carry

hfind7: pop     di                      ; restore registers
        pop     cx
        pop     bx
        pop     ax
        ret                             ; return to caller

hfind   endp

;
; HCOAL:        Private subroutine for HFREE and HREALLOC;
;               coalesces adjacent free blocks in heap
;
; Call with:    Nothing
;
; Returns:      Nothing
;
; Destroys:     Nothing
;
hcoal   proc    near

        push    ax                      ; save registers
        push    bx
        push    si
        push    di

        mov     si,hbase                ; get heap base address
        mov     di,si
        add     di,hsize                ; get heap end address

hcoal1: mov     bx,si                   ; point to block header

hcoal2: mov     ax,[bx]                 ; get length from header
        add     bx,2
        mov     si,ax                   ; calc address of next block
        and     si,-2
        add     si,bx
```

(continued)

Figure 11-3. *continued*

```
            cmp     si,di                   ; end of heap reached?
            je      hcoal3                  ; yes, exit

            test    ax,1                    ; not last block, is it free?
            jnz     hcoal1                  ; not free if bit 0 set, jump

            test    word ptr [si],1         ; next block free also?
            jnz     hcoal1                  ; no, jump

            add     ax,[si]                 ; merge two blocks together
            add     ax,2
            sub     bx,2
            mov     [bx],ax                 ; update header of first block
            jmp     hcoal2                  ; try for another merge

hcoal3:     pop     di                      ; restore registers
            pop     si
            pop     bx
            pop     ax
            ret                             ; return to caller

hcoal       endp

            if      chkptrs
;
; HVALID:       Tests whether a heap pointer is valid
;
; Call with:    DS:SI = questionable pointer to block
;
; Returns:      If pointer is valid:
;               Carry = clear
;
;               If pointer is invalid:
;               Carry = set
;
; Destroys:     Nothing
;
            public  hvalid
hvalid      proc    near

            push    ax                      ; save registers
            push    bx
            push    di

            test    word ptr [si-2],1       ; be sure already allocated
            je      hval2                   ; no, pointer invalid

            mov     bx,hbase                ; get heap base address
            mov     di,bx
```

(continued)

Figure 11-3. *continued*

```
        add     di,hsize                ; get heap end address

hval1:  mov     ax,[bx]                 ; get length of this block
        add     bx,2
        cmp     bx,si                   ; do pointers match?
        je      hval3                   ; yes, jump (carry is clear)
        and     ax,-2                   ; strip in-use bit and
        add     bx,ax                   ; advance to next block
        cmp     bx,di                   ; end of heap?
        jne     hval1                   ; no, try again
hval2:  stc                             ; end of heap, pointer invalid

hval3:  pop     di                      ; restore registers
        pop     bx
        pop     ax
        ret                             ; return to caller

hvalid  endp
        endif

_TEXT   ends

        end
```

Your program must call HINIT during its initialization sequence, supplying the base address (as an offset from DS) and size (in bytes) of the area that the heap manager can use for its memory pool. Your program can then call HALLOC to allocate blocks of memory, HREALLOC to resize previously allocated blocks, and HFREE to release blocks back to the heap.

The operation of the heap manager is straightforward. A header word, which gives the size of the block in bytes, precedes each allocated or available block of memory in the heap. The blocks are thus implicitly chained together. The end of the chain is also implicit from the base address and length originally provided to HINIT. The length of each block is an even number of bytes; if an odd size is requested, it is rounded up to the next even number. The least significant bit of a block's header word indicates the block's status: It is clear if the block is available or set if the block is allocated.

When HALLOC is called to allocate a new block, it scans down through the memory pool, leaping from one block to another by the size field until it finds an unassigned block large enough to satisfy the request. If that block is larger than the block requested, it is subdivided, and the excess becomes a new unassigned block. If no suitable block is found, HALLOC returns an error flag.

HREALLOC is used to resize a block that was previously allocated with HALLOC. If the new requested size is smaller than the old, the block is subdivided, and the excess becomes an unassigned block. If the new size is larger than the old size, HREALLOC first attempts to get the additional space from the subsequent block (if it is not allocated). Otherwise, HREALLOC searches the rest of the heap for a block of sufficient size, copies the previous block to the new one, and then releases the original block.

The HFREE routine is the simplest of the four. It is called with a pointer and returns nothing. Its only action is to clear the bit in the header word that precedes the memory block, to show that the block is available. Before it exits, HFREE makes a pass over the heap and coalesces all free blocks.

Here is an example of code that initializes a heap and then allocates, resizes, and frees a heap block:

```
blkptr   dw      0                   ; pointer to block allocated
                                     ; from heap

heapsiz  equ     1000                ; size of heap
heap     db      heapsize dup (?)    ; this memory contains heap
         .
         .
         .
         mov     si,seg heap         ; first create heap
         mov     ds,si
         mov     si,offset heap      ; DS:SI = heap base address
         mov     ax,heapsiz          ; AX = heap size
         call    hinit               ; call heap manager
         jc      error               ; jump, heap creation failed
         .
         .
         .
                                     ; allocate block from heap
         mov     ax,100              ; AX = size requested
         call    halloc              ; call heap manager
         jc      error               ; jump if allocation failed
         mov     blkptr,si           ; save offset of heap block

                                     ; resize block from heap
         mov     ax,200              ; AX = new size requested
         mov     si,blkptr           ; DS:SI = heap block address
         call    hrealloc            ; call heap manager
         jc      error               ; jump if resize failed
         mov     blkptr,si           ; save new offset of block

                                     ; release block back to heap
         mov     si,blkptr           ; DS:SI = heap block address
         call    hfree               ; call heap manager
```

You can modify the equate named CHKPTRS in HEAP.ASM to trade speed for error checking. As you develop your application, set CHKPTRS to true so that each pointer fed to HREALLOC or HFREE is validated before the associated memory block is resized or released. After your code is proven, change CHKPTRS to false so that the heap manipulation routines execute as fast as possible.

Linked Lists

Now that you have an elementary heap manager, you need a way to keep track of blocks the program is actively using in the heap. One possible approach is to maintain a big array of pointers: You could stick the addresses of heap blocks into the array as they are allocated and delete the addresses from the array when the blocks are released (Figure 11-4). But this simple scheme is not a smart way to manage memory: Why go to all the trouble of creating a heap manager if you must fall back on a static data structure to keep track of the memory blocks obtained from the heap manager? In addition, allocating more blocks than the number of slots in the pointer array is asking for trouble—and using a considerably smaller number of blocks than the number of slots in the array wastes memory again. And the pointer array can really get messy if you want to maintain a sorted view of the data.

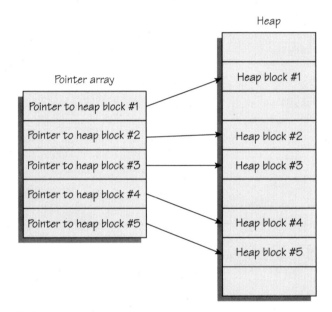

Figure 11-4.

Keeping track of heap blocks with a pointer array.

One possible solution is to maintain the heap blocks in a sorted linked list. Each time you allocate a new block and fill it with data, the program allocates enough extra space in the block to hold some list pointers. It traverses the existing list of blocks, finds the new block's proper location between two existing blocks according to the value of the data, and inserts the block into the list by simply updating the pointers in the two adjacent blocks and in the new block (Figure 11-5). Very little data movement is involved, and the memory that is required to hold the pointers and thus implement the list structure is, like everything else, allocated dynamically from the heap.

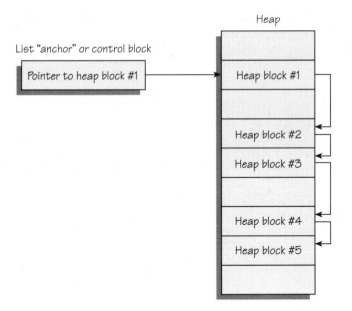

Figure 11-5.
Keeping track of heap blocks by linking them into a list.

To conserve as much memory as possible, you can create a one-way linked list that uses only one pointer in each heap block. For additional flexibility and data integrity, you can create a two-way linked list, which requires two pointers in each heap block but allows the program to traverse the list in either direction and also allows it to recover if a single block in the list is corrupted.

The routines in LIST.ASM (Figure 11-6) implement a simple manager for sorted, two-way linked lists of strings. The routines fall into three groups: list creation and destruction; list member addition and deletion; and list traversal. The list manager relies on the heap manager (HEAP.ASM) introduced earlier in this chapter. Your program must call HINIT in the HEAP module to initialize a heap before it uses any of the routines in the LIST module.

```
;
; LIST.ASM -- Simple list manager for MASM programs.
;             Uses routines in HEAP.ASM, STRINGS1.ASM,
;             STRINGS2.ASM, and STRINGS3.ASM.  Relies
;             on previous heap initialization by caller.
;             Assumes direction flag is clear!
;
; Copyright (C) 1991 Ray Duncan
```

Figure 11-6. *(continued)*
LIST.ASM, a simple linked list manager for MASM programs.

Figure 11-6. *continued*

```
;
; Format of list anchor blocks:
;
;    Offset  Size  Contents
;      0      2    Head of list pointer, or zero
;      2      2    Tail of list pointer, or zero
;      4      2    Current position pointer (cleared by all
;                    functions other than LFIRST, LNEXT, LPREV)
;
; Format of individual list records:
;
;    Offset  Size  Contents
;      0      2    Backward list link, or zero if head of list
;      2      2    Forward list link, or zero if tail of list
;      4      1    Count byte for string (n)
;      5      n    Record contents (ASCII string)
;


_TEXT   segment word public 'CODE'

        extrn   halloc:near
        extrn   hfree:near
        extrn   strcmpi:near

        assume  cs:_TEXT


;
; LINIT:       Initializes list
;
; Call with:   Nothing  (Heap must have been previously
;                         initialized by application call to HINIT)
;
; Returns:     If function successful:
;              Carry = clear
;              AX    = list handle
;
;              If function unsuccessful:
;              Carry = set
;
; Destroys:    AX if function unsuccessful
;
        public  linit
linit   proc    near

        push    si                      ; save registers
        mov     ax,6                    ; allocate anchor block
        call    halloc                  ; for new list
        jc      linit1                  ; error, no heap space
        mov     word ptr [si],0         ; initialize anchor block
        mov     word ptr [si+2],0
```

(continued)

Figure 11-6. *continued*

```
        mov     word ptr [si+4],0       ; return address of anchor
        mov     ax,si                   ; block as list handle

linit1: pop     si                      ; carry = clear if successful
        ret                             ; carry = set if failed

linit   endp

;
; LKILL:        Destroys list, releasing all its memory
;
; Call with:    BX    = list handle
;
; Returns:      If function successful:
;               Carry = clear
;
;               If function unsuccessful:
;               Carry = set
;
; Destroys:     Nothing
;
        public  lkill
lkill   proc    near

        push    si                      ; save register
        or      bx,bx                   ; be sure handle is valid
        jnz     lkill1
        stc
        jmp     lkill4                  ; null handle, error

lkill1: mov     si,[bx]                 ; get head of list
        or      si,si
        jz      lkill3                  ; jump, nothing there

lkill2: push    [si+2]                  ; push forward link
        call    hfree                   ; release this list record
        jc      lkill4                  ; jump, bad heap pointer
        pop     si                      ; retrieve link
        or      si,si                   ; end of list yet?
        jnz     lkill2                  ; no, loop

lkill3: mov     word ptr [bx],0         ; zero out anchor block
        mov     word ptr [bx+2],0       ; in case somebody tries
        mov     word ptr [bx+4],0       ; to use handle later
        mov     si,bx                   ; release anchor block
        call    hfree                   ; return HFREE status

lkill4: pop     si                      ; restore register
        ret                             ; and exit
```

(continued)

Figure 11-6. *continued*

```
lkill   endp

;
; LADD:       Adds string to sorted list
;
; Call with:  DS:SI = segment:offset of string
;             AX    = length of string
;             BX    = list handle
;
; Returns:    If function successful:
;             Carry = clear
;
;             If function unsuccessful:
;             Carry = set
;
; Destroys:   Nothing
;
        public  ladd
ladd    proc    near

        push    bx                      ; save registers
        push    cx
        push    dx
        push    di
        push    bp
        push    es
        push    ax
        push    si

        add     ax,5                    ; add size of control info
        call    halloc                  ; allocate memory for record
        jnc     ladd1                   ; proceed, allocation OK
        jmp     ladd7                   ; jump, no heap space

ladd1:  mov     bp,si                   ; save addr of new record
        mov     di,si                   ; also dest addr for move
        push    ds                      ; be sure ES = DS
        pop     es
        pop     si                      ; retrieve address and length
        pop     cx                      ; of string for new record
        push    cx
        push    si
        mov     [di+4],cl               ; length into new record
        add     di,5
        rep     movsb                   ; string into new record

        test    word ptr [bx],-1        ; empty list?
        jnz     ladd2                   ; no, jump

        mov     word ptr ds:[bp],0      ; zero out forward and back
```

(continued)

Figure 11-6. *continued*

```
        mov     word ptr ds:[bp+2],0     ; links in new record
        mov     [bx],bp                  ; set head = tail in list
        mov     [bx+2],bp                ; anchor block
        jmp     ladd7                    ; all done with this case

ladd2:  mov     ax,[bx]                  ; nonempty list, init current
        mov     [bx+4],ax                ; record in anchor block

ladd3:  push    bx                       ; save anchor block pointer
        mov     di,[bx+4]                ; ES:DI = current record
        mov     dl,[di+4]                ; DX = length of string
        xor     dh,dh
        add     di,5                     ; ES:DI = current string
        mov     si,bp                    ; DS:SI = new record
        mov     bl,[si+4]                ; BX = length of string
        xor     bh,bh
        add     si,5                     ; DS:SI = new string
        call    strcmpi                  ; compare case insensitive
        pop     bx                       ; restore anchor block pointer
        jle     ladd5                    ; new record <= current record

        mov     si,[bx+4]                ; current = tail of list?
        cmp     si,[bx+2]
        je      ladd4                    ; yes, jump
        mov     si,[si+2]                ; no, get forward link
        mov     [bx+4],si                ; update current record
        jmp     ladd3

ladd4:                                   ; add new record as tail
        mov     [si+2],bp                ; update forward link in current
        mov     ds:[bp],si               ; update backward link in new
        mov     word ptr ds:[bp+2],0     ; update forward link in new
        mov     [bx+2],bp                ; update tail in anchor block
        jmp     ladd7                    ; all done with this case

ladd5:                                   ; insert new rec before current
        mov     si,[bx+4]                ; current = head of list?
        cmp     si,[bx]
        jne     ladd6                    ; no, jump

        mov     [si],bp                  ; update backward link in current
        mov     word ptr ds:[bp],0       ; update backward link in new
        mov     word ptr ds:[bp+2],si    ; update forward link in new
        mov     [bx],bp                  ; update head in anchor block
        jmp     ladd7                    ; all done with this case

ladd6:  mov     di,[si]                  ; SI = current, DI = previous
        mov     [si],bp                  ; update backward link in current
        mov     [di+2],bp                ; update forward link in previous
```

(continued)

Figure 11-6. *continued*

```
        mov     ds:[bp],di              ; update backward link in new
        mov     ds:[bp+2],si            ; update forward link in new
        clc                             ; clear carry flag

ladd7:  pop     si                      ; restore registers
        pop     ax
        pop     es
        pop     bp
        pop     di
        pop     dx
        pop     cx
        pop     bx
        mov     word ptr [bx+4],0       ; no current record
        ret

ladd    endp


;
; LDEL:         Deletes string from sorted list
;
; Call with:    DS:SI = segment:offset of string
;               AX    = length of string
;               BX    = list handle
;
; Returns:      If function successful:
;               Carry = clear
;
;               If function unsuccessful:
;               Carry = set
;
; Destroys:     Nothing
;
        public  ldel
ldel    proc    near

        push    bx                      ; save registers
        push    cx
        push    dx
        push    di
        push    es
        push    ax
        push    si
        push    ds                      ; be sure ES = DS
        pop     es

        test    word ptr [bx],-1        ; empty list?
        jnz     ldel1                   ; no, proceed
        stc
        jmp     ldel8                   ; yes, error
```

(continued)

Figure 11-6. *continued*

```
ldel1:  mov     ax,[bx]                 ; current = head of list
        mov     [bx+4],ax

ldel2:  pop     di                      ; retrieve address and
        pop     dx                      ; length of string for
        push    dx                      ; record to be deleted
        push    di
        push    bx                      ; save anchor block pointer
        mov     si,[bx+4]               ; pointer to current record
        mov     bl,[si+4]               ; length of string
        xor     bh,bh
        add     si,5                    ; address of string
        call    strcmpi                 ; compare target to current
        pop     bx                      ; restore anchor block pointer
        je      ldel3                   ; found matching record

        mov     si,[bx+4]               ; current = tail of list
        cmp     si,[bx+2]
        mov     si,[si+2]               ; update current
        mov     [bx+4],si
        jne     ldel2                   ; loop, not tail yet

        stc                             ; whole list searched
        jmp     ldel8                   ; exit with error

ldel3:                                  ; matching record found
        mov     si,[bx+4]               ; pointer to current record
        mov     di,[si+2]               ; DI = next record
        mov     si,[si]                 ; SI = previous record

        mov     ax,si                   ; current = head = tail?
        or      ax,di
        jnz     ldel4                   ; no, jump

        mov     word ptr [bx],0         ; yes, update anchor block
        mov     word ptr [bx+2],0
        jmp     ldel7                   ; go release memory

ldel4:  or      si,si                   ; current = head?
        jnz     ldel5                   ; no, jump

        mov     [bx],di                 ; update head in anchor block
        mov     word ptr [di],0         ; update backward link in next
        jmp     ldel7                   ; go release memory

ldel5:  or      di,di                   ; current = tail?
        jnz     ldel6                   ; no, jump

        mov     [bx+2],si               ; update tail in anchor block
```

(continued)

Figure 11-6. *continued*

```
        mov     word ptr [si+2],0       ; update forward pointer in prev
        jmp     ldel7                   ; go release memory

ldel6:                                  ; current != head != tail
        mov     [si+2],di               ; update forward link in prev
        mov     [di],si                 ; update backward link in next

ldel7:  mov     si,[bx+4]               ; release memory for record
        call    hfree                   ; return status from HFREE

ldel8:  pop     si                      ; restore registers
        pop     ax
        pop     es
        pop     di
        pop     dx
        pop     cx
        pop     bx
        mov     word ptr [bx+4],0       ; no current record
        ret

ldel    endp


;
; LFIRST:       Returns first record in list
;
; Call with:    BX    = list handle
;
; Returns:      If function successful:
;               Carry = clear
;               DS:SI = segment:offset of string
;               AX    = length of string
;
;               If function unsuccessful:
;               Carry = set
;
; Destroys:     SI if function unsuccessful
;
        public  lfirst
lfirst  proc    near

        mov     si,[bx]                 ; get head of list
        mov     [bx+4],si               ; update current position
        or      si,si                   ; anything there?
        jz      lfirs1                  ; jump, error
        add     si,4                    ; point to count byte
        lodsb                           ; get count byte, clear
        xor     ah,ah                   ; carry, point to string
        jmp     lfirs2                  ; return success

lfirs1: stc                             ; common error exit point
```

(continued)

Figure 11-6. *continued*

```
lfirs2: ret                          ; return to caller

lfirst  endp


;
; LNEXT:       Returns next record in list
;
; Call with:   BX    = list handle
;
; Returns:     If function successful:
;              Carry = clear
;              DS:SI = segment:offset of string
;              AX    = length of string
;
;              If function unsuccessful:
;              Carry = set
;
; Destroys:    SI if function unsuccessful
;
        public  lnext
lnext   proc    near

        mov     si,[bx+4]            ; get current position
        or      si,si               ; anything there?
        jz      lnext1              ; jump, error
        mov     si,[si+2]           ; get list forward link
        or      si,si               ; anything there?
        jz      lnext1              ; jump, error
        mov     [bx+4],si           ; update current position
        add     si,4                ; point to count byte
        lodsb                       ; get count byte, clear
        xor     ah,ah               ; carry, point to string
        jmp     lnext2              ; return success

lnext1: stc                         ; common error exit point

lnext2: ret                         ; return to caller

lnext   endp


;
; LPREV:       Returns previous record in list
;
; Call with:   BX    = list handle
;
; Returns:     If function successful:
;              Carry = clear
;              DS:SI = segment:offset of string
;              AX    = length of string
```

(continued)

Figure 11-6. *continued*

```
;
;                   If function unsuccessful:
;                   Carry = set
;
; Destroys:    SI if function unsuccessful
;
            public  lprev
lprev       proc    near

            mov     si,[bx+4]           ; get current position
            or      si,si               ; anything there?
            jz      lprev1              ; jump, error
            mov     si,[si]             ; get list backward link
            or      si,si               ; anything there?
            jz      lprev1              ; jump, error
            mov     [bx+4],si           ; update current position
            add     si,4                ; point to count byte
            lodsb                       ; get count byte, clear
            xor     ah,ah               ; carry, point to string
            jmp     lprev2              ; return success

lprev1: stc                            ; common error exit point

lprev2: ret                            ; return to caller

lprev       endp

_TEXT       ends

            end
```

The procedure LINIT is called to initialize a list. It allocates a control block from the heap each time a list is created and returns the address of the control block as a handle for the list that must be used for all subsequent access to the list. The control block, sometimes called an *anchor block,* has the following format:

Offset	Length	Contents
0	2	Pointer to head of list, or zero if list is empty
2	2	Pointer to tail of list, or zero if list is empty
4	2	Current record pointer position

The routine LKILL destroys a list. Its only parameter is a list handle. LKILL first traverses the list, releasing the heap blocks for all existing list members, and then releases the list control block. As you can see, the use of list handles and control blocks allows your program to maintain multiple sorted lists in the same heap with very little additional work.

The routine LADD adds a member to a sorted list. It is called with a list handle and the address and length of a string. It first allocates a block from the heap to hold the string and the list pointers and copies the string into the block. Next, LADD traverses the list, inspecting the strings in each block until it finds the proper location for the new block. LADD then updates the pointers to link the new block into the list and returns to the caller. A typical call to LADD would look like this:

```
mystr     db    'test string'
mystr_len equ   $-mystr

hlist     dw    0                  ; list handle
          .
          .
          .
          mov   si,seg mystr       ; DS:SI = string address
          mov   ds,si
          mov   si,offset mystr
          mov   ax,mystr_len        ; AX = string length
          mov   bx,hlist            ; BX = list handle
          call  ladd
          jc    error               ; jump, can't add to list
```

LADD uses the STRCMPI routine from Chapter 5 to make case-insensitive comparisons, maintaining the order of the list without respect to the case of the strings, and allows more than two members of the list to contain the same strings. You can easily alter the source code to change these behaviors—for example, to maintain the list in case-sensitive order, replace the call to STRCMPI with a call to STRCMP.

LDEL deletes a member from a sorted list. It is called with a list handle and the address and length of a string in exactly the same style as LADD. LDEL traverses the list until it finds a block whose data matches the specified string, removes the block from the list by linking the two neighbor blocks, and finally releases the block that held the list member back to the heap. (Note that the routines in this module are for demonstration purposes only; to make them really useful in your own applications, you need to modify them so that extra memory is allocated for each list member to hold data or pointers to other data. The string portions of the list members will then serve as record keys.)

The routines LFIRST, LNEXT, and LPREV allow your program to traverse a linked list for purposes of debugging or displaying the list contents. The routines maintain a context or current list position in the third slot of the list control block. The routine LFIRST is called to initialize the context to the first member of the list. The routines LNEXT and LPREV can then be called to move forward and backward in the list. All three routines return the address and length of the string in the current list member.

The disadvantage of a sorted linked list such as the one maintained by LIST.ASM is that access to the elements of the list is strictly sequential. As the linked list becomes very large, the process of adding, deleting, or finding a particular list member can become very slow: The time required to add, delete, or find a list member is directly proportional to the list size. A more efficient data structure would allow you to take shortcuts to specific items.

Binary Trees

What would be really helpful is a fancier sort of ordered data structure that could be maintained by manipulating pointers but in which the time required to find an item does not grow proportionately to the number of items. One such structure is called a *binary tree.* Each entry, or *node,* in a binary tree consists of a chunk of data (usually a key and a pointer to other information associated with the key) and a linkage to "left" and "right" subtrees (each of which might be a null link if that subtree is empty). The first entry in the tree is called the root; by convention, its left link points to the subtree containing all nodes with lesser keys, and its right link points to the subtree containing all nodes with greater keys. (See Figure 11-7.)

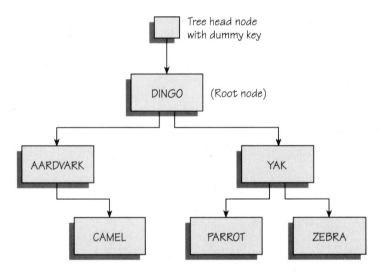

Figure 11-7.
A binary tree. The root node contains the key for the first record added to the tree. Its linkages point to two subtrees: The left subtree holds the nodes with lesser keys, and the right subtree holds the nodes with greater keys.

To find a specific piece of data, a program traverses a binary tree, starting at the root. As it reaches each node, it compares the key of interest to the key in the node. If the key doesn't match, one branch of the node's subtree is selected, based on the result of the comparison. This process continues until the desired key is found or until an empty subtree is reached. As you might imagine, algorithms that work with binary trees are easiest to implement in languages that support recursion.

Binary trees are an efficient way to implement indexes for the sorted random access data files discussed in Chapter 10. In a binary tree file index, the physical order of entries in the index file is irrelevant, and it is easy to update the index dynamically.

When a new record is added to the main data file, a corresponding index node can be physically added at the end of the index file. Its linkage fields and those of the node that becomes its parent are then updated. The entire operation is very fast and requires almost no data movement. Similarly, nodes can be logically deleted from a binary tree merely by adjusting some linkages, or by "lazy deletion," in which the node is marked as deleted and the entire tree is rebuilt when the space occupied by deleted nodes exceeds some predetermined threshold.

Ordinary binary trees are not problem-free, however. When keys are not randomly distributed, or when they are added to the tree in a nonrandom fashion, the tree can become asymmetric, leading in turn to wide variations in tree traversal times. The computer scientists' answer to this problem is the *balanced binary tree* (sometimes called a *B-tree*), in which all subtrees of the nodes at a particular tree level are the same length (Figure 11-8).

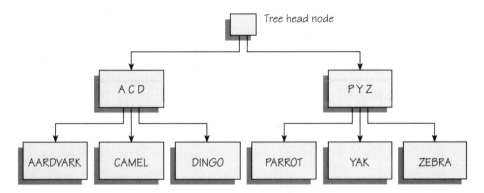

Figure 11-8.

A balanced binary tree. This index resembles the tree in Figure 11-7 but contains two kinds of nodes: internal nodes, which point only to other nodes; and external nodes, which point to actual data records. In a balanced tree, the number of nodes that must be examined to find a specific index entry is a constant.

Balanced tree indexes are implemented with two types of nodes rather than one. *Internal nodes* point only to other nodes, and *external nodes* point to the records being indexed. Internal nodes must be able to contain more than one key, and they can have multiple linkages to the next lower level. Balanced trees are widely used because of their excellent performance on worst-case key distributions. Unfortunately, this chapter cannot adequately cover the complexities of creating and maintaining balanced trees; for additional information, refer to Chapters 15 and 18 of Sedgewick's *Algorithms* (2d ed.).

The module TREE.ASM (Figure 11-9 on the next page) presents a simple binary tree manager that you can experiment with in your programs. It contains routines to initialize and destroy binary trees, routines to add nodes to or delete nodes from a binary tree, and a routine to find a specific node in a tree. This tree manager maintains trees of ASCII strings only, but you can easily extend it to associate record keys or other data with the strings. (The strings then serve as record "keys.") Like the list manager LIST.ASM, the routines in TREE.ASM rely on the heap manager in HEAP.ASM (Figure 11-3). Your program must call HINIT in the HEAP module to initialize a heap before calling any of the routines in the TREE module.

```
;
; TREE.ASM -- Simple binary tree manager for MASM programs.
;             Uses routines in HEAP.ASM, STRINGS1.ASM,
;             STRINGS2.ASM, and STRINGS3.ASM.  Relies
;             on previous heap initialization by caller.
;             Assumes direction flag is clear!
;
; Copyright (C) 1991 Ray Duncan
;
; Format of binary tree anchor block:
;
;    Offset  Size  Contents
;       0     2    Root node pointer
;       2     2    Current position pointer
;
; Format of individual tree records:
;
;    Offset  Size  Contents
;       0     2    Parent node pointer
;       2     2    Left subtree pointer, or zero
;       4     2    Right subtree pointer, or zero
;       6     1    Count byte for string (n)
;       7     n    Record contents (ASCII string)
;

_TEXT   segment word public 'CODE'

        extrn   halloc:near
        extrn   hfree:near
        extrn   strcmpi:near

        assume  cs:_TEXT


;
; TINIT:        Initializes binary tree
;
; Call with:    Nothing  (Heap must have been previously
;                         initialized by application call to HINIT)
;
; Returns:      If function successful:
;               Carry = clear
;               AX    = tree handle
```

Figure 11-9.   (continued)

TREE.ASM, a simple binary tree manager for MASM programs.

Figure 11-9. *continued*

```
;
;               If function unsuccessful:
;               Carry = set
;
; Destroys:     AX if function unsuccessful
;
        public  tinit
tinit   proc    near

        push    si                      ; save registers
        mov     ax,4                    ; allocate anchor block
        call    halloc                  ; for new list
        jc      tinit1                  ; error, no heap space
        mov     word ptr [si],0         ; initialize anchor block
        mov     word ptr [si+2],0       ; return address of anchor
        mov     ax,si                   ; block as list handle

tinit1: pop     si                      ; carry = clear if successful
        ret                             ; carry = set if failed

tinit   endp


;
; TKILL:        Destroys binary tree, releasing all its memory
;
; Call with:    BX   = tree handle
;
; Returns:      If function successful:
;               Carry = clear
;
;               If function unsuccessful:
;               Carry = set
;
; Destroys:     Nothing
;
        public  tkill
tkill   proc    near

        push    si                      ; save register
        or      bx,bx                   ; be sure handle is valid
        jnz     tkill1
        stc
        jmp     tkill3                  ; null handle, error

tkill1: mov     si,[bx]                 ; get root node of tree
        call    tkill4                  ; release all nodes

tkill2: mov     word ptr [bx],0         ; zero out anchor block
        mov     word ptr [bx+2],0       ; for extra safety
```

(continued)

Figure 11-9. *continued*

```
        mov     si,bx                   ; release anchor block
        call    hfree                   ; return HFREE status

tkill3: pop     si                      ; restore register and exit
        ret

tkill4: or      si,si                   ; valid node?
        jnz     tkill5                  ; yes, proceed
        ret                             ; no, exit

tkill5: push    si                      ; save pointer to this node
        push    [si+4]                  ; save pointer to right subtree

        mov     si,[si+2]               ; release left subtree
        call    tkill4

        pop     si                      ; release right subtree
        call    tkill4

        pop     si                      ; release this node
        call    hfree
        ret

tkill   endp

;
; TADD:         Adds record to binary tree
;
; Call with:    DS:SI = segment:offset of string
;               AX    = length of string
;               BX    = tree handle
;
; Returns:      If function successful:
;               Carry = clear
;
;               If function unsuccessful:
;               Carry = set
;
; Destroys:     Nothing
;
        public  tadd
tadd    proc    near

        push    bx                      ; save registers
        push    cx
        push    dx
        push    di
        push    bp
        push    es
```

(continued)

Figure 11-9. *continued*

```
            push    ax
            push    si

            add     ax,7                        ; add size of control info
            call    halloc                      ; allocate memory for node
            jnc     tadd1                       ; allocation OK, proceed
            jmp     tadd6                       ; jump, no heap space

tadd1:      mov     bp,si                       ; save addr of new node
            mov     di,si                       ; also dest addr for move
            push    ds                          ; be sure ES = DS
            pop     es
            pop     si                          ; retrieve address and length
            pop     cx                          ; of string for new node
            push    cx
            push    si
            mov     [di+6],cl                   ; length into new node
            add     di,7
            rep     movsb                       ; string into new node

            mov     word ptr ds:[bp],0          ; assume the worst, zero out
            mov     word ptr ds:[bp+2],0        ; all parent and subtree
            mov     word ptr ds:[bp+4],0        ; pointers in new node

            test    word ptr [bx],-1            ; previously empty tree?
            jnz     tadd2                       ; no, jump

            mov     [bx],bp                     ; set anchor block ptr to root
            jmp     tadd6                       ; all done with this case

tadd2:      mov     ax,[bx]                     ; nonempty list, init current
            mov     [bx+2],ax                   ; record in anchor block

tadd3:      push    bx                          ; save anchor block pointer
            mov     di,[bx+2]                   ; ES:DI = current node
            mov     dl,[di+6]                   ; DX = length of string
            xor     dh,dh
            add     di,7                        ; ES:DI = current string
            mov     si,bp                       ; DS:SI = new record
            mov     bl,[si+6]                   ; BX = length of string
            xor     bh,bh
            add     si,7                        ; DS:SI = new string
            call    strcmpi                     ; compare case insensitive
            pop     bx                          ; restore anchor block pointer
            je      tadd5                       ; new record = current record
            jg      tadd4                       ; new record > current record

                                                ; new record < current record
            mov     si,[bx+2]                   ; get pointer to current node
            mov     di,[si+2]                   ; get left subtree pointer
```

(continued)

Figure 11-9. *continued*

```
        mov     [bx+2],di           ; update current in anchor block
        or      di,di               ; is there any left subtree?
        jnz     tadd3               ; yes, keep looking
        mov     [si+2],bp           ; no, this node is new subtree
        mov     ds:[bp],si          ; parent pointer into new node
        jmp     tadd6               ; all done with this case

tadd4:                              ; new record > current record
        mov     si,[bx+2]           ; get pointer to current node
        mov     di,[si+4]           ; get right subtree pointer
        mov     [bx+2],di           ; update current in anchor block
        or      di,di               ; is there any right subtree?
        jnz     tadd3               ; yes, keep looking
        mov     [si+4],bp           ; no, this node is new subtree
        mov     ds:[bp],si          ; parent pointer into new node
        jmp     tadd6               ; all done with this case

tadd5:                              ; node with matching name
        mov     si,bp               ; already exists, release
        call    hfree               ; memory allocated for new
        stc                         ; node and return error

tadd6:  pop     si                  ; restore registers and exit
        pop     ax
        pop     es
        pop     bp
        pop     di
        pop     dx
        pop     cx
        pop     bx
        ret

tadd    endp

;
; TFIND:      Finds record in binary tree
;
; Call with:  DS:SI = segment:offset of string
;             AX    = length of string
;             BX    = tree handle
;
; Returns:    If function successful:
;             Carry = clear
;             DS:SI = string in tree
;             AX    = length of string
;
;             If function unsuccessful:
;             Carry = set
;
```

(continued)

Figure 11-9. *continued*

```
; Destroys:      Nothing
;
        public  tfind
tfind   proc    near

        push    bx                      ; save registers
        push    cx
        push    dx
        push    di
        push    bp
        push    es

        push    ax                      ; save address and length
        push    si                      ; of target string

        push    ds                      ; be sure ES = DS
        pop     es

        test    word ptr [bx],-1        ; empty tree?
        jnz     tfind1                  ; no, proceed
        stc
        jmp     tfind5                  ; yes, exit with error

tfind1: mov     ax,[bx]                 ; current = head of list
        mov     [bx+2],ax

tfind2: pop     di                      ; retrieve address and
        pop     dx                      ; length of string for
        push    dx                      ; record to be found
        push    di
        push    bx                      ; save anchor block pointer
        mov     si,[bx+2]               ; pointer to current record
        mov     bl,[si+6]               ; length of string
        xor     bh,bh
        add     si,7                    ; address of string
        call    strcmpi                 ; compare target to current
        pop     bx                      ; restore anchor block pointer
        je      tfind4                  ; current node = target
        jg      tfind3                  ; current > target

                                        ; current < target
        mov     si,[bx+2]               ; get pointer to current
        mov     si,[si+4]               ; get right subtree pointer
        mov     [bx+2],si               ; update current node
        or      si,si                   ; is there any left subtree?
        jnz     tfind2                  ; yes, try left child node
        stc
        jmp     tfind5                  ; exit, no match found
```

(continued)

Figure 11-9. *continued*

```
tfind3:                                 ; current > target
        mov     si,[bx+2]               ; get pointer to current
        mov     si,[si+2]               ; get left subtree pointer
        mov     [bx+2],si               ; update current node
        or      si,si                   ; is there any right subtree?
        jnz     tfind2                  ; yes, try right child node
        stc
        jmp     tfind5                  ; exit, no match found

tfind4:                                 ; current = target
        mov     si,[bx+2]               ; get address and length of
        mov     al,[si+6]               ; string within the node
        xor     ah,ah
        add     si,7
        add     sp,4                    ; discard original string
        jmp     tfind6                  ; address and length on stack

tfind5: pop     si                      ; if no match, restore address
        pop     ax                      ; and length of original string

tfind6: pop     es                      ; restore registers and exit
        pop     bp
        pop     di
        pop     dx
        pop     cx
        pop     bx
        ret

tfind   endp

;
; TDEL:         Deletes record from binary tree
;
; Call with:    DS:SI = segment:offset of string
;               AX    = length of string
;               BX    = tree handle
;
; Returns:      If function successful:
;               Carry = clear

;               If function unsuccessful:
;               Carry = set
;
; Destroys:     Nothing
;
        public  tdel
tdel    proc    near

        push    bx                      ; save registers
        push    cx
```

(continued)

Figure 11-9. *continued*

```
            push    dx
            push    di
            push    bp
            push    es
            push    ax
            push    si
            push    ds                      ; be sure ES = DS
            pop     es

            test    word ptr [bx],-1        ; empty tree?
            jnz     tdel1                   ; no, proceed
            stc
            jmp     tdel17                  ; yes, exit with error

tdel1:  mov     ax,[bx]                 ; current = head of list
            mov     [bx+2],ax

tdel2:  pop     di                      ; retrieve address and
            pop     dx                      ; length of string for
            push    dx                      ; record to be deleted
            push    di
            push    bx                      ; save anchor block pointer
            mov     si,[bx+2]               ; pointer to current record
            mov     bl,[si+6]               ; length of string
            xor     bh,bh
            add     si,7                    ; address of string
            call    strcmpi                 ; compare target to current
            pop     bx                      ; restore anchor block pointer
            je      tdel4                   ; current node = target
            jg      tdel3                   ; current > target

                                            ; current < target
            mov     si,[bx+2]               ; get pointer to current
            mov     si,[si+4]               ; get right subtree pointer
            mov     [bx+2],si               ; update current node
            or      si,si                   ; is there any left subtree?
            jnz     tdel2                   ; yes, try left child node
            stc
            jmp     tdel17                  ; exit, no match found

tdel3:                                      ; current > target
            mov     si,[bx+2]               ; get pointer to current
            mov     si,[si+2]               ; get left subtree pointer
            mov     [bx+2],si               ; update current node
            or      si,si                   ; is there any right subtree?
            jnz     tdel2                   ; yes, try right child node
            stc
            jmp     tdel17                  ; exit, no match found
```

(continued)

Figure 11-9. *continued*

```
tdel4:                                  ; current = target
        mov     bp,[bx+2]               ; BP = pointer to current
        mov     di,ds:[bp]              ; DI = pointer to parent
        mov     si,ds:[bp+2]            ; are there any children?
        or      si,ds:[bp+4]            ; if no children, just zap
        jz      tdel7                   ; parent's link to this node

        test    word ptr ds:[bp+2],-1   ; left subtree empty?
        jnz     tdel6                   ; no, jump
        mov     si,ds:[bp+4]            ; move right subtree to parent
        mov     [si],di                 ; update parent link in child
        jmp     tdel7

tdel6:  test    word ptr ds:[bp+4],-1   ; right subtree empty?
        jnz     tdel10                  ; no, jump
        mov     si,ds:[bp+2]            ; move left subtree to parent
        mov     [si],di                 ; update parent link in child

tdel7:                                  ; update parent subtree link
        or      di,di                   ; was this root node?
        jnz     tdel8                   ; no, continue
        mov     [bx],si                 ; yes, new root into anchor block
        jmp     tdel16                  ; done with this case

tdel8:  cmp     [di+2],bp               ; was this left child or right?
        jne     tdel9                   ; jump, right
        mov     [di+2],si               ; update parent's left subtree
        jmp     tdel16                  ; done with this case

tdel9:  mov     [di+4],si               ; update parent's right subtree
        jmp     tdel16                  ; done with this case

tdel10:                                 ; neither subtree empty
        mov     si,ds:[bp+4]            ; is immediate right child
        test    word ptr [si+2],-1      ; smallest in right subtree?
        jnz     tdel11                  ; no, jump
        mov     di,ds:[bp+2]            ; yes, deleted node's left child
        mov     [si+2],di               ; becomes replacement's left child
        mov     [di],si                 ; update parent pointer in child
        jmp     tdel13                  ; go fix deleted node's parent

tdel11: mov     si,[si+2]               ; find smallest in right subtree
        test    word ptr [si+2],-1      ; is there a left child?
        jnz     tdel11                  ; yes, keep looking

        push    si                      ; save replacement node
        push    [si+4]                  ; graft right link of replacement
        mov     si,[si]                 ; into left link of its parent
        pop     [si+2]                  ; (which is guaranteed to be zero)
```

(continued)

Figure 11-9. *continued*

```
        pop     si                      ; retrieve ptr to replacement

        mov     di,ds:[bp+2]            ; copy left child pointer from
        mov     [si+2],di               ; deleted to replacement node
        or      di,di                   ; is there a left child?
        jz      tdel12                  ; no, jump
        mov     [di],si                 ; yes, update its parent node

tdel12: mov     di,ds:[bp+4]            ; copy right child pointer from
        mov     [si+4],di               ; deleted to replacement node
        or      di,di                   ; is there a right child?
        jz      tdel13                  ; no, jump
        mov     [di],si                 ; yes, update its parent node

tdel13: mov     di,ds:[bp]              ; copy parent pointer from
        mov     [si],di                 ; deleted to replacement node
        or      di,di                   ; was there a parent?
        jnz     tdel14                  ; jump, parent exists
        mov     [bx],si                 ; deleted node was root
        jmp     tdel16                  ; update anchor block instead

tdel14: cmp     [di+2],bp               ; was deleted node left child?
        jne     tdel15                  ; no, jump
        mov     [di+2],si               ; yes, update parent's left link
        jmp     tdel16

tdel15: mov     [di+4],si               ; update parent's right link

tdel16: mov     si,[bx+2]               ; release memory for record
        call    hfree                   ; return status from HFREE

tdel17: pop     si                      ; restore registers and exit
        pop     ax
        pop     es
        pop     bp
        pop     di
        pop     dx
        pop     cx
        pop     bx
        ret

tdel    endp

_TEXT   ends

        end
```

The procedure TINIT is called to initialize a binary tree. It allocates an anchor (control) block from the heap each time a tree is created, and it returns the address of the anchor block as a handle for the tree that must be used for all subsequent access to the tree. The anchor block has the following format:

Offset	Length	Contents
0	2	Pointer to root node, zero if tree is empty
2	2	Current pointer position

The routine TKILL destroys a binary tree by releasing the heap blocks for all existing nodes in the tree and then releasing the anchor block for the tree. The code in TKILL is a compact example of the type of recursion typically used to process binary trees.

The routine TADD adds a node to a binary tree. It is called with a tree handle and the address and length of a string. It allocates a block from the heap to hold the node and copies the string into the block. TADD then traverses the tree, finds the proper location for the new node, and links the node into the tree. More specifically, TADD begins at the root, compares the string to be added to the tree with the current node, and then selects the left or right subtree according to the results of the comparison. If the subtree is empty, TADD adds the new node and updates all the appropriate pointers; otherwise, it follows the pointer to the next node and repeats the comparison. Here is an example of a call to TADD:

```
mystr       db    'test string'
mystr_len equ   $-mystr

htree       dw    0                  ; handle for binary tree
            .
            .
            .
            mov   si,seg mystr   ; DS:SI = string address
            mov   ds,si
            mov   si,offset mystr
            mov   ax,mystr_len    ; AX = string length
            mov   bx,htree        ; BX = tree handle
            call tadd
            jc    error           ; jump, can't add to list
```

TADD uses the STRCMPI routine from Chapter 5 to make case-insensitive comparisons and does not allow two nodes of the tree to have the same strings or keys. (You can easily change these characteristics in your own programs if you want.)

TDEL deletes a node from a tree. It is called with a tree handle and the address and length of a string in the same way TADD is called. TDEL traverses the tree until it finds a node whose data matches the specified string, removes the node from the tree by adjusting pointers, and finally releases the block that held the node back to the heap. The code for TDEL is considerably more complex than the code for TADD. Most of the code for TDEL is required for the case in which the node to be deleted has children in both the left and right subtrees. In order to keep the tree sorted,

TDEL must search the tree to find an appropriate node to substitute for the deleted node and must then update the pointers in the parents and children of both the deleted node and the replacement node.

Finally, the routine TFIND accepts a tree handle and the address and length of a string and searches the tree for a node with a matching string. Although this routine is not terribly useful in its present form, TFIND can be used to "look up" records in a tree if you change TADD so that it stores data or pointers to data in the nodes in addition to the strings.

PROCEDURES INTRODUCED IN THIS CHAPTER

Procedure Name	Action	Parameters	Results
HALLOC	Allocates block from local heap	AX = requested block size	If function successful: Carry = clear DS:SI = address of allocated block If function unsuccessful: Carry = set
HFREE	Releases heap block	DS:SI = segment:offset of heap block	Nothing (unless debugging routines enabled)
HINIT	Initializes local heap	DS:SI = segment:offset of heap base AX = heap size in bytes	If function successful: Carry = clear If function unsuccessful: Carry = set
HREALLOC	Resizes previously allocated heap block	DS:SI = segment:offset of existing heap block AX = new requested block size	If function successful: Carry = clear DS:SI = address of resized block (might have been moved) If function unsuccessful: Carry = set
LADD	Adds string to sorted list	DS:SI = segment:offset of string AX = length of string BX = list handle	If function successful: Carry = clear If function unsuccessful: Carry = set
LDEL	Deletes string from sorted list	DS:SI = segment:offset of string AX = length of string BX = list handle	If function successful: Carry = clear If function unsuccessful: Carry = set

(continued)

PROCEDURES INTRODUCED IN THIS CHAPTER *continued*

Procedure Name	Action	Parameters	Results
LFIRST	Returns first list record	BX = list handle	If function successful: Carry = clear DS:SI = segment:offset of string AX = length of string If function unsuccessful: Carry = set
LINIT	Initializes sorted list	Nothing	If function successful: Carry = clear AX = length of string If function unsuccessful: Carry = set
LKILL	Destroys sorted list	BX = list handle	If function successful: Carry = clear If function unsuccessful: Carry = set
LNEXT	Returns next list record	BX = list handle	If function successful: Carry = clear DS:SI = segment:offset of string AX = length of string If function unsuccessful: Carry = set
LPREV	Returns previous list record	BX = list handle	If function successful: Carry = clear DS:SI = segment:offset of string AX = length of string If function unsuccessful: Carry = set
TADD	Adds record to binary tree	DS:SI = segment:offset of string AX = length of string BX = tree handle	If function successful: Carry = clear If function unsuccessful: Carry = set
TDEL	Deletes record from binary tree	DS:SI = segment:offset of string AX = length of string BX = tree handle	If function successful: Carry = clear If function unsuccessful: Carry = set

(continued)

PROCEDURES INTRODUCED IN THIS CHAPTER *continued*

Procedure Name	Action	Parameters	Results
TFIND	Finds matching node in binary tree	DS:SI = segment:offset of string AX = length of string BX = tree handle	If function successful: Carry = clear DS:SI = segment:offset of string in matching node AX = length of string If function unsuccessful: Carry = set
TINIT	Initializes binary tree	Nothing	If function successful: Carry = clear AX = tree handle If function unsuccessful: Carry = set
TKILL	Destroys binary tree	BX = tree handle	If function successful: Carry = clear If function unsuccessful: Carry = set

Companion Disk

The companion disk directory \CH11 contains the programs and modules that are listed below.

Routines Presented in This Chapter

HEAP.ASM	Heap manager
LIST.ASM	Linked list manager
TREE.ASM	Binary tree manager

Routines Previously Discussed

HTOL.ASM	Converts a hexadecimal ASCII string to a double-precision (32-bit) unsigned integer
ITOH.ASM	Converts a single-precision (16-bit) unsigned integer to a hexadecimal ASCII string
STRINGS1.ASM	MASM string package #1
STRINGS2.ASM	MASM string package #2
STRINGS3.ASM	MASM dstring package #3

Note that only the routine STRCMPI in STRINGS3.ASM is called directly by routines in LIST.ASM and TREE.ASM, but that STRCMPI in turn depends on procedures in STRINGS1.ASM and STRINGS2.ASM.

Demonstration Programs

TRYHEAP	MAKE file for TRYHEAP.EXE
TRYHEAP.ASM	Interactive demonstration of the HEAP.ASM heap manager
TRYLIST	MAKE file for TRYLIST.EXE
TRYLIST.ASM	Interactive demonstration of the LIST.ASM list manager
TRYTREE	MAKE file for TRYTREE.EXE
TRYTREE.ASM	Interactive demonstration of the TREE.ASM binary tree manager

The interactive program TRYHEAP.ASM demonstrates use of the heap manager routines in HEAP.ASM. To build TRYHEAP.EXE, enter this command:

```
C>MAKE TRYHEAP  <Enter>
```

TRYHEAP accepts several commands. You can allocate blocks from the heap, resize previously allocated blocks, and release blocks back to the heap. Each time you execute one of these commands, the status of the heap is displayed as a list of the base addresses and sizes of all currently allocated blocks.

The demonstration program TRYLIST.ASM illustrates use of the list manager routines in LIST.ASM. To build TRYLIST.EXE, enter this command:

```
C>MAKE TRYLIST  <Enter>
```

TRYLIST prompts you to enter a string, inserts the string into the linked list, and then displays the current contents of the heap and of the list. This cycle repeats until the heap space is exhausted or until you press the Enter key in response to the prompt.

The interactive program TRYTREE.ASM demonstrates use of the binary tree manager routines in TREE.ASM. To build TRYTREE.EXE, enter this command:

```
C>MAKE TRYTREE  <Enter>
```

TRYTREE is very similar to TRYLIST. It prompts you to enter a string, inserts the string into the binary tree, and then displays the current contents of the heap and of the binary tree. This cycle repeats until the heap space is exhausted or until you press the Enter key in response to the prompt.

12

Multiple-Precision Integer Arithmetic

Programmers who use high-level languages rarely need to concern themselves with the mechanisms of arithmetic in their applications. They simply declare their variables as signed or unsigned, short or long, integer or real, and trust the compiler to translate the arithmetic operators in their source code into the proper machine instructions, sequences of instructions, or calls to library routines. They can even mix data types and rely on the compiler to convert (or "coerce") the type of one piece of data to match another.

MASM programmers, in contrast, continually confront the issues of computer arithmetic and data typing. To be a successful MASM programmer, you must have a solid grasp of binary data formats, signed and unsigned two's complement arithmetic, the CPU's built-in support for basic arithmetic operations, and the algorithms by which more complex arithmetic operations can be built from the available machine instructions. No shortcuts are possible.

This chapter begins with the Intel 80x86's native support for single-precision and double-precision integer arithmetic, takes a look at the classical algorithms for the four basic arithmetic operations, and finally develops a library of multiple-precision arithmetic routines that you can use in your own programs. As usual, the emphasis is on practical rather than theoretical considerations. (References to more detailed discussions are listed in the Bibliography at the end of this book.)

Integer Data Formats

You will discover that two pairs of terms pop up repeatedly during any discussion of integer arithmetic: *single-precision* and *double-precision* integers, and *signed* and *unsigned* integers.

A single-precision integer varies in size from machine to machine, but it is always a number that fits into a general register and that can be operated on conveniently with single machine instructions. It is also typically a power-of-2 multiple of bytes.

On the 8086, the 8088, the 80286, and the 80386/486 running in real mode or 16-bit protected mode, a single-precision integer is 16 bits, or 2 bytes. On the 80386/486 in 32-bit protected mode, a single-precision integer is 32 bits, or 4 bytes.

A double-precision integer, as you might expect from its name, is twice the size of a single-precision number for a given machine—again, always a power-of-2 multiple of bytes. On the 8086, the 8088, the 80286, and the 80386/486 in real mode or 16-bit protected mode, a double-precision integer is 32 bits. A double-precision integer is 64 bits on the 80386/486 in 32-bit protected mode. Most double-precision integer operations enjoy only primitive support in the 80x86 instruction set and—in the absence of a numeric coprocessor—must be carried out with sometimes lengthy sequences of machine instructions.

The distinction between signed and unsigned integers is straightforward. In a signed integer, the most significant bit is reserved for the arithmetic sign (the bit will be 0 if the number is positive, 1 if the number is negative); the remaining bits indicate the number's magnitude. The range of a 16-bit signed integer, for example, is −32,768 (8000H) through 32,767 (7FFFH). In an unsigned integer, all bits indicate magnitude. The range of a 16-bit unsigned integer is 0 through 65,535 (FFFFH).

Of course, for any given chunk of data, bits are merely bits, and the "signedness" or "unsignedness" of a given bit pattern depends on your point of view. But picking the right point of view is very important: A logical error in which a signed value is treated as unsigned, or vice versa, can cause some subtle and difficult program bugs, as you'll see later.

You must also understand how the bytes of a multibyte arithmetic value are laid out in memory. On Intel CPUs, the least significant byte of a value is always stored at the lowest memory address, followed by the next most significant byte at the next higher address, and so on until the most significant byte of the value, which is stored at the highest address occupied by the value, is reached. The sign bit of the value is the most significant bit of the byte at the highest address. For example, consider the 32-bit integer 12345678H, which is composed of 4 bytes laid out in memory as follows:

Lowest address			Highest address
78H	56H	34H	12H

CPUs that organize the bytes of a multibyte value in this manner are sometimes referred to as "Little-Endians," to distinguish them from "Big-Endian" CPUs (such as the Motorola 680x0 family), which store the most significant byte at the lowest address. Interestingly, the 80486 processor has a new instruction, called BSWAP, whose only purpose is to transform a 32-bit data value in a register from "Big-Endian" format to "Little-Endian" format and back again. In other words, it performs the same function for 32-bit values as the XCHG instruction performs for 16-bit values. For example, if you have a 32-bit value in register EAX, the instruction

```
bswap eax
```

is equivalent to (but much faster than) this sequence:

```
xchg ah,al
rol  eax,16
xchg ah,al
```

Such an instruction might seem pretty exotic, but it could be handy if your program needs to read data files created by a program running on a "Big-Endian" CPU.

Single-Precision Integer Arithmetic

The 80x86 CPU family supports single-precision integer addition, subtraction, multiplication, and division with the following instructions:

ADD	Single-precision addition
SUB	Single-precision subtraction
MUL	Unsigned single-precision multiplication
IMUL	Signed single-precision multiplication
DIV	Unsigned single-precision division
IDIV	Signed single-precision division

These instructions serve as your fundamental weapons against the family of single-precision integers, and you must be thoroughly familiar with their behavior and their idiosyncrasies.

Related but less important instructions include the following:

NEG	Two's complement (multiply by −1)
CMP	Compare single-precision integers
CBW	Sign-extend 8 bits to 16 bits

ADD, SUB, NEG, and CMP set the CPU's flags (the most important being carry, sign, overflow, and zero) according to the result of the operation. CMP, in fact, can be seen as a sort of nondestructive SUB that does nothing but set the CPU flags. (This is an easy way to remember the order of CMP's operands.)

The ADD, SUB, and CMP instructions do not come in signed and unsigned varieties. In these particular cases, the signed or unsigned nature of the result is solely in the eye of the beholder. If you want to regard the result as unsigned, you test the carry flag; if you prefer to think of the result as signed, you test the sign and overflow flags. The 80x86 family has an astonishingly diverse battery of conditional jumps to provide for such contingencies.

For example, if you want to perform a conditional branch after comparing two addresses (which are unsigned values), you would use the JB, JBE, JA, or JAE instruction. After comparing two dollar amounts (signed values), you would use the JL, JLE, JG, or JGE instruction. Testing the wrong flag or selecting the wrong type of conditional jump can often cause obscure program bugs, especially when addresses are being calculated or compared. Such bugs can lie in wait for a long time, unmasked only when a completely unrelated part of the program is changed or when the program's modules are relinked in a different order.

The multiply and divide instructions are a little more interesting and a little less regular. MUL and IMUL affect only the carry and overflow flags, leaving the other flags undefined; DIV and IDIV leave the state of all flags undefined. The signed instructions—IMUL and IDIV—have slightly less range because they render special treatment to the sign bit. Obviously, you should always use the unsigned instructions—MUL and DIV—when you are working with addresses.

The multiply and divide instructions are indeed single-precision arithmetic operations, but the complete truth is not so simple. The multiply instructions accept two single-precision operands, but they produce a double-precision result. One of the arguments must always be in register AX, whereas the other can be in any other register or in memory; the result always appears in registers DX and AX, with the most significant part in DX. The conventional notation for this latter situation is DX:AX. (On the 80386/486 in 32-bit protected mode, EAX and EDX are used instead of AX and DX.)

The divide instructions accept a double-precision dividend and a single-precision divisor, and they produce a single-precision quotient and remainder. The dividend is always taken from DX:AX; the divisor can be in any other register or in memory. The quotient is always left in register AX, and the remainder appears in register DX. (Again, on the 80386/486 in 32-bit protected mode, EAX and EDX are used instead of AX and DX.)

Why this mixing of single-precision and double-precision arguments and results, and why this special treatment of DX and AX? You must be able to use the multiply and divide instructions to scale a single-precision value (by multiplying and then dividing) through a double-precision intermediate without losing any precision. Using dedicated registers to provide arguments or accept results is an explicit trade of instruction set orthogonality for more compact opcodes and therefore for smaller programs.

Incidentally, the 80286, the 80386, and the 80486 support an odd, but handy, form of the IMUL instruction not found on the 8086 and 8088. It is one of the few instructions in the entire 80x86 family with three operands: The destination is always a register; one of the source operands is a register or memory address; and the other is an immediate, or literal, value. This form of IMUL is also aberrant in other ways: The result of the operation is a single-precision rather than a double-precision value; the result can go to a register other than DX and AX; a register argument need not be in AX or DX; and the operation does not necessarily destroy one of the arguments. For example, to multiply the contents of CX by 10 and leave the result in register BX, you would write the following:

```
imul bx,cx,10
```

MUL, IMUL, DIV, and IDIV additionally support half-precision operations (operating on or returning 8-bit values). These are rarely used in normal application programming, however.

Double-Precision Integer Arithmetic

The 80x86 family's support for double-precision operations is discouragingly paltry. Besides the arithmetic instructions already listed, it includes only the following:

ADC	Single-precision addition with carry
SBB	Single-precision subtraction with carry (borrow)

These (in essence) allow you to propagate the carry bit through the piecewise addition and subtraction of multiple-precision values. For example, the following adds a double-precision value in DX:AX to a double-precision value in SI:DI, leaving the result in DX:AX:

```
add   ax,di      ; lower half
adc   dx,si      ; upper half
```

Similarly, to subtract a double-precision value in SI:DI from a double-precision value in DX:AX, leaving the result in DX:AX, you could write this code:

```
sub   ax,di      ; lower half
sbb   dx,si      ; upper half
```

Other loosely related instructions, useful primarily for converting single-precision values to double-precision, include the following:

CWD	Sign-extend 16 bits to 32 bits
CDQ	Sign-extend 32 bits to 64 bits (80386/486 only)
MOVSX	Sign-extend 8 bits or 16 bits to 16 bits or 32 bits (80386/486 only)
MOVZX	Zero-extend 8 bits or 16 bits to 16 bits or 32 bits (80386/486 only)

To take the two's complement of a double-precision number, you can use the time-tested technique of flipping all the bits and then adding 1. For example, to change the sign of a double-precision number in DX:AX, you can use these instructions:

```
not   dx
not   ax
add   ax,1
adc   dx,0
```

A slightly faster technique relies on the fact that NEG sets the carry flag:

```
neg    dx
neg    ax
sbb    dx,0
```

What about double-precision multiplication and division? If you take as a guide the single-precision native MUL, IMUL, DIV, and IDIV instructions, you know that a useful double-precision multiply must process two double-precision arguments to produce a quad-precision result. Similarly, a fully generalized double-precision divide must accept a quad-precision dividend and a double-precision divisor, yielding a double-precision quotient and remainder.

At this point, your intuition as an 80x86 programmer is probably whispering that you are about to run short of registers. The problems go far deeper, however. You might hope, for example, that the built-in single-precision multiply and divide instructions could be useful building blocks for efficient double-precision (or multiple-precision) multiply and divide routines. But the harsh reality is that the hardware's single-precision multiply instruction is only marginally helpful when used for stepwise multiple-precision multiplication operations in the obvious manner, because MUL and IMUL are quite slow on the older 8086 and 8088 processors. As for multiple-precision divides, the hardware's built-in divide instruction is (for all practical purposes) useless; although a multiple-precision divide constructed on single-precision divides is feasible, it is complex and—worse yet—not very fast.

The Classical Algorithms

When you want to perform arithmetic to a degree of precision not supported by the CPU's native machine instructions, you are led directly to the so-called classical algorithms for addition, subtraction, multiplication, and division. The classical algorithms are the underpinnings of the stepwise, methodical procedures you learned in grade school for performing arithmetic with paper and pencil on numbers with more than one digit. These algorithms are called "classical" because their history extends far back before the computer age. In fact, the term *algorithm* originally referred only to the formalized procedures for these four arithmetic operations and is a corruption of the name of al Khowarizmi, an Arab mathematician renowned for his writings on the subject.

The ultimate resource for programmers on the classical algorithms is Donald Knuth's *The Art of Computer Programming* (specifically, vol. 2, *Seminumerical Algorithms*, pp. 229–45). Knuth's sample programs are rendered in MIX, the assembly language of a hypothetical CPU for which simulators exist only in the halls of academia. I have translated his listings into C-like pseudocode, which is shown in Figures 12-1, 12-2, 12-3, and 12-4.

```
int m;                      // number of digits
int i;                      // index variable
int b;                      // base
int k                       // carry

array u[m], v[m];           // holds arguments
array w[m];                 // receives results

k = 0;                      // initialize carry

for(i = 0; i < m; i++)      // add digit by digit
{
    w[i] = (u[i] + v[i] + k) mod b;
    k    = (u[i] + v[i] + k) / b;
}
```

Figure 12-1.
Multiple-precision addition in C-like pseudocode. In this simplified presentation, both arguments and the result are assumed to be nonnegative. The carry k *always takes the value 0 or 1.*

```
int m;                      // number of digits
int i;                      // index variable
int b;                      // base
int k;                      // carry

array u[m], v[m];           // holds arguments
array w[m];                 // receives results

k = 0;                      // initialize carry

for(i = 0; i < m; i++)      // subtract digit by digit
{
    w[i] = (u[i] - v[i] + k) mod b;
    k    = (u[i] - v[i] + k) / b;
}
```

Figure 12-2.
Multiple-precision subtraction in C-like pseudocode. In this simplified presentation, both arguments and the result are assumed to be nonnegative, and the argument in array u[] *is assumed to be greater than or equal to the argument in* v[]. *The carry* k *always takes the value 0 or −1.*

```
int m;                        // number of arg digits
int i, j;                     // index variables
int b;                        // base
int k;                        // carry
int t;                        // scratch variable

array u[m], v[m];             // holds arguments
array w[m * 2];               // receives product

for(i = 0; i < m * 2; i++)    // initialize product
{
    w[i] = 0;
}

for(i = 0; i < m; i++)        // sum partial products
{
    k = 0;                    // initialize carry

    for(j = 0; j < m; j++)    // find this partial product
    {
        t         = u[j] * v[i] + w[i + j] + k;
        w[i + j]  = t mod b;  // digit of partial product
        k         = t / b;    // calculate carry
    }
    w[i + m] = k;             // highest digit of
}                             // partial product
```

Figure 12-3.
C-like pseudocode for a multiple-precision multiplication that exploits the CPU's native multiply instruction. The square of the base must be less than or equal to 1 plus the largest product that can be generated by the hardware's unsigned multiply. In this simplified presentation, both of the arguments and the result are assumed to be nonnegative, and both arguments are the same size. The value of the carry k always satisfies the condition $0 <= k < b$, where b is the base.

```
int m;                        // number of digits
int i;                        // index variable
int b;                        // base
int c = 0;                    // normalization loops
int k;                        // borrow flag
int z;                        // trial quotient
```

Figure 12-4.   *(continued)*
Multiple-precision division in C-like pseudocode. This simplified presentation assumes that the unsigned dividend and divisor have been previously placed right-aligned in the arrays u[] and v[] and padded with leading-zero digits as needed, that the dividend has twice as many digits as the divisor, and that overflow and divide by zero conditions have already been checked.

Figure 12-4. *continued*

```
array u[m * 2 + 1];          // holds dividend
array v[m];                  // holds divisor
array q[m + 1];              // receives quotient
array r[m];                  // receives remainder

while[v[0] == 0)             // normalize divisor
{                            // and dividend
    v[] = v[] * b;
    u[] = u[] * b;
    c++;                     // count normalizing loops
}

for(i = 0; i <= m; i++)      // for all quotient digits
{
    if(u[i] = v[0])          // calculate trial quotient
        z = b - 1;
    else
        z = (u[i] * b) + u[i + 1] - (z * v[0]);
    while((v[1] * z) > ((u[i] * b) + u[i + 1] - (z * v[0])))
        z = z - 1;
                             // multiply and subtract
    u[i ... i + m] = u[i ... i + m] - v[0 ... m - 1] * z;

    if(u[i ... i + m] < 0)   // force result positive
    {
        u[i ... i + m] = u[i ... i + m] + b ^ (m + 1);
        k = true;
    }
    else k = false;

    q[i] = z;                // accumulate quotient digits

    if(k)                    // add back if previous borrow
    {
        q[i] = q[i] - 1;
        u[i ... i + m] = u[i ... i + m] + v[0 ... m - 1];
    }
}

r[] = r[] / (b * c);         // unnormalize remainder
```

In Figures 12-1 through 12-4, *u[]* and *v[]* are arrays that hold arguments in base *b*, one digit per array element. The physical size of each array element is irrelevant as long as the element is large enough to hold a number of magnitude *b − 1*. The value *m* is the maximum number of digits in each argument, and the result is formed in array *w[]*. The variable *k* represents the carry and is set to the excess when the result of an operation can't fit into a single digit.

To illustrate how these arrays and variables are used, consider what happens when you add the first digits of two multiple-precision numbers. The value of the first result digit and the resulting carry are found as follows:

```
w[0] = (u[0] + v[0]) mod b;
k    = (u[0] + v[0]) / b;
```

Subsequent digits (1 through $m - 1$) in the result are found in the same way, except that the previous value of k is included:

```
w[i] = (u[i] + v[i] + k) mod b;
k    = (u[i] + v[i] + k) / b;
```

The classical algorithms apply equally well to numbers of any base. You can choose to view your arguments and results as bit arrays (base 2), or you can group the bits and work on octal numbers (base 8) or hexadecimal numbers (base 16). You can even allow the natural byte or word size of the CPU to be an individual "digit."

The multiplication algorithm shown in Figure 12-3 differs from the traditional longhand technique in that the partial products are accumulated on the fly. When you perform multiplication with pencil and paper, you probably find the partial products first and then add them together at the end of the calculation. One especially nice feature of this multiplication algorithm is that it allows you to exploit the CPU's native hardware multiply if one is available. You merely need to pick a base such that the square of the base is less than or equal to 1 plus the largest product that can be generated by the CPU's unsigned multiply instruction.

As you can see in Figure 12-4, the classical algorithm for radix-independent division is relatively complex and subtle. Long division requires normalizations, groupings, and trial divides that do not readily reduce into a simple, easily understood piece of radix-independent pseudocode. Luckily, when you are working in binary (radix = 2), the classical division algorithm degenerates to a considerably simpler form, which is typically implemented as a shift-and-subtract loop. The multiple trial divides that can be needed for each forward step in the generalized form of the algorithm—not to mention the logic necessary to pick trial divisors intelligently—disappear completely. Similarly, the classical algorithm used for binary multiplication can be simplified to a short shift-and-add loop.

"Ah, yes," I can almost hear you saying, "the good old shift-and-add and shift-and-subtract methods for multiplication and division." Most MASM programmers know about these types of routines and also feel instinctively that we understand how they work, based on our day-to-day experiences with using a left shift for a fast multiply by 2, a right shift for a fast divide by 2, the common shortcut for multiplication by 10 that relies on a couple of shifts and an add, and so on. But few programmers are ever called on to write one of these multiplication or division routines. In practice, they are not quite as obvious as you might imagine. Accordingly, the following sections provide "cookbook" methods for writing multiplication and division routines that will serve you well on any reasonable CPU (one that uses two's complement arithmetic and has a carry flag). We'll then illustrate the methods with working code.

Multiplication by the Shift-and-Add Method

Here we assume that you are multiplying two arguments (sometimes called the *multiplier* and *multiplicand*), which are the same length in bytes, to obtain a *product* that is twice the length of either argument. The arguments and product are assumed to be unsigned; handling arithmetic signs and checking for zero arguments are best done in an external shell routine. We also assume that your CPU has a carry flag under direct program control, as well as right and left shift instructions that work with the carry flag to let you remove a bit from one byte and insert it in another. (The Intel 80x86 CPUs boast both a carry flag and a fine repertoire of shift instructions, so we are in business.)

Here's the recipe for multiplication by shifting and adding:

1. Initialize to zero the high half of the buffer that will receive the product. (Because the low half will be discarded by shifting, its original value is unimportant.)

2. Initialize the loop counter to the value that is eight times the length of each argument (in bytes) plus 1.

3. Clear the carry flag.

4. Perform a logical right shift on the buffer containing the partial product by one bit position; the value in the carry flag now becomes the most significant bit of the product.

5. Perform a logical right shift on the buffer containing the second argument (the multiplier) by one bit position; the "lost" bit shifted out is saved in the carry flag.

6. If the carry flag is clear (that is, the bit shifted out of the multiplier was 0), go to step 8.

7. If the carry flag is set (that is, the bit shifted out of the multiplier was 1), add the first argument (the multiplicand) to the high half of the partial product. Any overflow of this addition is saved in the carry flag.

8. Decrement the loop counter, preserving the carry flag; if the loop counter is nonzero, go to step 4.

This procedure is illustrated by the routine DMUL.ASM in Figure 12-5.

```
;
; DMUL.ASM  --  Double-precision unsigned multiply
;               for 8086, 8088, 80286, 80386, and
;               80486 in real mode/16-bit protected mode.
;               This version uses the classic bit-by-bit
;               shift-and-add technique.
```

Figure 12-5. *(continued)*
DMUL.ASM, a routine that uses the shift-and-add algorithm to multiply two 32-bit unsigned integers, yielding a 64-bit unsigned result.

Figure 12-5. *continued*

```
;
; Copyright (C) 1991 Ray Duncan
;
; Call with:    DX:AX      = double-precision argument 1
;               CX:BX      = double-precision argument 2
;
; Returns:      DX:CX:BX:AX = quad-precision product
;
; Destroys:     Nothing

_TEXT   segment word public 'CODE'

        assume  cs:_TEXT

        public  dmul
dmul    proc    near

        push    si                      ; save registers
        push    di
        push    bp                      ; set up stack frame

        mov     bp,33                   ; initialize loop counter
        xor     si,si                   ; initialize upper half
        xor     di,di                   ; of product SI:DI:DX:AX

dmul1:  rcr     si,1                    ; shift partial product
        rcr     di,1                    ; and multiplier right by
        rcr     dx,1                    ; 1 bit, putting lost bit
        rcr     ax,1                    ; of multiplier into carry

        jnc     dmul2                   ; jump if lost bit is 0

        add     di,bx                   ; add multiplicand to high
        adc     si,cx                   ; half of partial product

dmul2:  dec     bp                      ; decrement counter and loop
        jnz     dmul1

        mov     bx,dx                   ; position result
        mov     cx,di
        mov     dx,si

        pop     bp                      ; restore registers
        pop     di
        pop     si
        ret                             ; and exit

dmul    endp

_TEXT   ends

        end
```

What's going on in this routine? Think back to the technique you learned years ago for longhand multiplication of decimal numbers. Each digit of the multiplicand is multiplied by each digit of the multiplier to obtain a set of partial products, which are added, after appropriate shifting, to form the final product. In binary multiplication, each digit of the multiplier can be only 0 or 1. Thus, each partial product to be accumulated is either 0 or the appropriately shifted value of the multiplicand. The remainder is merely trickery to make everything end up in the correct position. (The routine DMUL1, which uses a byte-by-byte algorithm, is included on the companion disk but is not reproduced here.)

Division by the Shift-and-Subtract Method

The next procedure assumes that you are dividing an unsigned *dividend* by an unsigned *divisor* to get an unsigned *quotient* and an unsigned *remainder*. The dividend is further assumed to be twice the length (in bytes) of the divisor; both remainder and quotient are the same length as the divisor. Again, handling of signs, zero divisors, overflow, and other odd conditions are preferably handled in an external shell routine, allowing programs that have control over their arguments (or that must work with unsigned quantities such as memory addresses) to call the unsigned routine directly for best performance. We additionally assume that the characteristics demanded of the CPU for the shift-and-add multiplication routine (shifts and carry flag control) also apply for the shift-and-subtract divide routine.

Here's the recipe for division by shifting and subtracting:

1. Set the loop counter to the value that is eight times the length of the divisor (in bytes); this is the number of bits of quotient and remainder that you need to generate. (The initial value in the buffer that receives the quotient is unimportant because it will be discarded by shifting during the procedure.)

2. Clear the carry flag.

3. Shift the quotient left by one bit position; the previous value of the carry flag is now inserted into the quotient as the least significant bit.

4. Shift the dividend left by one bit position; the bit shifted out is saved in the carry flag.

5. If the carry flag is clear, go to step 7.

6. Subtract the divisor from the upper half of the dividend. Set the carry flag and go to step 8.

7. If the upper half of the dividend is larger than the divisor, go to step 6; otherwise, clear the carry flag and go to step 8.

8. Decrement the loop counter, preserving the state of the carry flag; if the loop counter is nonzero, go to step 3.

9. Shift the quotient left by one bit position, bringing the carry flag into the quotient as the final least significant bit. (Moving this last shift outside the main loop is not necessary but allows you to use a more efficient control structure.) The remainder is whatever is left in the high half of the dividend.

This procedure is illustrated by the routine DDIV.ASM in Figure 12-6.

```
;
; DDIV.ASM -- Double-precision unsigned divide
;             for 8086, 8088, 80286, 80386, and
;             80486 in real mode/16-bit protected mode.
;
; Copyright (C) 1991 Ray Duncan
;
; Call with:    DX:CX:BX:AX = quad-precision dividend
;               SI:DI       = double-precision divisor
;
; Returns:      DX:AX       = double-precision quotient
;               CX:BX       = double-precision remainder
;
; Destroys:     SI, DI

_TEXT   segment word public 'CODE'

        assume  cs:_TEXT

        public  ddiv
ddiv    proc    near

        push    bp                      ; save register
        mov     bp,cx                   ; BP = 3rd word of dividend
        mov     cx,32                   ; initialize loop counter
        clc                             ; carry flag initially clear

ddiv1:  rcl     ax,1                    ; test this bit of dividend
        rcl     bx,1
        rcl     bp,1
        rcl     dx,1
        jnc     ddiv3                   ; jump if bit was clear

ddiv2:  sub     bp,di                   ; subtract divisor from dividend
        sbb     dx,si
        stc                             ; force carry flag set and
        loop    ddiv1                   ; shift it into quotient
        jmp     ddiv5

ddiv3:  cmp     dx,si                   ; dividend > divisor?
        jc      ddiv4                   ; no, jump
        jne     ddiv2                   ; yes, subtract divisor
        cmp     bp,di
        jnc     ddiv2                   ; yes, subtract divisor
```

Figure 12-6.   (continued)

DDIV.ASM, a routine that uses the shift-and-subtract algorithm to divide a 64-bit unsigned dividend by a 32-bit unsigned divisor, yielding a 32-bit unsigned quotient and remainder.

Figure 12-6. *continued*

```
ddiv4:  clc                             ; force carry flag clear and
        loop    ddiv1                   ; shift it into quotient

ddiv5:  rcl     ax,1                    ; bring last bit into quotient
        rcl     bx,1

        mov     cx,bp
        xchg    dx,bx                   ; put quotient in DX:AX
        xchg    cx,bx                   ; put remainder in CX:BX

        pop     bp                      ; restore register
        ret                             ; and exit

ddiv    endp

_TEXT   ends

        end
```

It is helpful to draw analogies with longhand decimal division. Again, when you choose to view each bit as a single digit, trial divides are not necessary—either the divisor fits into the portion of the dividend you are looking at or it doesn't. You use shifting as a shortcut to inspecting groups of the dividend's digits that are the same length as the divisor. The rest is simply bookkeeping and positioning the results.

Multiple-Precision Arithmetic Routines

The final listings in this chapter contain the source code for a complete battery of multiple-precision arithmetic routines:

MPNEG	Multiple-precision two's complement (changes sign)
MPABS	Multiple-precision absolute value
MPADD	Multiple-precision addition
MPSUB	Multiple-precision subtraction
MPMUL	Multiple-precision unsigned multiplication
MPIMUL	Multiple-precision signed multiplication
MPDIV	Multiple-precision unsigned division
MPIDIV	Multiple-precision signed division

All of these routines can process integers of any length from 1 byte through 255 bytes. They are patterned conceptually after the native CPU instructions for addition, subtraction, sign inversion, absolute value, multiplication, and division. All assume that their arguments and results are stored in "Little-Endian" byte-order—that is, with the least significant byte at the lowest address and the most significant byte (including the sign bit) at the highest address.

The routines MPNEG (Figure 12-7) and MPABS (Figure 12-8) are designed to be symmetric with the monadic CPU instructions NEG and ADD. The two routines accept identical parameters: a pointer to the argument in registers DS:SI, and the length of the argument in register CX. All registers are returned unchanged, and the result replaces the argument. MPNEG uses the familiar trick of taking the one's complement of the argument and then adding 1; MPABS simply tests the sign bit of the value and calls MPNEG if the value is negative.

For example, to change the sign of the multibyte value in the array *myint*, you could use the following code:

```
intsize equ    n                      ; define size of integer

myint   db     intsize dup (?)        ; storage for integer
        .
        .
        .
        mov    si,seg myint           ; DS:SI = address of integer
        mov    ds,si
        mov    si,offset myint
        mov    cx,intsize             ; CX = length of integer
        call   mpneg                  ; change sign of integer
```

```
;
; MPNEG.ASM -- Multiple-precision two's complement routine
;             for Intel 8086, 8088, 80286, 80386, and
;             80486 in real mode/16-bit protected mode.
;
; Copyright (C) 1991 Ray Duncan
;
; Call with:   DS:SI = address of argument
;              CX    = argument length in bytes
;
;              Assumes direction flag is clear at entry
;
; Returns:     DS:SI = address of result
;
; Destroys:    Nothing

_TEXT   segment word public 'CODE'

        assume  cs:_TEXT

        public  mpneg
mpneg   proc    near
```

Figure 12-7.   *(continued)*

MPNEG.ASM, a general-purpose two's complement routine to change the sign of a multiple-precision integer.

Figure 12-7. *continued*

```
        push    cx                      ; save two copies of
        push    cx                      ; length of value

mpneg1: not     byte ptr [si]           ; one's complement this digit
        inc     si                      ; advance through value
        loop    mpneg1                  ; until all digits inverted

        pop     cx                      ; retrieve length of argument
        sub     si,cx                   ; restore first-byte address
        stc                             ; set carry to add 1

mpneg2: adc     byte ptr [si],0         ; add 1 to one's complement
        inc     si                      ; to get two's complement
        loop    mpneg2                  ; until all digits finished

        pop     cx                      ; restore operand length
        sub     si,cx                   ; restore first-byte address
        ret                             ; back to caller

mpneg   endp

_TEXT   ends

        end
```

```
;
; MPABS.ASM -- Multiple-precision integer absolute value
;               for Intel 8086, 8088, 80286, 80386, and
;               80486 in real mode/16-bit protected mode.
;
; Copyright (C) 1991 Ray Duncan
;
; Call with:    DS:SI = address of argument
;               CX    = argument length in bytes
;
;               Assumes direction flag is clear at entry
;
; Returns:      DS:SI = address of result
;
; Destroys:     Nothing

_TEXT   segment word public 'CODE'
```

Figure 12-8.   *(continued)*

MPABS.ASM, a general-purpose routine to find the absolute value of a multiple-precision integer. MPABS calls MPNEG (Figure 12-7).

Figure 12-8. *continued*

```
        assume  cs:_TEXT

        extrn   mpneg:near

        public  mpabs
mpabs   proc    near

        push    si                      ; save address of value

        add     si,cx                   ; calc address of high byte
        test    byte ptr [si-1],80h     ; test sign bit

        pop     si                      ; restore address of value
        jz      mpabs1                  ; jump, it was positive

        call    mpneg                   ; it was negative, flip sign

mpabs1: ret                             ; back to caller

mpabs   endp

_TEXT   ends

        end
```

The two routines MPADD (Figure 12-9) and MPSUB (Figure 12-10) carry out multiple-precision addition and subtraction, respectively. The logic of these routines closely follows the flow of the pseudocode listings for addition and subtraction in Figure 12-1 and Figure 12-2. Like the CPU's native ADD and SUB instructions, the arguments for MPADD and MPSUB are referred to as the *source* and *destination* arguments, and the results are returned by overwriting the destination. For the sake of both simplicity and speed, the returned result is the same length as each argument, and overflow is ignored.

MPADD and MPSUB have identical calling sequences. DS:SI points to the source argument, ES:DI points to the destination, and register CX contains the length of each argument. When MPADD or MPSUB returns, all registers are unchanged, with ES:DI conveniently pointing to the result, which can then be used as an argument in another multiple-precision operation. For example, to add the two values in the arrays *myint1* and *myint2*, leaving the result in *myint2*, you would write the following code:

```
intsize equ     n                       ; define size of integer

myint1  db      intsize dup (?)         ; source operand
myint2  db      intsize dup (?)         ; destination operand
        .
        .
        .
```

```
        mov    si,seg myint1      ; DS:SI = address of
        mov    ds,si              ; source operand
        mov    si,offset myint1
        mov    di,seg myint2      ; ES:DI = address of
        mov    es,di              ; destination operand
        mov    di,offset myint2
        mov    cx,intsize         ; CX = operand length
        call   mpadd              ; now add operands
```

```
;
; MPADD.ASM -- Multiple-precision integer addition
;              for Intel 8086, 8088, 80286, 80386, and
;              80486 in real mode/16-bit protected mode.
;
; Copyright (C) 1991 Ray Duncan
;
; Call with:    DS:SI = address of source operand
;               ES:DI = address of destination operand
;               CX    = operand length in bytes
;
;               Assumes direction flag is clear at entry
;
; Returns:      ES:DI = address of result
;
; Destroys:     Nothing

_TEXT   segment word public 'CODE'

        assume  cs:_TEXT

        public  mpadd
mpadd   proc    near

        push   ax                 ; save registers
        push   si
        push   di
        push   cx
        clc                       ; initialize carry flag

mpadd1: lodsb                     ; next byte from source
        adc    byte ptr es:[di],al ; accumulate sum
        inc    di
        loop   mpadd1             ; until all bytes processed

        pop    cx                 ; restore registers
        pop    di
        pop    si
```

Figure 12-9.   *(continued)*

MPADD.ASM, a general-purpose addition routine for multiple-precision integers.

Figure 12-9. *continued*

```
        pop     ax
        ret                             ; back to caller

mpadd   endp

_TEXT   ends

        end
```

```
;
; MPSUB.ASM -- Multiple-precision integer subtraction
;               for Intel 8086, 8088, 80286, 80386, and
;               80486 in real mode/16-bit protected mode.
;
; Copyright (C) 1991 Ray Duncan
;
; Call with:    DS:SI = address of source operand
;               ES:DI = address of destination operand
;               CX    = operand length in bytes
;
;               Assumes direction flag is clear at entry
;
; Returns:      ES:DI = address of result (destination - source)
;
; Destroys:     Nothing

_TEXT   segment word public 'CODE'

        assume  cs:_TEXT

        public  mpsub
mpsub   proc    near

        push    ax                      ; save registers
        push    cx
        push    si
        push    di
        clc                             ; initialize carry flag

mpsub1: lodsb                           ; next byte from source
        sbb     byte ptr es:[di],al     ; subtract from destination
        inc     di
        loop    mpsub1                  ; until all bytes processed

        pop     di                      ; restore registers
```

Figure 12-10.   *(continued)*
MPSUB.ASM, a general-purpose subtraction routine for multiple-precision integers.

Figure 12-10. *continued*

```
        pop    si
        pop    cx
        pop    ax
        ret                              ; back to caller

mpsub   endp

_TEXT   ends

        end
```

Figures 12-11 and 12-12 contain the source code for two versions of the MPMUL routine to perform unsigned multiplication. MPMUL in Figure 12-11 follows the classical algorithm faithfully and uses the CPU's native multiply instruction to obtain partial products that are accumulated on the fly. MPMUL in Figure 12-12 carries out multiplication by the shift-and-add method described earlier. Both accept the address of the multiplier in registers DS:SI, the address of the multiplicand in registers ES:DI, and the length of each operand in register CX. All registers are returned unchanged, with ES:DI pointing to the product.

```
;
; MPMUL.ASM -- Multiple-precision unsigned multiply
;              for Intel 8086, 8088, 80286, 80386, and
;              80486 in real mode/16-bit protected mode.
;
; Copyright (C) 1991 Ray Duncan
;
; Call with:    DS:SI = address of source operand
;               ES:DI = address of destination operand
;               CX    = operand length in bytes
;
;               Assumes direction flag is clear at entry
;               Assumes DS = ES <> SS
;               Assumes CX <= 255
;
; Returns:      ES:DI = address of product
;
;               NOTE: Buffer for the destination operand must
;               be twice as long as the actual operand because
;               it will receive a double-precision result.
;
```

Figure 12-11. *(continued)*

MPMUL.ASM, a general-purpose unsigned multiplication routine for multiple-precision integers. This version uses the CPU's native hardware multiply to carry out multiplication in a bytewise fashion. (Compare Figure 12-12.)

Figure 12-11. *continued*

```
; Destroys:      Nothing
;
; Usage:         DS:SI = u[0] base address source operand
;                SS:BP = v[0] base address destination operand
;                ES:DI = w[0] base address of product
;                BX    = i    index for outer loop
;                CX    = j    index for inner loop
;                DH    = m    operand length in bytes
;                DL    = k    remainder of partial products


_TEXT   segment word public 'CODE'

        assume  cs:_TEXT

        public  mpmul
mpmul   proc    near

        push    ax                      ; save registers
        push    bx
        push    dx
        push    bp
        sub     sp,cx                   ; make buffer on stack
        mov     bp,sp                   ; for destination operand
        mov     dh,cl                   ; save operand length (m)

        push    cx
        push    si                      ; copy destination operand
        push    di                      ; to temporary storage in
        push    es                      ; stack frame because result
        push    ss                      ; will be built in destination
        pop     es                      ; operand's buffer
        mov     si,di
        mov     di,bp
        rep movsb
        pop     es
        pop     di
        pop     si
        pop     cx

        push    di                      ; initialize destination buffer
        xor     ax,ax                   ; to receive result (it better be
        rep stosw                       ; twice the size of the operands)
        pop     di

        xor     bx,bx                   ; i = 0

mpmul1: xor     dl,dl                   ; k = 0
        xor     cx,cx                   ; j = 0
```

(continued)

Figure 12-11. *continued*

```
mpmul2: xchg    bx,cx
        mov     al,[si+bx]              ; get u[j]
        xchg    bx,cx

        xchg    bp,di
        mov     ah,ss:[di+bx]           ; get v[i]
        xchg    bp,di

        mul     ah                      ; t = u[j] * v[i]
        add     al,dl                   ;     + k
        adc     ah,0
        add     bx,cx
        add     al,[bx+di]              ;     + w[i + j]
        adc     ah,0
        mov     [bx+di],al              ; w[i + j] = t mod b
        mov     dl,ah                   ; k        = t / b
        sub     bx,cx                   ; restore i

        inc     cx                      ; j++
        cmp     cl,dh                   ; j = m?
        jne     mpmul2                  ; no, repeat inner loop

        push    bx
        add     bl,dh                   ; w[i + m] = k
        adc     bh,0
        mov     [di+bx],ah
        pop     bx

        inc     bx                      ; i++
        cmp     bl,dh                   ; i = m?
        jne     mpmul1                  ; no, repeat outer loop

        add     sp,bx                   ; discard operand buffer
        pop     bp                      ; restore registers
        pop     dx
        pop     bx
        pop     ax
        ret                             ; back to caller

mpmul   endp

_TEXT   ends

        end
```

```
;
; MPMUL.ASM -- Multiple-precision unsigned multiply
;               for Intel 8086, 8088, 80286, 80386, and
;               80486 in real mode/16-bit protected mode.
;               This version uses the shift-and-add method.
;
; Copyright (C) 1991 Ray Duncan
;
; Call with:    DS:SI = address of source operand
;               ES:DI = address of destination operand
;               CX    = operand length in bytes
;
;               Assumes direction flag is clear at entry
;               Assumes DS = ES <> SS
;               Assumes 0 < CX <= 255
;
; Returns:      ES:DI = address of product
;
;               NOTE: Buffer for the destination operand must be
;               twice as long as the actual operand because
;               it will receive a double-precision result.
;
; Destroys:     Nothing
;
_TEXT   segment word public 'CODE'

        assume  cs:_TEXT


        public  mpmul
mpmul   proc    near

        push    ax                      ; save registers
        push    bx
        push    cx
        push    dx
        push    bp

        push    di                      ; save addr of dest argument
        mov     dx,cx                   ; save bytes/operand

        add     di,cx                   ; find address of high half
        mov     bp,di                   ; of product, save it in BP

        xor     al,al                   ; initialize high half of
        rep stosb                       ; partial product to zero
```

Figure 12-12. *(continued)*

MPMUL.ASM, a general-purpose unsigned multiplication routine for multiple-precision integers. This version uses a binary shift-and-add approach that does not exploit the CPU's native hardware multiply. (Compare Figure 12-11.)

Figure 12-12. *continued*

```
        pop     di                          ; retrieve addr of dest arg

        mov     cx,dx                       ; CX = bits per argument + 1
        shl     cx,1
        shl     cx,1
        shl     cx,1
        inc     cx

        clc                                 ; initialize carry

mpmul1: pushf                               ; save carry flag
        mov     bx,dx                       ; BX = bytes in product - 1
        shl     bx,1
        dec     bx
        popf                                ; restore carry flag

mpmul2: rcr     byte ptr es:[di+bx],1       ; shift partial product and
        dec     bx                          ; dest operand right 1 bit
        jns     mpmul2                      ; loop while BX >= 0

        jnc     mpmul4                      ; jump if bit shifted out = 0

                                            ; bit shifted out = 1
        xchg    bp,di                       ; DI = high half of product
        push    cx                          ; save bit counter
        mov     cx,dx                       ; CX = bytes per argument
        xor     bx,bx                       ; init index (also clears carry)

mpmul3: mov     al,[si+bx]                  ; add source argument to high
        adc     es:[di+bx],al               ; half of partial product
        inc     bx
        loop    mpmul3

        pop     cx                          ; restore bit counter
        xchg    bp,di                       ; restore dest operand pointer

mpmul4: loop    mpmul1                      ; loop until all bits processed

        pop     bp                          ; restore registers
        pop     dx
        pop     cx
        pop     bx
        pop     ax
        ret                                 ; back to caller

mpmul   endp

_TEXT   ends

        end
```

You might find it instructive to run some timing comparisons of the two versions of MPMUL. When running such benchmarks, however, you must remember that the cost of a hardware multiply differs drastically as you progress from the 8086/8088 to the 80386 and 80486. In other words, both the relative speed and the absolute speed of the two versions of this routine depend heavily on the host CPU.

Here is a typical invocation of MPMUL:

```
intsize equ    n                       ; define size of integer

myint1  db     intsize dup (?)         ; source operand
myint2  db     intsize*2 dup (?)       ; destination operand
         .
         .
         .
        mov    si,seg myint1           ; DS:SI = address of
        mov    ds,si                   ; source operand
        mov    si,offset myint1
        mov    di,seg myint2           ; ES:DI = address of
        mov    es,di                   ; destination operand
        mov    di,offset myint2
        mov    cx,intsize              ; CX = operand length
        call   mpmul                   ; now find product
```

The procedure MPIMUL (Figure 12-13) carries out signed multiplication. MPIMUL checks the signs of the arguments to determine the sign of the eventual result, calls MPABS to make both arguments positive, calls MPMUL to do the hard work of multiplication, and finally calls MPNEG (if necessary) to apply the sign to the result. The register calling convention for MPIMUL is exactly the same as for MPMUL.

CAUTION: When calling the multiple-precision multiply routines, you must always ensure that the buffer holding the destination operand is twice as large as the operand itself so that the buffer will be large enough to hold the product of the two operands.

```
;
; MPIMUL.ASM -- Multiple-precision signed multiply
;           for Intel 8086, 8088, 80286, 80386, and
;           80486 in real mode/16-bit protected mode.
;           Also requires MPNEG.ASM (multiple-precision
;           two's complement), MPABS.ASM (multiple-precision
;           absolute value), and MPMUL.ASM (multiple-
;           precision unsigned integer multiply).
```

Figure 12-13.   (continued)
MPIMUL.ASM, a general-purpose signed multiplication routine for multiple-precision integers. MPIMUL calls MPABS (Figure 12-8), MPMUL (Figure 12-11 or Figure 12-12), and MPNEG (Figure 12-7).

Figure 12-13. *continued*

```
;
; Copyright (C) 1991 Ray Duncan
;
; Call with:    DS:SI = address of source operand
;               ES:DI = address of destination operand
;               CX    = operand length in bytes
;
;               Assumes direction flag is clear at entry
;               Assumes DS = ES <> SS
;               Assumes CX <= 255
;
; Returns:      ES:DI = address of product
;
;               NOTE: Buffer for the destination operand must
;               be twice as long as the actual operand because
;               it will receive a double-precision result.
;
; Destroys:     Nothing

_TEXT   segment word public 'CODE'

        extrn   mpmul:near
        extrn   mpneg:near
        extrn   mpabs:near


        assume  cs:_TEXT

        public  mpimul
mpimul  proc    near

        push    ax                      ; save registers
        push    bx

        mov     bx,cx                   ; take exclusive OR of
        mov     al,[si+bx-1]            ; signs of operands
        xor     al,[di+bx-1]
        pushf                           ; save sign of result

        call    mpabs                   ; force source operand positive

        xchg    si,di                   ; force destination operand
        call    mpabs                   ; positive too
        xchg    si,di

        call    mpmul                   ; perform unsigned multiply

        popf                            ; retrieve sign of result
        jns     mpim1                   ; jump, result is positive
```

(continued)

Figure 12-13. *continued*

```
              xchg     si,di               ; operand signs were not same
              add      cx,cx               ; so make result negative
              call     mpneg
              xchg     si,di
              shr      cx,1

mpim1:        pop      bx                  ; restore registers
              pop      ax
              ret                          ; back to caller

mpimul        endp

_TEXT         ends

              end
```

The division operations are the most complex of the lot. Figure 12-14 contains the source code for the unsigned multiple-precision integer division procedure named MPDIV.ASM. The MPDIV routine uses the shift-and-subtract technique explained earlier. It is called with DS:SI pointing to the divisor, ES:DI pointing to the dividend, and CX containing the divisor length in bytes. MPDIV returns all registers unchanged. DS:SI points to the quotient (which has overwritten the original divisor), and ES:DI points to the remainder (which has overwritten the original dividend).

A typical call to MPDIV would be coded like this:

```
    intsize equ     n                       ; define size of integer

    myint1  db      intsize dup (?)         ; source operand
                                            ; or divisor
    myint2  db      intsize*2 dup (?)       ; destination operand
                                            ; or dividend
            .
            .
            mov     si,seg myint1           ; DS:SI = address of
            mov     ds,si                   ; source operand
            mov     si,offset myint1
            mov     di,seg myint2           ; ES:DI = address of
            mov     es,di                   ; destination operand
            mov     di,offset myint2
            mov     cx,intsize              ; CX = operand length
            call    mpdiv                   ; find quotient, remainder
```

```
;
; MPDIV.ASM -- Multiple-precision unsigned divide
;               using the shift-and-subtract method
;               for Intel 8086, 8088, 80286, 80386, and
;               80486 in real mode/16-bit protected mode.
;
; Copyright (C) 1991 Ray Duncan
;
; Call with:    DS:SI = address of divisor
;               ES:DI = address of dividend
;               CX    = divisor length in bytes
;                       (dividend length = 2 * divisor length)
;
;               Assumes direction flag is clear at entry
;               Assumes DS = ES <> SS
;               Assumes 0 < CX <= 255
;
; Returns:      ES:DI = address of quotient
;               DS:SI = address of remainder
;
;               NOTE: The dividend is assumed to be twice as long
;               as the divisor.  The returned remainder and quotient
;               are the same size as the divisor.
;
; Destroys:     Nothing

_TEXT   segment word public 'CODE'

        assume  cs:_TEXT

        public  mpdiv
mpdiv   proc    near

        push    ax                      ; save registers
        push    bx
        push    cx
        push    dx
        push    si
        push    di
        push    bp

        mov     dx,cx                   ; save divisor length in DX

        mov     bp,cx                   ; BP will be outer loop
        shl     bp,1                    ; counter, set it to number
        shl     bp,1                    ; of bits in divisor
        shl     bp,1
```

Figure 12-14. *(continued)*

*MPDIV.ASM, a general-purpose unsigned division routine for multiple-precision
integers, which carries out the operation in binary using a shift-and-subtract loop.*

Figure 12-14. *continued*

```
        clc                         ; initially clear carry

mpdiv1: push    di                  ; save pointer to dividend
        mov     cx,dx               ; CX = bytes in dividend

mpdiv2: rcl     word ptr [di],1     ; shift carry flag into
        inc     di                  ; low bit of quotient
        inc     di                  ; shift high bit of dividend
        loop    mpdiv2              ; into carry flag

        pop     di                  ; restore pointer to dividend

        jnc     mpdiv5              ; jump if high bit was clear

mpdiv3: push    si                  ; save pointer to divisor
        push    di                  ; save pointer to dividend

        add     di,dx               ; DI = addr high half of dividend
        mov     cx,dx               ; CX = bytes in divisor
        clc                         ; initially clear carry

mpdiv4: mov     al,[si]             ; subtract divisor from high
        sbb     [di],al             ; half of dividend
        inc     si
        inc     di
        loop    mpdiv4

        pop     di                  ; restore pointer to dividend
        pop     si                  ; restore pointer to divisor

        stc                         ; shift bit = 1 into quotient
        dec     bp                  ; all bits of answer generated?
        jnz     mpdiv1              ; no, loop
        jmp     mpdiv7              ; yes, go clean up and exit

mpdiv5: push    si                  ; save pointer to divisor
        push    di                  ; save pointer to dividend

        add     di,dx               ; point to high half of dividend
        mov     cx,dx               ; CX = bytes in divisor
        clc                         ; initially clear carry

mpdiv6: mov     al,[di]             ; high half of dividend > divisor?
        sbb     al,[si]
        inc     si
        inc     di
        loop    mpdiv6
```

(continued)

Figure 12-14. *continued*

```
              pop     di                  ; restore pointer to dividend
              pop     si                  ; restore pointer to divisor

              jnc     mpdiv3              ; jump, high dividend > divisor

              clc                         ; shift bit = 0 into quotient
              dec     bp                  ; all bits of answer generated?
              jnz     mpdiv1              ; no, loop again

mpdiv7: mov   cx,dx                       ; CX = bytes in quotient

mpdiv8: rcl   byte ptr [di],1             ; bring final bit into quotient
        inc   di
        loop  mpdiv8

              xchg    si,di               ; copy remainder to final address
              mov     cx,dx
              rep movsb

              pop     bp                  ; restore registers
              pop     di
              pop     si
              pop     dx
              pop     cx
              pop     bx
              pop     ax
              ret                         ; back to caller

mpdiv   endp

_TEXT   ends

        end
```

The register calling convention for the signed integer division routine MPIDIV (Figure 12-15 on the following page) is exactly the same as for MPDIV. Like its counterpart MPIMUL, MPIDIV saves the signs of the original operands, makes both operands positive by calling MPABS, and then calls the unsigned routine MPDIV to do the actual work of division. After the return from MPDIV, MPIDIV calls MPNEG if necessary to apply the proper signs to the quotient and remainder. For symmetry with the CPU's native IDIV instruction, the sign of the quotient is positive if the signs of the dividend and divisor are the same, and negative otherwise; the sign of the remainder is always the same as the sign of the divisor.

```
;
; MPIDIV.ASM -- Multiple-precision signed division
;                 for Intel 8086, 8088, 80286, 80386, and
;                 80486 in real mode/16-bit protected mode.
;                 Also requires MPNEG.ASM (multiple-precision
;                 two's complement), MPABS.ASM (multiple-precision
;                 absolute value), and MPDIV.ASM (multiple-
;                 precision unsigned integer divide).
;
; Copyright (C) 1991 Ray Duncan
;
; Call with:      DS:SI = address of divisor
;                 ES:DI = address of dividend
;                 CX    = divisor length in bytes
;                         (dividend length = 2 * divisor length)
;
;                 Assumes direction flag is clear at entry
;                 Assumes DS = ES <> SS
;                 Assumes 0 < CX <= 255
;
; Returns:        DS:SI = address of remainder
;                 ES:DI = address of quotient
;
;                 NOTE: The dividend is assumed to be twice as long
;                 as the divisor.  The returned remainder and quotient
;                 are the same size as the divisor.
;
;                 The sign of the quotient is positive if the
;                 signs of the dividend and divisor are the same,
;                 negative if they are different.  The sign of the
;                 remainder is the same as the sign of the dividend.
;
; Destroys:       Nothing

_TEXT   segment word public 'CODE'

        extrn   mpdiv:near
        extrn   mpneg:near
        extrn   mpabs:near

        assume  cs:_TEXT

        public  mpidiv
mpidiv  proc    near
```

Figure 12-15.   (continued)

*MPIDIV.ASM, a general-purpose signed division routine for multiple-precision
integers. MPIDIV calls MPABS (Figure 12-8), MPDIV (Figure 12-14), and MPNEG
(Figure 12-7).*

Figure 12-15. *continued*

```
        push    ax                      ; save registers
        push    bx

        mov     bx,cx                   ; get exclusive OR of
        mov     al,[si+bx-1]            ; signs of operands
        add     bx,bx
        xor     al,[di+bx-1]
        pushf                           ; save sign of result

        mov     al,[di+bx-1]            ; test sign of dividend
        or      al,al
        pushf                           ; save sign of remainder

        call    mpabs                   ; force divisor positive

        xchg    si,di                   ; force dividend positive
        add     cx,cx
        call    mpabs
        xchg    si,di
        shr     cx,1

        call    mpdiv                   ; perform unsigned divide

        popf                            ; retrieve sign of remainder
        jns     mpid1                   ; jump, remainder is positive

        call    mpneg                   ; flip sign of remainder

mpid1:  popf                            ; retrieve sign of result
        jns     mpid2                   ; jump, result is positive

        xchg    si,di                   ; save pointer to remainder
        call    mpneg                   ; flip sign of quotient
        xchg    si,di                   ; restore pointer to remainder

mpid2:  pop     bx                      ; restore register
        pop     ax
        ret                             ; back to caller

mpidiv  endp

_TEXT   ends

        end
```

PROCEDURES INTRODUCED IN THIS CHAPTER

Procedure Name	Action	Parameters	Results
DDIV	Double-precision (64 x 32) unsigned division	DX:CX: BX:AX = dividend SI:DI = divisor	DX:AX = quotient CX:BX = remainder
DMUL	Double-precision (32 x 32) unsigned multiplication	DX:AX = *value1* CX:BX = *value2*	DX:CX:BX:AX = product
MPABS	Multiple-precision integer absolute value	DS:SI = segment:offset of value CX = length of value	DS:SI = segment:offset of result
MPADD	Multiple-precision integer addition	DS:SI = segment:offset of *value1* ES:DI = segment:offset of *value2* CX = length of value	ES:DI = segment:offset of result
MPDIV	Multiple-precision unsigned integer division	DS:SI = segment:offset of divisor ES:DI = segment:offset of dividend CX = length of value	DS:SI = segment:offset of remainder ES:DI = segment:offset of quotient
MPIDIV	Multiple-precision signed integer division	Same as MPDIV	Same as MPDIV
MPIMUL	Multiple-precision signed integer multiplication	Same as MPMUL	Same as MPMUL
MPMUL	Multiple-precision unsigned integer multiplication	DS:SI = segment:offset of *value1* ES:DI = segment:offset of *value2* CX = length of value	ES:DI = address of product
MPNEG	Multiple-precision integer two's complement	DS:SI = segment:offset of value CX = length of value	DS:SI = segment:offset of result
MPSUB	Multiple-precision integer subtraction	DS:SI = segment:offset of *value1* ES:DI = segment:offset of *value2* CX = length of value	ES:DI = segment:offset of result (*value2 – value1*)

Companion Disk

The companion disk directory \CH12 contains the programs and modules that are listed below.

Routines Presented in This Chapter

DDIV.ASM	Double-precision unsigned division
DMUL.ASM	Double-precision unsigned multiplication, using a bit-by-bit shift-and-add algorithm
MPABS.ASM	Multiple-precision absolute value
MPADD.ASM	Multiple-precision addition
MPDIV.ASM	Multiple-precision unsigned division
MPIDIV.ASM	Multiple-precision signed division
MPIMUL.ASM	Multiple-precision signed multiplication
MPMUL1.ASM	Multiple-precision unsigned multiplication, using a byte-by-byte multiply-and-accumulate algorithm
MPMUL2.ASM	Multiple-precision unsigned multiplication, using a bit-by-bit shift-and-add algorithm
MPNEG.ASM	Multiple-precision two's complement (changes sign)
MPSUB.ASM	Multiple-precision subtraction

Routines Previously Discussed

HTOL.ASM	Converts a hexadecimal ASCII string to a double-precision (32-bit) unsigned integer
HTOQ.ASM	Converts a hexadecimal ASCII string to a quad-precision (64-bit) unsigned integer
ITOH.ASM	Converts a single-precision (16-bit) unsigned integer to a hexadecimal ASCII string

Interactive Demonstration Programs

TRYDMUL	MAKE file for TRYDMUL.EXE
TRYDMUL.ASM	Interactive demonstration program
TRYDDIV	MAKE file for TRYDDIV.EXE
TRYDDIV.ASM	Interactive demonstration program
TRYMPMUL	MAKE file for TRYMPMUL.EXE
TRYMPMUL.ASM	Interactive demonstration program
TRYMPDIV	MAKE file for TRYMPDIV.EXE
TRYMPDIV.ASM	Interactive demonstration program

The program TRYDMUL.ASM demonstrates use of the routine DMUL.ASM. To build TRYDMUL.EXE, enter this command:

```
C>MAKE TRYDMUL   <Enter>
```

When you run TRYDMUL.EXE, it prompts you for two 32-bit hex integers, converts the ASCII strings to their binary equivalents, multiplies the arguments, and then displays the 64-bit result in hexadecimal. Press the Enter key at any prompt to exit the program.

Similarly, the interactive program TRYDDIV.ASM demonstrates use of the routine DDIV.ASM. To build TRYDDIV.EXE, enter this command:

```
C>MAKE TRYDDIV   <Enter>
```

When you execute TRYDDIV.EXE, it prompts you for a 64-bit hex dividend and a 32-bit hex divisor, converts the ASCII strings to their binary equivalents, carries out the division operation, and then displays the 32-bit quotient and remainder in hex ASCII. Press the Enter key at any prompt to exit the program.

The demonstration programs TRYMPMUL.ASM and TRYMPDIV.ASM are more sophisticated, generalized versions of the TRYDMUL and TRYDDIV programs. They illustrate use of the various routines MPABS.ASM, MPNEG.ASM, MPMUL1.ASM or MPMUL2.ASM, MPIMUL.ASM, MPDIV.ASM, and MPIDIV.ASM. To build these two demonstration programs, enter the following:

```
C>MAKE TRYMPMUL   <Enter>
C>MAKE TRYMPDIV   <Enter>
```

Both programs can use either signed or unsigned math, depending on whether you respond with *s* or *u* at the initial prompt. Both accept two hexadecimal arguments and display their results in hexadecimal. Press the Enter key at any prompt to exit the programs.

13

Using the Intel Numeric Coprocessors

In the preceding chapter, we looked at the classical algorithms for the four basic integer operations and devised a set of MASM subroutines for multiple-precision integer addition, subtraction, multiplication, and division. It's now time to leave the relatively shallow and safe waters of integer arithmetic behind and venture into the deeper, more treacherous reaches of real numbers and floating-point arithmetic.

Grade-school students are introduced to real numbers in stages: first the "counting numbers" (positive integers), then the negative numbers (completing the set of all integers), and finally fractions and their decimal equivalents. To demonstrate these concepts, teachers often use a "number line"—a horizontal line with arrows at both ends (pointing to negative infinity on the left and positive infinity on the right) and a hashmark in the middle signifying 0. Once the integers

    ... −3, −2, −1, 0, 1, 2, 3 ...

are charted on the number line, it's a fairly easy leap to the notion of "numbers between the numbers" (for example, the fraction ½, symbolized by a dot on the number line halfway between 0 and 1) and then to understanding that an infinite number of numbers can be found between any two points on the number line, with the whole comprising the set of real numbers.

Later on in high school, if our hypothetical students choose algebra, chemistry, or physics, they are taught scientific, or exponential, notation—a tool that allows them to write real numbers of any size or precision. For example, the fraction ¼ can be expressed in scientific notation as

    $2.5 * 10^{-1}$

The 2.5 portion of the number is called the *mantissa, fraction,* or *significand;* one nonzero digit always appears to the left of the decimal point, and the number of digits after the decimal point indicates the degree of precision to which the number's value is known. (A mantissa in this form is said to be *normalized*.) The 10^{-1} portion of the number is called the *exponent,* or *characteristic;* it specifies the location of the decimal point in the number. Most teachers also present students with a cookbook full of rules for operations on numbers written in scientific notation, including instructions such as "To find the product of two numbers, multiply the mantissas and sum the powers of the exponents."

Having mastered real numbers and the means to manipulate them, our high-school whiz kids might be tempted to adopt a somewhat smug attitude toward matters mathematical. Of course, this prematurely optimistic outlook will be demolished when they are confronted with imaginary numbers, irrational numbers, complex numbers, infinitesimals, and all the other counterintuitive mathematical monsters—but that is another story.

Floating-Point Arithmetic on Computers

Although the methods used to fondle floating-point numbers on computers are certainly based on those fundamental rules and algorithms that you were taught in school, several distinctions are important.

To begin with, most computers and high-level language libraries support only a limited number of floating-point formats (typically only two), and these formats naturally have a finite precision and range. Thus, you cannot possibly represent every real number as a floating-point number on your computer; in fact, the number of numbers you *can't* express is infinitely larger than the number of numbers you *can* represent. The designers of your CPU or compiler picked a floating-point data format or formats that seemed sufficient for most normal applications and that could be implemented efficiently. If the requirements of your application program fall outside the bounds foreseen by those designers, you must either roll your own floating-point routines or do without.

In addition, your computer's floating-point numbers do not map onto real numbers in a uniform way. For example, when you plot the numbers that can be represented by a 32-bit integer onto the real-number line, you see a set of points marching monotonically down the line from $-2{,}147{,}483{,}648$ (-2^{31}) to $2{,}147{,}483{,}647$ $(2^{31}-1)$. But if you plot the numbers that can be represented by a 32-bit floating-point number onto the real-number line, you get a surprise: The number of numbers that can be represented in the floating-point format is exactly the same as for the integer format, but the floating-point numbers are densely clustered around 0 and grow increasingly sparse as the distance from 0 increases. Of course, the smallest and largest floating-point numbers are far smaller or larger than the smallest and largest integers, but this dynamic range is gained at the expense of precision.

Finally, people undeniably prefer to compute in base 10, whereas computers find base 2 more to their liking. Because application designers and programmers like to keep everyone happy, numbers must be converted from decimal to binary, or vice versa, each time they are input or output. This conversion rarely causes problems with integers, but it becomes a thorny issue when you work with floating-point numbers because some decimal numbers cannot be expressed exactly in binary floating-point form. (One such number is $1.0 * 10^{-1}$.)

Binary Floating-Point Data Formats

After a decimal floating-point number is converted to a normalized binary floating-point number, you can think of it as having the following form, where each bit b in the mantissa is 0 or 1:

$$1.bbbbb... * 2^n$$

The mantissa is normalized by adjusting the exponent so that the most significant 1 bit is to the left of the binary point; in other words, the mantissa is always greater than or equal to 1 and less than 2.

But how are floating-point numbers actually stored in memory? In the early days of computing, nearly every compiler and CPU used a different floating-point data format, which made it difficult to transport data from one machine to another or even from a program written in one high-level language to a program written in another. In the late 1970s, an effort to standardize binary floating-point arithmetic began, first under the auspices of the ACM and then under the IEEE Computer Society. This undertaking drew upon several proposals (the most important being the so-called KCS proposal, written by Kahan, Connen, and Stone in 1978), which represented the integration of concepts and techniques dating back to the earliest days of computer science. In 1981, the IEEE published the draft IEEE 754 Standard for Binary Floating-Point Arithmetic, which was modified and adopted as an official ANSI/IEEE standard in 1985 (and then recast in a generalized form as the IEEE 854 Standard for Radix-Independent Floating-Point Arithmetic in 1987).

The ANSI/IEEE 754 standard was principally directed at making floating-point calculations safe and predictable for programmers who lacked training in numerical analysis (nearly all of us!). It specified the degree of accuracy to which computations must be carried out, rounding behavior, error and exception handling, and the results of the basic floating-point arithmetic operations, comparisons, and conversions. And it also specified binary formats for floating-point numbers, which were rapidly adopted by the industry and are now widely supported in both hardware and software.

The two most important floating-point data formats described in the ANSI/IEEE 754 standard are shown in Figure 13-1 on the following page. The single-precision format occupies 32 bits (a doubleword on Intel CPUs). The double-precision format requires 64 bits (a quadword on Intel CPUs). Both formats consist of three fields: a sign bit (always the most significant bit), followed by the binary exponent, with the mantissa in the remaining, least significant bits. Single-precision numbers can take on values in the (approximate) range $\pm1.18 * 10^{-38}$ through $\pm3.40 * 10^{38}$; double-precision numbers lie in the range $\pm2.23 * 10^{-308}$ through $\pm1.80 * 10^{308}$.

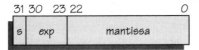

31 30   23 22   0

Single-precision floating-point format

63 62   52 51   0

| s | exp | mantissa |

Double-precision floating-point format

Figure 13-1.
The single-precision and double-precision floating-point formats specified in the ANSI/IEEE 754 standard.

The sign bit is 1 if the number is negative and 0 if the number is positive. The mantissa is unsigned and does not change with the sign of the floating-point number. Because the mantissa is left-normalized, its most significant bit is (by definition) always 1. Consequently, the IEEE 754 designers played a neat trick: They specified that the mantissa has an "implied leading bit," which is always 1 and is not present in the actual data. This allows an extra bit of precision to be squeezed out of each floating-point format.

The exponent field of both types of floating-point numbers is *biased* (offset from 0 by a fixed amount). For single-precision numbers, which have an 8-bit exponent, a value of 127 (7FH) in the exponent field corresponds to a true exponent value of 0. Double-precision numbers, which have an 11-bit exponent field, use an exponent bias of 1023 (3FFH). This bias allows the reciprocal of any normalized floating-point number to be represented without underflow. The relative sizes of the exponent fields in the two formats were chosen to allow a double-precision number to accommodate the product of as many as eight single-precision numbers without the possibility of overflow.

The exponent of an ANSI/IEEE 754 floating-point number can also take on two "magic" values that cause the number to be handled in a special way. If all bits of the exponent are 0, then the floating-point number is either 0 or a "denormalized" number—the result of a gradual underflow. If all bits of the exponent are set, then the floating-point number either represents infinity or a special signaling value called a NaN (Not a Number), as shown in Figure 13-2.

Let's look at some practical examples of binary floating-point data. Consider the 32-bit (4-byte) single-precision floating-point number shown on the next page:

The sign bit is 0, the biased exponent is 10000010B or 82H, and the mantissa (after restoring the implied leading bit) is 10100000000000000000000B, or A00000H. Correcting for the exponent bias yields 1.010B * 2^3, or 10 decimal. As another example, consider this 64-bit (8-byte) double-precision floating-point number:

The sign bit is 1, the biased exponent is 01111111110B or 3FEH, and the mantissa (after inserting the implied leading bit) is 10000000000000H. Correcting for the exponent bias yields −1.0B * 2^{-1}, or −0.5 decimal.

Exponent Bits	Mantissa Bits	Special Meaning
All 0	All 0	Floating-point zero
All 0	Nonzero	Denormalized floating-point number (usually result of gradual underflow)
All set	All 0	Infinity
All set	Nonzero	NaN (Not a Number) (various reserved mantissa values used to signal overflow, unrecoverable underflow, invalid operands, invalid result, inexact result, and so on)

Figure 13-2.
The interpretation of reserved exponent values in the ANSI/IEEE 754 standard. Floating-point numbers with all bits 0 or all bits set in the exponent field are trapped and receive special treatment.

Numeric Coprocessors

The influence of the ANSI/IEEE 754 standard was bolstered by Intel's 1980 release of the 8087 numeric coprocessor for the 8086 and 8088 CPUs. The 8087 implemented the entire (draft) ANSI/IEEE 754 standard in hardware—even its most esoteric aspects, such as supporting both affine and projective infinity—and the 8087 rapidly became the yardstick for measuring the compliance of all other CPUs, numeric coprocessors, and software floating-point libraries with the impending standard. The 8087 also brought unprecedented (and largely unforeseen) number-crunching power within the reach of microcomputer users and made it possible to migrate many demanding minicomputer and mainframe applications onto personal computers for the first time.

The 8087 was followed by the 80287 numeric coprocessor in 1983 and the 80387 numeric coprocessor in 1987. The 80287 was designed to work with the 80286 CPU and was the first Intel coprocessor to support memory protection and multitasking. The 80387 was designed to work with the 80386 CPU and incorporated support for demand paging, several new trigonometric instructions, and conformance with the ANSI/IEEE 754 standard (as it was finally approved in 1985). The 80387 is the last of its line; the 80486 has all the logic of the 80387 built in, and it does not require a separate numeric coprocessor. Of course, each successive chip supported a larger memory address space and also benefited from the technological advances in large-scale integration that accrued from 1980 to 1987, with a corresponding increase in clock speeds and a decreased number of machine cycles per floating-point operation. The performance of the 20 MHz 80386/387 combination on a typical floating-point instruction mix is about 16 times better than that of a 5 MHz 8086/8087 duo (Figure 13-3).

Processor/Coprocessor	Typical Speed	First Shipped	Relative Performance
8086 + 8087	5 MHz	1980	1
80286 + 80287	8 MHz	1983	2.5
80386 + 80387	20 MHz	1987	16
80486 (embedded 80387)	25 MHz	1989	64

Figure 13-3.
The speed, date of first shipment, and relative performance of the various combinations of Intel CPUs and coprocessors.

The 8087, 80287, and 80387 chips are called coprocessors because they are closely coupled to the system's CPU, have a highly specialized instruction set, and cannot function alone. The coprocessors share the same data and address bus as the main CPU, and they monitor the CPU's instruction stream as it is fetched from memory and flows by on the data bus. Floating-point instructions begin with a special escape code that is recognized and acted on by the numeric coprocessor; the CPU essentially ignores the floating-point instructions except to perform any necessary address calculations on behalf of the numeric coprocessor.

The shared instruction stream—and the hundreds of cycles that can be required for many of the more complex coprocessor instructions to complete—allow a certain amount of concurrent processing. For example, a program can load a floating-point number onto the coprocessor, issue a floating-point square root instruction, and then execute several dozen CPU instructions during the more than 100 cycles the square root operation needs to complete. The program can then resynchronize with the coprocessor and unload the result of the square root operation into memory or use the result as an argument for the next floating-point operation.

This type of concurrent programming demands careful scheduling of operations and counting of cycles so that both processors are kept busy and do not waste time waiting for each other. Such coding is also extremely environment dependent because instruction timing varies drastically among the different models of CPUs and numeric coprocessors.

The 80x87 series were not the first floating-point arithmetic chips available for use with microprocessors. A number of early 8080, Z-80, and even 8086/8088-based microcomputers had sockets for the AMD (Advanced Micro Devices) 9511 and 9512 chips, which supported 32-bit and 64-bit floating-point operations, respectively. But the AMD products were not coprocessors (like a peripheral device, they were addressed through an 8-bit I/O port), they used nonstandard data formats, they were slow and clumsy to program, and they enjoyed little or no support in commercial, mass-market software packages. The 80x87 chips were the first hardware number-crunchers cheap enough and pervasive enough (thanks to the 8087 socket built into the first PC motherboard) to motivate mass-market software publishers to check for the presence of a floating-point chip in their programs and to use the chip if it was available.

80x87 Architecture

The instructions understood by the 80x87 processors fall into six basic categories: data transfer, arithmetic, comparison, transcendental, constants, and processor control (Figure 13-4). The instruction sets of the 80287 and 80387 are proper supersets

Instruction	Description
Data Transfer	
FLD, FST, FSTP	Loads or stores floating-point value
FILD, FIST, FISTP	Loads or stores integer value
FBLD, FBSTP	Loads or stores binary-coded-decimal (BCD) value
FXCH	Exchanges two coprocessor registers

Figure 13-4. *(continued)*
A summary of the instruction set of the 8087, 80287, and 80387 numeric coprocessors. Mnemonics ending with P pop one operand off the coprocessor's floating-point register stack; mnemonics ending with PP pop two operands.

Figure 13-4. *continued*

Instruction	Description
Arithmetic	
FADD, FADDP, FIADDP	Floating-point add
FSUB, FSUBP, FISUB	Floating-point subtract
FSUBR, FSUBRP, FISUBR	Floating-point subtract reversed
FMUL, FMULP, FIMUL	Floating-point multiply
FDIV, FDIVP, FIDIV	Floating-point divide
FDIVR, FDIVRP, FIDIVR	Floating-point divide reversed
FSQRT	Floating-point square root
FSCALE	Scales one value by another
FPREM, FPREM1	Partial remainder (FPREM1 on 80387 only)
FRNDINT	Rounds to integer
FXTRACT	Extracts exponent and mantissa from value
FABS	Absolute value
FCHS	Changes sign of value
Comparison	
FCOM, FCOMP, FCOMPP	Compares two ordered values
FUCOM, FUCOMP, FUCOMPP	Compares two unordered values (80387 only)
FTST	Compares value to zero, sets flags
FXAM	Tests type of value, sets flags
Transcendental	
FPTAN, FPATAN	Tangent and arctangent (partial on 8087 and 80287; generalized on 80387)
FSIN, FCOS, FSINCOS	Sine and cosine (80387 only)
F2XM1	Raises 2 to power and subtracts 1
FYL2X	Multiplies value times $\log_2$ of another value
FYL2XP1	Multiplies value times $\log_2$ of another value plus 1
Constants	
FLDZ	Loads the value 0
FLD1	Loads the value 1
FLDPI	Loads the value *pi*
FLDL2T	Loads the value $\log_2(10)$
FLDL2E	Loads the value $\log_2(e)$
FLDLG2	Loads the value $\log_{10}(2)$
FLDLN2	Loads the value $\log_e(2)$

(continued)

Figure 13-4. *continued*

Instruction	Description
Processor Control	
FINIT	Initializes coprocessor
FSTSW	Stores status word (FSTSW AX form not available on 8087)
FLDCW, FSTCW	Loads or stores control word
FCLEX	Clears coprocessor exception (error) flags
FLDENV, FSTENV	Loads or stores coprocessor environment
FSAVE, FRSTOR	Saves or restores coprocessor state
FINCSTP, FDECSTP	Increments or decrements coprocessor stack pointer
FFREE	Marks floating-point register as empty
FNOP	Coprocessor "no-operation"
FENI, FDISI	Enables or disables coprocessor error interrupts (8087 only; ignored on 80287 and 80387)

of the 8087; the 80287 and the 80387 will run 8087 application code without modification. You can, however, generate better performance and more programs if you modify the source code to take advantage of the 80287's and the 80387's improved synchronization characteristics and instruction set, particularly the generalized tangent, arctangent, sine, and cosine instructions that are unique to the 80387.

The basic on-chip resources common to all members of the 80x87 family are eight floating-point registers, a control word register, a status word register, and a tag word register (Figure 13-5 on the following page). Each floating-point register is 80 bits wide and is generally used as a push-down stack, although each one can be addressed directly by the programmer when necessary. The tag word is divided into eight 2-bit fields, each corresponding to a floating-point register and indicating whether the number in that register is a valid floating-point value, zero, infinity, or invalid or whether the register is empty.

The status word, which is read-only, contains the condition codes for the most recent floating-point operation as well as error indicators. It also specifies which of the floating-point registers is the current top of stack (Figure 13-6 on page 287). If you push too many numbers onto the 80x87 stack and the top-of-stack pointer wraps, an exception is generated. The control word is read/write and determines the rounding mode of the chip, the precision to which operations are carried out, and which types of errors are allowed to generate an interrupt (Figure 13-7 on page 288).

In addition, special coprocessor instruction pointer and data pointer registers located directly on the CPU chip are associated with the coprocessor's execution of floating-point instructions. When a coprocessor error interrupt occurs, the interrupt

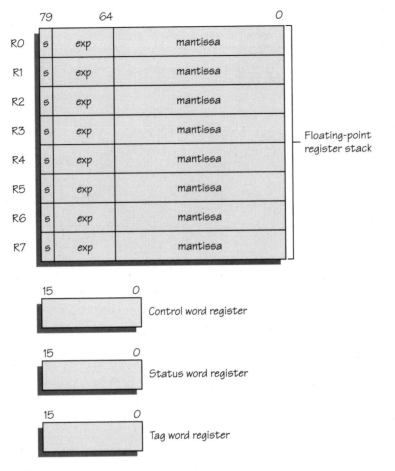

Figure 13-5.
Processor resources common to all members of the 80x87 family. They include eight 80-bit floating-point registers, which can be addressed randomly or as a push-down stack; a 16-bit status word register; a 16-bit control word register; and a 16-bit tag word register, which is divided into eight 2-bit fields that indicate the type of value in each floating-point register. Special coprocessor instruction pointer and data pointer registers are located on the CPU chip for use by floating-point error handlers (not shown).

handler can examine these registers to determine the location and the type of the floating-point instruction or operand that caused the problem. (Because the CPU and the coprocessor run asynchronously for the most part, the values in the CPU's own instruction pointer and data pointer registers are not likely to be helpful.)

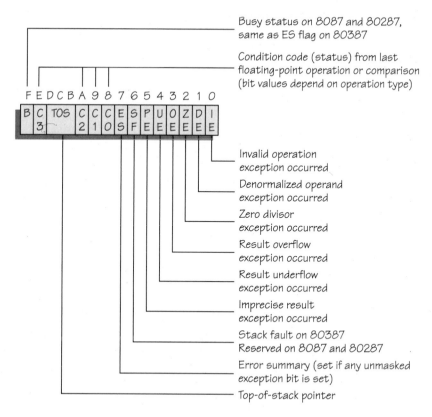

Figure 13-6.

The coprocessor status word register, which is read-only and can be examined by programs to determine the result of the most recent floating-point operation or the cause of the most recent floating-point exception (error).

Before you can use a coprocessor in an application program, you must first be sure that it exists, and then you must configure it for the desired rounding, precision, and error-handling modes. One method of doing this is illustrated in the procedure INIT87.ASM (Figure 13-8 on page 289). The routine first executes the no-wait form of the coprocessor initialization instruction FINIT (more about waits later in this chapter) and then attempts to transfer the status word from the coprocessor into a memory word that has been initialized to FFFFH with the FSTSW instruction. If the coprocessor exists, the procedure sets the desired modes by loading the coprocessor control word and then returns a status code in the CPU's zero flag.

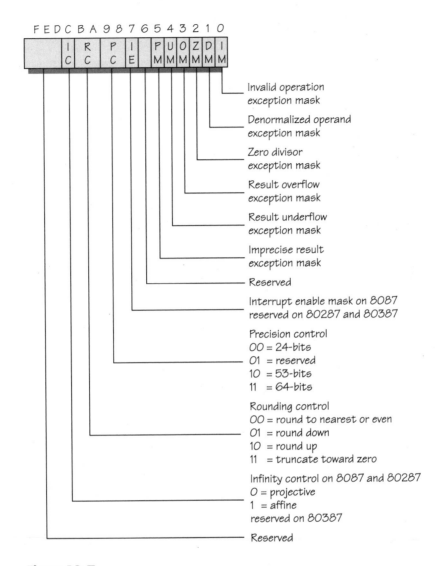

Figure 13-7.
The coprocessor control word register, which can be read or written by application programs to query or set the current rounding mode and precision mode and to control error handling. When the exception mask bit for an error type is set to 1, that error type will not generate an interrupt, and the value of the result is set to a special bit pattern called a NaN (Not a Number).

```
;
; INIT87.ASM -- Initializes 80x87 numeric coprocessor.
;
; Copyright (C) 1991 Ray Duncan
;
; Call with:     AX = control word for desired rounding
;                     mode, precision, exception mask
;
; Returns:       If coprocessor present:
;                Z flag = true (1)
;
;                If coprocessor not found:
;                Z flag = false (0)
;
; Destroys:      Nothing

_TEXT   segment word public 'CODE'

        assume  cs:_TEXT

        public  init87
init87  proc    near

        push    bx                      ; save registers
        push    ax

        mov     ax,-1                   ; put FFFFH on stack
        push    ax
        mov     bx,sp                   ; make it addressable

        fninit                          ; try to initialize coprocessor
        fnstsw  ss:[bx]                 ; try to get status word

        pop     ax                      ; if low 8 bits are 0
        or      al,al                   ; coprocessor is present

        jnz     initx                   ; jump if no coprocessor

        fldcw   ss:[bx+2]               ; load coprocessor control word

initx:  pop     ax                      ; restore registers
        pop     bx
        ret                             ; and return result in Z flag

init87  endp

_TEXT   ends

        end
```

Figure 13-8.
*INIT87.ASM, a routine to test for the existence of an 80x87 numeric coprocessor
and initialize it if it is present.*

80x87 Data Formats

Intel CPUs and coprocessors communicate, in essence, by means of shared memory—if a number you want to use in a calculation happens to reside in a CPU register, the only way to get that number to the coprocessor is to store it in RAM first. No direct register-to-register communication exists between the CPU and the coprocessor (with one exception: the FSTSW instruction on the 80287 and 80387, which will be discussed later).

The coprocessor family supports seven data types in memory: 16-bit, 32-bit, and 64-bit integers; 80-bit packed binary-coded-decimal (BCD) numbers; and 32-bit, 64-bit, and 80-bit floating-point numbers. The 32-bit and 64-bit floating-point formats are identical to those defined by the ANSI/IEEE 754 standard (Figure 13-1 on page 280). The remaining formats are shown in Figure 13-9. Note that the 16-bit and 32-bit integer formats are identical to those supported by the entire 80x86 family and that the 64-bit integer format is the same as the double-precision integers used by the 80386 when it is running in 32-bit protected mode. Regardless of a number's format in memory, however, when it is loaded into a coprocessor floating-point register it is always converted to the 80-bit extended-precision floating-point format (also called the temporary real data type in some Intel manuals).

Using the extended-precision floating-point format for all operations internal to the coprocessor has interesting implications. First, because the dynamic range of the 80-bit format is so much greater than that of the 32-bit or 64-bit format typically used in program variables, an overflow or underflow of a final result is rare as long as all intermediate results are maintained on the chip. Second, converting a number from one data type to another in memory is easy: Simply load the original data from memory onto the coprocessor, and then unload it again in the desired format.

Let's take a closer look at the coprocessor's extended floating-point data type, which corresponds to the optional double-extended format of the ANSI/IEEE 754 standard. The dynamic range of these numbers is approximately $\pm 3.4 * 10^{-4932}$ through $\pm 1.2 * 10^{4932}$. The 80 bits are divided into three fields: a sign bit, a 15-bit exponent, and a 64-bit mantissa.

The sign bit is 1 if the number is negative and 0 if the number is positive. The mantissa is unsigned and does not change with the sign of the floating-point number. Because the mantissa is left-normalized, its most significant bit is always 1 unless the number is 0 or the result of an operation that underflowed or had invalid operands. Unlike the single-precision and double-precision floating-point data formats, no implied leading bit is used in the mantissa of the extended-precision format.

The exponent of the extended-precision format is biased—offset from 0—by the value 16,383 (3FFFH). For example, a value of 16,386 in the exponent fields corresponds to an exponent of 3; in other words, the mantissa is multiplied by 2^3. The exponent can also take on the "magic" values that were discussed earlier and summarized in Figure 13-2 on page 281.

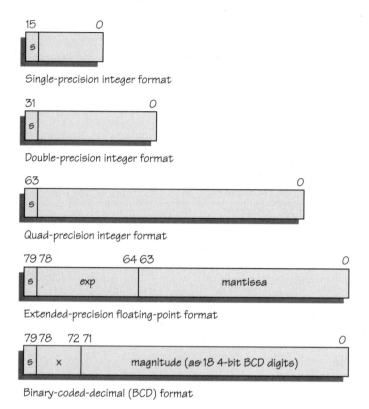

15   0

s

Single-precision integer format

31   0

s

Double-precision integer format

63   0

s

Quad-precision integer format

79 78   64 63   0

s   exp   mantissa

Extended-precision floating-point format

79 78   72 71   0

s   x   magnitude (as 18 4-bit BCD digits)

Binary-coded-decimal (BCD) format

Figure 13-9.
The data formats (in addition to those shown in Figure 13-1) supported by the Intel 80x87 numeric coprocessor family in memory. The BCD format packs 2 digits per byte, for a total of 18 digits plus a sign bit in an 80-bit format (with 7 unused bits). The 16-bit, 32-bit, and 64-bit integers are normal two's complement binary integers with the sign in the most significant bit. Whatever a number's format in memory, it is always converted to the extended (80-bit) floating-point format when it is loaded into a floating-point register on the coprocessor.

Working with Stack Machines

One reason the Intel coprocessors have a reputation for being difficult to program is that they are true *stack machines*. The eight floating-point registers, named ST(0) through ST(7), are organized as a push-down stack and lie, in effect, in a separate address space. This is in sharp contrast to the CPU stack, which is located in normal memory. You can bypass the PUSH and POP instructions to address arbitrary CPU stack elements directly, but your access to the coprocessor's stack is much more restricted. Only the topmost cell of the stack—ST(0), sometimes abbreviated ST—is "visible" for load and store operations.

The general approach to carrying out calculations on a stack machine is familiar to Forth programmers and to anyone who owns a Hewlett-Packard calculator. First you load values onto the stack, and then you execute an operation that removes its arguments from the stack and pushes a result onto the stack. The result can be left on the stack and used as an argument for the next operation, or it can be unloaded from the stack into a variable.

Stack machines perform chained calculations efficiently because most parameter passing occurs within (what amounts to) a relatively fast local memory. Stack machine code is also compact because the location of arguments and results for most instructions is implicit; bulky offsets and complex address calculations are required only when the coprocessor makes its infrequent references to external RAM. In addition, stack machines are well suited to multitasking environments because stack machine code is naturally re-entrant: In most cases, only a few special-purpose registers must be saved across a context switch.

But stack machines also have unique disadvantages. Keeping mental track of the location of more than two or three items on the stack at any one time is difficult even for experienced programmers. Stack machine programming demands a "reverse Polish" or "postfix" syntax that is painful to write, read, and debug for software developers familiar with the infix syntax of more traditional languages. Finally, the stacks are usually comparatively shallow. For a stack machine to be fast, the stacks must be implemented on the processor chip, and stack memory (like the general registers of a conventional CPU) requires lots of transistors and silicon real estate. Consequently, when designing your code, you must be careful to avoid stack overflows because any kind of recovery from an overflow is difficult.

Coprocessor Data Movement

The coprocessor has a bewildering variety of load and store instructions that are used to move data from RAM to the floating-point register stack and back again (Figure 13-10). The assembler chooses the proper opcode based on both the mnemonic and the type of the operand.

Let's look at transferring numbers from RAM to the coprocessor (ignoring synchronization issues for the moment). The following code loads a 32-bit floating-point number from a variable onto the coprocessor floating-point stack:

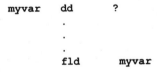

```
myvar    dd       ?
           .
           .
           .
         fld     myvar
```

Figure 13-11 on page 294 shows the status of the floating-point stack before and after this code executes. When indirect addressing is used, you must use the PTR operator to supply the assembler with the type information it needs. For example, to load the first two elements from an array of 32-bit floating-point numbers, you might write the following:

```
myvar    dd       4 dup (0)
          .
          .
          .
         mov      bx,offset myvar
         fld      dword ptr [bx]
         fld      dword ptr [bx+4]
```

You use the same technique to load 64-bit or 80-bit floating-point numbers onto the coprocessor, except that you declare the variables with the DQ or DT directive or use QWORD PTR or TBYTE PTR in the operand.

Integer values are loaded from memory onto the coprocessor with the FILD instruction, and FBLD is used with binary-coded-decimal (BCD) values. For example, to load a 32-bit integer from a memory variable, you could write this code:

```
myvar    dd       ?
          .
          .
          .
         fild     myvar
```

Remember that even though the value is stored in memory as an integer, it is

converted to an 80-bit floating-point number when it is loaded onto the coprocessor. Now let's assume that the value you want to transfer to the coprocessor is in CPU registers DX:AX. You must first transfer the number to memory before you can get it

Data Type	Load	Store
16-bit integer	FILD WORD PTR	FIST WORD PTR FISTP WORD PTR
32-bit integer	FILD DWORD PTR	FIST DWORD PTR FISTP DWORD PTR
64-bit integer	FILD QWORD PTR	FISTP DWORD PTR
32-bit floating-point number	FLD DWORD PTR	FST DWORD PTR FSTP DWORD PTR
64-bit floating-point number	FLD QWORD PTR	FST QWORD PTR FSTP QWORD PTR
80-bit floating-point number	FLD TBYTE PTR	FSTP TBYTE PTR
80-bit binary-coded-decimal (BCD) number	FBLD	FBSTP

Figure 13-10.

Coprocessor instructions used to transfer data from RAM onto the floating-point register stack or vice versa. Instruction mnemonics ending with P pop the coprocessor stack after storing the number on top of the stack into memory. Note the three "missing" instruction forms: The operand for FST cannot be an extended (80-bit) floating-point number; the operand for FIST cannot be a quad (64-bit) integer; and there is no BCD store instruction that does not pop the coprocessor stack.

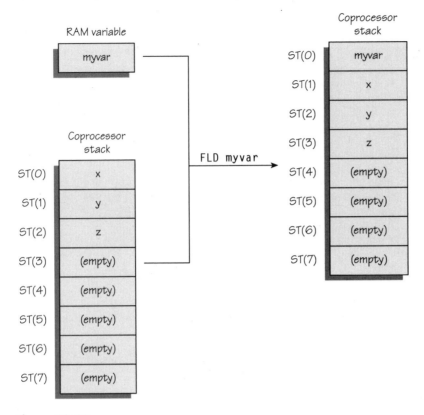

Figure 13-11.
The coprocessor stack before and after an FLD instruction.

to the coprocessor, being sure to store the less significant word of the value at the lower address:

```
myvar    dd       ?
         .
         .
         .
         mov      word ptr myvar,ax
         mov      word ptr myvar+2,dx
         fild     myvar
```

What if you don't want to waste memory in your data segment on a statically allocated variable? You can borrow a page from C's book and create a temporary variable on the CPU's stack for the data and then transfer the value from the CPU stack to the coprocessor:

```
         mov      bp,sp
         sub      sp,4
         mov      [bp-4],ax
         mov      [bp-2],dx
         fild     dword ptr [bp-4]
```

If you prefer, you can accomplish the same job more quickly with the following:

```
push    dx
push    ax
mov     bp,sp
fild    dword ptr [bp]
```

On the 80386 and later CPUs, you can write more elegant code for such temporary variables because the 80386 (unlike the 8086 and 80286) supports indexed addressing via the ESP register. For example, to transfer a 32-bit integer value from register EAX to the coprocessor, you could write this code:

```
push    eax
fild    dword ptr [esp]
```

To unload the result of a coprocessor operation into memory as a floating-point number, you ordinarily use the FSTP instruction. For example, to store the number that is on top of the coprocessor stack into a variable as a 64-bit floating-point number, you would write the following code:

```
myvar   dq      ?
          .
          .
          .
        fstp    myvar
```

The FSTP instruction pops the coprocessor stack when it transfers the value from the top of the stack to memory; the number that was previously the second number on the coprocessor stack (next-on-stack) becomes the new top-of-stack (Figure 13-12 on the following page). FISTP and FBSTP are used to store numbers into memory as integer and BCD data and then to pop the stack. If the size of the data is not explicit by reference to a typed variable, you must supply it with a PTR modifier on the operand, as you must with the various load instructions.

```
myvar   dq      ?
          .
          .
          .
        mov     bx,offset myvar
        fstp    qword ptr [bx]
```

To unload a number into memory without popping the coprocessor stack, you can use the FST and FIST instructions. These instructions are appropriate when you want to save an intermediate result from a calculation and also leave a copy of the number on the coprocessor stack for use in subsequent floating-point operations. Interestingly, three "holes" are found in the coprocessor instruction set in this area: There is no BCD store instruction that does not pop the stack; FST cannot be used to store an 80-bit floating-point number; and FIST cannot be used to store a 64-bit integer.

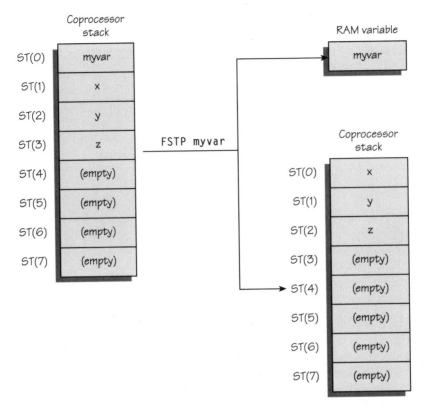

Figure 13-12.
The coprocessor stack before and after an FSTP instruction.

The FLD, FST, and FSTP instructions can also be used to move numbers around within the coprocessor stack, in addition to transferring numbers between RAM and the coprocessor stack. Here we can borrow many useful concepts from Forth. For instance, 20 years of Forth evolution have demonstrated that five primitive stack operations account for nearly all of the nonarithmetic stack manipulations in a typical program:

DUP	Duplicates the number on top of the stack
DROP	Discards the number on top of the stack
SWAP	Interchanges the top two numbers on the stack
OVER	Copies the second number on the stack to the top of the stack
ROT	Rotates the third number on the stack to the top of the stack

All five can be easily expressed in terms of the coprocessor's load, store, and exchange (FXCH) instructions (Figure 13-13).

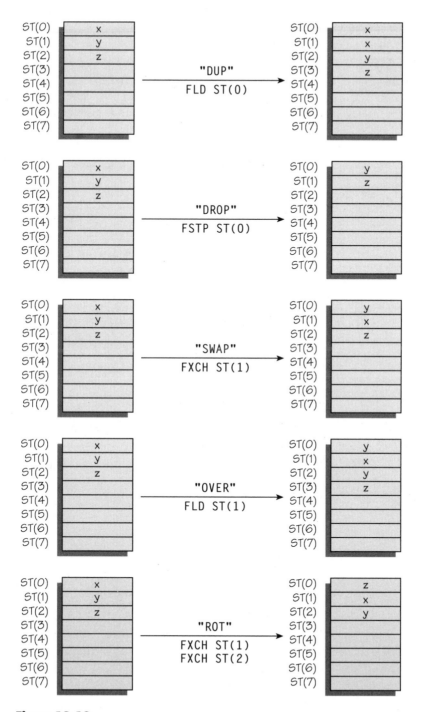

Figure 13-13.

The five fundamental nonarithmetic stack operations: DUP, DROP, SWAP, OVER, and ROT.

To Wait or Not to Wait

One of the subtler aspects of coprocessor programming is enforcing proper synchronization between the CPU and the coprocessor. The CPU and the coprocessor share a single instruction stream—which is controlled by and fetched from memory by the CPU—but they can execute asynchronously much of the time. The CPU can complete several or even dozens of its instructions in the time required for the coprocessor to complete a floating-point operation.

Although asynchronous execution is a powerful tool, a programmer must sometimes bring both the CPU and the coprocessor to a known state before permitting further instructions to execute on one or the other. The primary software means of synchronizing the CPU and the coprocessor is the FWAIT instruction. If an FWAIT is encountered in the instruction stream and the coprocessor is busy, the CPU goes into a wait state until the coprocessor finishes its current operation.

On the original 8087 chip, the synchronization problem is general: All synchronization is obtained by properly positioned FWAIT instructions. Not even a minimum degree of automatic synchronization is built into the hardware. If a floating-point instruction is encountered in the instruction stream before the coprocessor has finished its previous operation, the coprocessor simply becomes confused and returns erroneous results or hangs. Thus, the only safe approach to 8087 programming is to put an FWAIT before every floating-point instruction.

To make the proper placement of FWAITs for 8087 chips less painful to the programmer, Intel decided to have the "normal" forms of the 8087 mnemonics generate FWAIT prefixes automatically. For example, take a look at the machine code generated by this source code:

```
fld     dword ptr [bp]
fld     dword ptr [bp+4]
```

You'll find that what is actually being produced is the opcodes for the following:

```
fwait
fld     dword ptr [bp]
fwait
fld     dword ptr [bp+4]
```

If you don't want the assembler to put an automatic FWAIT opcode before a floating-point instruction, you must use the FN form of the mnemonic, such as FNLD. (The N stands for No wait.)

On the 80287 and 80387 chips, the hardware is somewhat smarter and will stall a floating-point instruction if the coprocessor is still busy, without needing an explicit FWAIT. Thus, if you know that your program will be executing only on an 80287 or 80387, you can use the FN forms and obtain more compact code. Although you might expect the assembler to disable the generation of FWAITs for the normal directives when a .287 or .387 directive is in effect, the assembler unfortunately is not that logical.

In certain situations, you must program FWAITs explicitly, regardless of which coprocessor you are using. In general, you must supply FWAITs when you are transferring data between RAM and the coprocessor, to ensure that the CPU will not access the memory locations until it is "safe" to do so. Consider the following code, which loads a 32-bit real number onto the coprocessor stack from a variable and then sets the value of the variable to 0:

```
myvar    dd       0
         .
         .
         .
         fld      myvar
         fwait
         mov      word ptr myvar,0
         mov      word ptr myvar+2,0
```

If the FWAIT did not follow the FLD (causing the CPU to stall until the FLD is completed), the CPU might store zeros in the variable before the coprocessor finishes loading the variable, and the value that arrives at the coprocessor might therefore be partially or completely incorrect. Of course, in a real program, you try to defer the FWAIT and the CPU's modification of the variable as long as possible, sandwiching other instructions in between to minimize the chance of the FWAIT actually stalling the CPU for a significant number of cycles. You can omit the explicit FWAIT if you can arrange your code so that another floating-point instruction is executed after the FLD but before the CPU again writes to the variable.

Similarly, when you unload a number from the coprocessor stack into RAM, you must be sure that the number has completely arrived before you try to access it with the CPU. The following code stores the number on top of the coprocessor stack into a variable as a 32-bit integer and then loads the 32-bit integer into DX:AX:

```
myvar    dd       0
         .
         .
         .
         fistp    myvar
         fwait
         mov      ax,word ptr myvar
         mov      dx,word ptr myvar+2
```

In this case, if the FWAIT did not precede the CPU's reference to the variable, the program might end up with a bogus value in DX:AX.

Lack of an explicit FWAIT in the proper place can lead to very subtle bugs. Examine the following code, for example, which transfers a 64-bit floating-point number from the CPU's stack to the coprocessor's stack:

```
         mov      bx,sp
         fld      qword ptr ss:[bx]
         add      sp,8
```

This code fails, though only sporadically. At unpredictable intervals, a timer interrupt or other interrupt occurs immediately after the ADD instruction is executed but before the coprocessor has finished fetching the 64-bit number from RAM. Service of the interrupt causes the CPU's flag register, CS, and IP to be pushed onto the stack, overwriting the three most significant words of the floating-point number. Once it is found, this particular bug is fixed easily enough by putting an FWAIT before the ADD. But it's better to program defensively and avoid this sort of bug altogether.

Basic Arithmetic Operations

The coprocessor instructions for the four basic arithmetic operations—addition, subtraction, multiplication, and division—fall into three categories, as shown in Figure 13-14. Although all these machine instructions have two operands (a source and a destination), one or both of the operands might be implicit in the machine code or in the source code. The result always replaces the destination operand.

Arithmetic Operation	ST(0) with ST(n) or Floating-Point Value in Memory	ST(0) with ST(n), and Pop ST(0)	ST(0) with Integer Value in Memory
Add	FADD	FADDP	FIADD
Subtract	FSUB	FSUBP	FISUB
Subtract reversed	FSUBR	FSUBRP	FISUBR
Multiply	FMUL	FMULP	FIMUL
Divide	FDIV	FDIVP	FIDIV
Divide reversed	FDIVR	FDIVRP	FIDIVR

Figure 13-14.
The three categories of coprocessor arithmetic instructions.

The instructions in the second column of Figure 13-14 work on two floating-point numbers. The source operand can be either a floating-point register or a floating-point number in a memory variable; the destination operand is always in a floating-point register. One of the operands must be ST(0); in most cases, it is convenient to make ST(0) the destination.

The instructions in the third column of Figure 13-14 also work on two floating-point numbers, but they pop the stack after the operation is completed. If the two operands are in ST(0) and ST(1), these instructions allow you to discard the source operand and keep only the result in the destination operand, thereby implementing classic stack machine behavior.

The instructions in the fourth column of Figure 13-14 always have ST(0) as the implicit destination operand and an integer value in a memory value as an explicit source operand. The result is left in ST(0), and the value in the memory variable is unchanged.

Let's look at a few simple examples of these basic arithmetic instructions. The following code adds the floating-point numbers in the variables *myvar1* and *myvar2* and leaves the sum in *myvar3*:

```
myvar1   dd       ?
myvar2   dd       ?
myvar3   dd       ?
         .
         .
         .
         fld      var1
         fld      var2
         faddp    st(1),st(0)
         fstp     var3
         fwait
```

Interestingly, if you write a non-stack-popping arithmetic instruction without any operands, the assembler assumes that you want classic stack behavior and generates the pop form anyway. In other words, if you write

```
         fadd
```

the assembler generates this code:

```
         faddp    st(1),st(0)
```

Equivalent but somewhat faster code would look like this:

```
myvar1   dd       ?
myvar2   dd       ?
myvar3   dd       ?
         .
         .
         .
         fld      var1
         fadd     var2
         fstp     var3
         fwait
```

You're probably wondering about the operations called subtract reversed and divide reversed in Figure 13-14. To see why these exist, let's first consider the normal subtract and divide instructions. FSUB subtracts the source operand from the destination operand and leaves the result in the destination operand. FDIV divides the destination operand by the source operand and leaves the quotient in the destination operand. Both behave exactly as you would expect from your experience with the Intel CPUs' subtract and divide instructions.

The reversed instructions allow you to skip a load instruction or to exchange instructions before a subtract or divide if the wrong value of a pair happens to be in the desired destination. For example, the code

```
         fsubrp   st(1),st(0)
```

is exactly equivalent to this code:

```
        fxch    st(1)
        fsubp   st(1),st(0)
```

The importance of the reversed instructions is even more evident when one of the operands is in memory. For instance, the code

```
myvar   dd      ?
            .
            .
            .
        fdivr   myvar
```

has the same effect as the following code:

```
myvar   dd      ?
            .
            .
            .
        fld     myvar
        fxch    st(1)
        fdivp   st(1),st(0)
```

We should also mention three more simple coprocessor instructions:

FCHS	Changes the sign
FABS	Returns the absolute value
FSQRT	Returns the square root

All three instructions are written without operands; they always take their argument from ST(0) and return their result to ST(0).

The routines DIMUL87.ASM and DIDIV87.ASM (Figures 13-15 and 13-16) illustrate the basic principles of coprocessor arithmetic and data movement. They use the coprocessor to implement double-precision integer (32-bit) signed multiplication and division, and they can be incorporated into integer-based programs that would otherwise require extensive subroutines such as the MPIMUL and MPIDIV modules in Chapter 12. Note that because the coprocessor does not directly support unsigned integer multiplies or divides, use of the coprocessor to manipulate addresses requires great care.

```
;
; DIMUL87.ASM -- Double-precision signed integer multiply
;               for 80x87 coprocessor and 8086, 8088, 80286,
;               80386, or 80486 in real mode/16-bit protected mode.
```

Figure 13-15.   *(continued)*
DIMUL87.ASM, a routine to perform signed integer double-precision multiplication on the numeric coprocessor.

Figure 13-15. *continued*

```
;
;              Be sure to call INIT87 routine first to test for
;              coprocessor existence and to set rounding mode,
;              precision, and exception masks!
;
; Copyright (C) 1991 Ray Duncan
;
; Call with:   DX:AX        = double-precision argument 1
;              CX:BX        = double-precision argument 2
;
; Returns:     DX:CX:BX:AX = quad-precision product
;
; Destroys:    Nothing

_TEXT    segment word public 'CODE'

         assume  cs:_TEXT

         public  dimul
dimul    proc    near

         push    dx                      ; put argument 1 on stack
         push    ax

         push    cx                      ; put argument 2 on stack
         push    bx

         mov     bx,sp                   ; make arguments addressable

         fild    dword ptr ss:[bx]       ; load one argument
         fimul   dword ptr ss:[bx+4]     ; multiply it by the other

         fistp   qword ptr ss:[bx]       ; unload result
         fwait                           ; wait for it to arrive

         pop     ax                      ; retrieve result
         pop     bx
         pop     cx
         pop     dx
         ret                             ; and exit

dimul    endp

_TEXT    ends

         end
```

```
;
; DIDIV87.ASM -- Double-precision signed integer divide
;               for 80x87 coprocessor and 8086, 8088, 80286,
;               80386, or 80486 in real mode/16-bit protected mode.
;
;               Be sure to call INIT87 routine first to test for
;               coprocessor existence and to set rounding mode,
;               precision, and exception masks!
;
; Copyright (C) 1991 Ray Duncan
;
; Call with:    DX:CX:BX:AX = quad-precision dividend
;               SI:DI       = double-precision divisor
;
; Returns:      DX:AX       = double-precision quotient
;               CX:BX       = double-precision remainder
;
; Destroys:     Nothing

_TEXT   segment word public 'CODE'

        assume  cs:_TEXT

        public  didiv
didiv   proc    near

        push    dx                      ; put dividend on stack
        push    cx
        push    bx
        push    ax

        push    si                      ; put divisor on stack
        push    di

        mov     bx,sp                   ; make arguments addressable

        fild    dword ptr ss:[bx]       ; put divisor on coprocessor
        fild    qword ptr ss:[bx+4]     ; put dividend on coprocessor

        fld     st(1)                   ; make copies of both
        fld     st(1)

        fdivrp  st(1),st(0)             ; perform signed divide

        fistp   dword ptr ss:[bx]       ; unload quotient

        fprem                           ; calculate remainder
```

Figure 13-16.   (continued)

*DIDIV87.ASM, a routine to perform signed integer double-precision division
on the numeric coprocessor.*

Figure 13-16. *continued*

```
            fistp    dword ptr ss:[bx+4]        ; unload remainder
            fstp     st(0)                      ; discard stack top

            pop      ax                         ; quotient into DX:AX
            pop      dx

            pop      bx                         ; remainder into CX:BX
            pop      cx

            add      sp,4                       ; clean up stack
            ret                                 ; and exit

didiv       endp

_TEXT       ends

            end
```

Testing and Comparing Numbers

The coprocessor family's ability to compare and test floating-point numbers is based on seven instructions: FCOM, FCOMP, FCOMPP, FICOM, FICOMP, FTST, and FXAM. The 80387 offers three additional comparison instructions: FUCOM, FUCOMP, and FUCOMPP.

FCOM, FCOMP, and FCOMPP are the most important comparison instructions. All three compare the source operand to ST(0) and set the condition code bits in the coprocessor status word according to the result of the comparison. FCOMP pops one value off the stack after the comparison, whereas FCOMPP pops two. Obviously, FCOMPP is intended for use in classic stack programming, in which the top two values on the stack are compared destructively.

After the condition code bits are set, you can use the FSTSW instruction to store the coprocessor status word where the CPU can inspect it. On the 8087, you must unload the status word to memory and then load it into a CPU register:

```
status  dw       ?
            .
            .
            .
        fstsw    status
        fwait
        mov      ax,status
```

On the 80287 and 80387, you can transfer the status word directly to the AX register:

```
        fstsw    ax
```

(This is the single instance of direct register-to-register communication between the coprocessor and CPU alluded to earlier.)

When the status word has been retrieved, you might be tempted to use the CPU's AND or TEST instruction to evaluate the state of the condition code bits. Intel, however, provides a much faster (if obscure) method. The condition code bits in the coprocessor status word are positioned so that they can be shoved into the CPU's zero flag, parity flag, and carry flag with the SAHF (Store AH into Flags) instruction. After the CPU flags have been forced in this way, they can be exploited to control conditional jumps in the usual manner.

For example, the following code for an 80287 or 80387 compares the value in ST(0) to the number in ST(1), discards both, and then branches according to the result:

```
fcompp
fstsw    ax
sahf
ja       label1   ; if st(0) > st(1)
jmp      label2   ; if st(0) <= st(1)
```

When using this technique, be sure to restrict yourself to the conditional jump instructions JA, JAE, JB, JBE, JE, JNE, and their aliases. Using a conditional jump that also relies on the overflow flag, such as JG or JL, can lead to very strange results!

FCOM, FCOMP, and FCOMPP generate an exception if one or both of the numbers being compared are NaNs (because an earlier operation had an invalid operand or generated an invalid result) and the exception has not been masked by the program. If the exception is masked, the instructions return a special condition code indicating that the result is "unordered." The FUCOM, FUCOMP, and FUCOMPP instructions were added in the 80387 to allow more flexibility in exception handling; they never generate an exception, regardless of the value of their operands, but they can still return an unordered result.

The FTST and FXAM instructions nondestructively evaluate the number in ST(0) and set the condition code bits according to the result. Because FTST compares ST(0) to zero, it is used to determine whether a number is negative, zero, or positive. FXAM examines ST(0) to determine whether it contains a valid normalized floating-point number, zero, negative or positive infinity, denormal, NaN, and so on.

More About Stack Arithmetic

When you understand the basics of arithmetic on stack machines, you can play a number of tricks that take advantage of the stack architecture to speed up special cases of addition, multiplication, division, and raising numbers to powers. For example, to double a number that is already on top of the floating-point stack, you can write this code:

```
fadd     st(0),st(0)
```

If the number resides in a variable, you can use the following:

```
myvar    dd       0
         .
         .
         .
         fld     myvar
         fadd    st(0),st(0)
         fstp    myvar
         fwait
```

You could also write this:

```
myvar    dd       0
         .
         .
         .
         fld     myvar
         fadd    myvar
         fstp    myvar
         fwait
```

This method, however, involves more references to memory, increasing the contention for the memory bus between the CPU and the coprocessor, and thus runs more slowly. (The final synchronizing FWAIT instructions are shown in these examples, but remember that the FWAIT is not necessary if your program performs another floating-point instruction before the CPU accesses the result in the variable.)

To square a number that is already on top of the floating-point stack, you can write the following:

```
         fmul    st(0),st(0)
```

If the number resides in a variable, you can code as shown here:

```
myvar    dd       0
         .
         .
         .
         fld     myvar
         fmul    st(0),st(0)
         fstp    myvar
         fwait
```

You can easily raise a number to a (small) power with in-line code or a loop. For example, to obtain the cube of a value, you can write this code:

```
myvar    dd       0
         .
         .
         .
         fld     myvar
         fld     st(0)
```

(continued)

```
        fmul      st(0),st(0)
        fmulp     st(1),st(0)
        fstp      myvar
        fwait
```

Here is alternative coding:

```
myvar   dd        0
            .
            .
            .
        fld       myvar
        fmul      myvar
        fmul      myvar
        fstp      myvar
        fwait
```

Again, however, the alternative form involves more memory bus traffic and address calculations and therefore should be avoided. (Later in the chapter, we'll discuss a more general method for raising a number to a power.)

The coprocessor's built-in constants can often be used to advantage. To take the reciprocal of a number, you can write this code:

```
myvar   dd        0
            .
            .
            .
        fld1
        fdiv      myvar
        fstp      myvar
        fwait
```

As another simple example, consider the conversion of an angle's radians to degrees. The basic relationship between radians and degrees is the following:

360 degrees = 2π radians

Thus, if x is a value in degrees and y is a value in radians:

$$x = \frac{360 * y}{2\pi}$$

If an angle measured in radians is stored in a variable, you could use this sequence to convert the number of radians to an equivalent number of degrees and leave the result in the same variable:

```
myvar   dd        0
int360  dw        360
            .
            .
            .
        fld       myvar
        fimul     int360
```

```
        fldpi
        fadd        st(0),st(0)
        fdivp       st(1),st(0)
        fstp        myvar
        fwait
```

Rounding

The coprocessors support four rounding modes: round to nearest or even ("banker's method"), round toward positive infinity ("round up"), round toward negative infinity ("round down"), and truncate ("chop"). The active rounding mode comes into play when the result of a calculation cannot be contained in the 80-bit floating-point format that is used in the coprocessor registers or when a number is unloaded from the coprocessor stack into one of the shorter memory-resident data formats.

The current rounding mode is determined by bits in the coprocessor control word (Figure 13-7 on page 288). The default mode after coprocessor initialization with the FINIT or FNINIT instruction is "round to nearest or even." Your application program should always either initialize the coprocessor or explicitly set the rounding mode, to avoid unexpected results. This is especially important when you use the coprocessor for integer arithmetic, because "chop" mode is symmetric with the rounding performed by the CPU's native divide instruction; "round to nearest or even" is appropriate only for floating-point operations.

The "round up" and "round down" modes are rarely needed, but they can be handy for estimating the degree of uncertainty in an extended calculation. You can carry out the entire calculation twice, first with "round up" selected and again with "round down," and then compare the two results to determine the maximum potential error in the final result that might be caused by rounding intermediate values.

A final note with regard to rounding: If you use the coprocessor in a TSR, device driver, or interrupt handler, you must always be careful to save and restore the coprocessor rounding mode so that calculations by a foreground application are not disturbed. For example, to save the current rounding mode and then temporarily set it to truncate, you could code as follows:

```
oldmode dw          0
newmode dw          0
        .
        .
        .
        fstcw       oldmode
        fwait
        mov         ax,oldmode
        and         ax,0f3ffh
        or          ax,00c00h
        mov         newmode,ax
        fldcw       newmode
        fwait
```

(continued)

```
        .
        .
        .
        (other calculations here)
        .
        .
        .
        fldcw    oldmode
        fwait
```

It is often, however, not sufficient to save and restore the rounding mode in a TSR, device driver, or interrupt handler. You might also need to save and restore the coprocessor environment or even the entire coprocessor state, including the contents of the floating-point register stack, to ensure that your calculations are carried out successfully. This can require a great many storage and processor cycles as well as close attention to problems of re-entrancy.

Exception Handling

The coprocessor recognizes six basic types of exceptions (errors) for floating-point operations:

- Invalid operation
- Division by zero
- Denormalized operand
- Overflow
- Underflow
- Inexact result (precision)

When an exception occurs, the result depends on the state of the exception mask bits in the coprocessor control word (Figure 13-7 on page 288). If the mask bit for the exception is clear (0), the coprocessor sets the appropriate error bits in the coprocessor status word (Figure 13-6 on page 287) and triggers an interrupt. The interrupt number depends on the CPU model: On the 8086 and 8088, the interrupt is signaled via an 8259 programmable interrupt controller or the CPU's NMI line; on the 80286, 80386, and 80486 CPUs, an Int 10H is generated. Note that the interrupt does *not* occur at the time the error is detected by the coprocessor; rather, it occurs when the CPU next encounters an FWAIT or a floating-point instruction. The interrupt handler can use the FSTENV or FSAVE instruction to unload the state of the coprocessor into RAM, deduce the cause of the error, and take the appropriate recovery measures.

If the mask bit for the exception in the coprocessor control word is set (1), the coprocessor sets the error bit in the status word and "fixes up" the result of the operation that caused the exception, allowing calculations to continue. Depending on the type of error, the coprocessor returns zero, infinity, indefinite, a denormalized value, or one of several special bit patterns (NaNs). The error bits in the status word are "sticky" and remain set through subsequent floating-point operations until they are cleared by the execution of FCLEX, FRSTOR, or FLDENV or by initialization of the coprocessor. The fix-up result can be propagated through subsequent floating-point operations, or it can disappear, depending on its nature. A very small denormalized value, for example, if added to a large normalized value, essentially vanishes and is of no further concern in the calculation.

Aside from the Int 10H exceptions generated directly by the coprocessor, several other interrupts can occur as a result of a coprocessor operation. The most basic is Int 7H, which is generated when a floating-point instruction is executed but no coprocessor is present. The intent of Int 7H is to allow automatic traps to routines in an emulator library so that the identical object code can run on systems with or without coprocessors. For 80286, 80386, and 80486 processors running in protected mode, Int 09H (Segment Overrun), Int 0BH (Segment Not Present), Int 0CH (Stack Fault), or Int 0DH (General Protection Fault) can occur if an address used in a floating-point instruction lies partially or completely outside a valid segment. These protected mode interrupts are typically handled in an operating system rather than in an application. Finally, on the 80486, an Int 9H never occurs for a coprocessor instruction (an Int 0DH is produced instead), and an Int 11H is optionally generated in the event of coprocessor access to a nonaligned memory operand.

In general, handling coprocessor interrupts is a complicated business that is best left to systems programmers. Although detecting an exception interrupt is obviously simple, proper error recovery can be very difficult. In most application programs, it is preferable to mask all exceptions when the coprocessor is initialized and leave them masked, concentrating your energies on the algorithms and application design rather than on interrupt handlers. Your program can check the coprocessor status word at suitable intervals for an error flag, as well as testing the results of all calculations for unexpected infinity, indefinite, or NaN values.

Transcendental Functions

Although the coprocessor family does support transcendental functions such as logs, sines, cosines, tangents, and their inverses, this support is not as complete and straightforward as you might wish. On the 8087 and 80287, the transcendental functions are supplied as rather primitive operations with limited ranges (Figure 13-17 on the next page) that must be used as building blocks for more generalized procedures, and the derivation of the generalized routines is not intuitively clear.

Let's look first at logs and antilogs. The log to the base n of any number x, where x is greater than 0, can be found as shown here:

$\log_n(2) * \log_2(x)$

The instructions FYL2X ($y * \log_2(x)$) and FYL2XP1 ($y * \log_2(x + 1)$), together with the load constant instructions FLDLG2 (load $\log_{10}(2)$) and FLDLN2 (load $\log_e(2)$), allow common (base 10) and natural (base e) logs to be calculated efficiently. For

Instruction	Operation	Argument Range
FPTAN	Partial tangent	$0 <= x <= \frac{\pi}{4}$ $\|x\| < 2^{63}$ (80387)
FPATAN	Partial arctangent	$0 <= x <= y <=$ infinity
FSIN	Sine (80387)	$\|x\| < 2^{63}$
FCOS	Cosine (80387)	$\|x\| < 2^{63}$
FSINCOS	Sine and cosine (80387)	$\|x\| < 2^{63}$
F2XM1	$2^x - 1$	$0 <= x <= 0.5$ $-1 <= x <= 1$ (80387)
FYL2X	$y * \log_2(x)$	$0 <= x <= +$infinity $-$infinity $<= y <= +$infinity
FYL2XP1	$y * \log_2(x + 1)$	$0 <= x <= (1 - \frac{\sqrt{2}}{2})$ $-$infinity $<= y <= +$infinity

Figure 13-17.

Transcendental functions supported by the coprocessor family. The parenthetical notation (80387) designates operations that are available on the 80387 or 80486 but not on the 8087 or 80287.

instance, to obtain the common log of a number (after screening the number to ensure that it is valid and positive), you could write the following code:

```
myvar    dd       0
         .
         .
         .
         fldlg2
         fld      myvar
         fyl2x
         fstp     myvar
         fwait
```

When the argument is very close to 1, use the FYL2XP1 instruction in a similar sequence for a more precise result.

Finding antilogs is considerably more tedious. This is the general approach to finding the antilog to the base *n* of some number *x*:

$$n^x = 2^{x \cdot \log_2(n)}$$

Thus, to find common and natural antilogs, you need the instructions FLD1 (load constant 1), FLDL2E (load $\log_2(e)$), FLDL2T (load $\log_2(10)$), F2XM1 ($2^x - 1$), and FSCALE ($x * 2^y$). FSCALE raises 2 to a power by shifting, but it doesn't suffice because integer powers of 10 (or *e*) don't correspond to integer powers of 2. The argument must be decomposed into its integer portions and fractional portions with FRNDINT and FSUB and the relationship exploited:

$$2^{(y + z)} = 2^y \cdot 2^z$$

Figure 13-18 contains a somewhat simplified routine to find the common antilog of a number. In production code, you would also add logic to check for invalid arguments. Note that the routine temporarily forces the rounding mode for the duration of the FRNDINT instruction, to ensure that the fractional portion of the number lies within an acceptable range for F2XM1.

```
;
; FALOG.ASM -- Calculates common antilog on 80x87.
;
; Copyright (C) 1991 Ray Duncan
;
; Call with:     ST(0) = argument
;
; Returns:       ST(0) = antilog to base 10
;
; Uses:          CPU registers are preserved;
;                uses 3 cells of coprocessor stack
;
; Note: To obtain natural antilog, replace fldl2t instruction
;       with fldl2e.
;
; Be sure coprocessor has been properly initialized
; with a previous call to INIT87!

_TEXT    segment word public 'CODE'

         assume  cs:_TEXT

oldcw    equ     word ptr [bp-4]       ; original control word
newcw    equ     word ptr [bp-2]       ; new control word


         public  falog
falog    proc    near

         push    ax                    ; save registers and
         push    bp                    ; make stack frame
         mov     bp,sp                 ; for local variables
         sub     sp,4
         fldl2t                        ; load log2(10)
         fmulp   st(1),st(0)           ; log2(10) * argument
```

Figure 13-18. (*continued*)
FALOG.ASM, a routine that finds the common antilog of a floating-point number.

Figure 13-18. *continued*

```
        fld     st(0)           ; duplicate product
        fstcw   oldcw           ; get old control word
        fwait                   ; wait until it arrives
        mov     ax,oldcw        ; change rounding mode
        and     ax,0f3ffh       ; field to "round down"
        or      ax,0400h
        mov     newcw,ax
        fldcw   newcw           ; force rounding mode
        frndint                 ; get int part of product
        fldcw   oldcw           ; restore old rounding mode
        fld     st(0)           ; duplicate integer part
        fxch    st(2)           ; get original product
        fsubrp  st(1),st(0)     ; find fractional part
        fld1
        fchs
        fxch    st(1)           ; scale fractional part
        fscale
        fstp    st(1)           ; discard coprocessor junk
        f2xm1                   ; raise 2 to power - 1
        fld1
        faddp   st(1),st(0)     ; correct for the -1
        fmul    st(0),st(0)     ; square result
        fscale                  ; scale by int part
        fstp    st(1)           ; discard coprocessor junk
        add     sp,4            ; discard local variables
        pop     bp              ; restore registers and
        pop     ax              ; return result in ST(0)
        ret


falog   endp

_TEXT   ends

        end
```

Although the antilog code is messy, it is trivial compared to the contortions required to find sines, cosines, and tangents of arbitrary angles. The coprocessor support for these functions is a partial tangent instruction (FPTAN), which on the 8087 and 80287 can cope with arguments only in the range 0 through $\pi/4$ radians (0 through 45 degrees). Therefore, the angle must first be reduced into this range with the FPREM instruction before the standard trigonometric identities can be exploited to obtain the result. Figure 13-19 contains source code for generalized sine, cosine, and tangent functions. Again, in production code, you would add more extensive argument checking.

```
;
; FTRIG.ASM -- Calculates sine, cosine, and tangent for 8087 and
;              80287. These routines will also work on an 80387
;              but are not needed on that processor because of
;              its built-in FSIN, FCOS, FSINCOS, and generalized
;              FTAN functions.
;
; Copyright (C) 1991 Ray Duncan
;
; Procedure FSIN calculates sine(x)
; Procedure FCOS calculates cosine(x)
; Procedure FTAN calculates tangent(x)
;
; All three procedures have the same calling sequence:
;
; Call with:    ST(0) = argument in radians
;
; Returns:      ST(0) = result
;
; Uses:         AX, BX. Other registers preserved.
;
; Be sure coprocessor has been properly initialized
; with a previous call to INIT87!

_DATA    segment word public 'DATA'

piby2  dq      3ff921fb54442d18h       ; constant pi / 2
piby4  dq      3fe921fb54442d18h       ; constant pi / 4

plusinf dd     07f800000h              ; +infinity encoding
neginf  dd     0ff800000h              ; -infinity encoding

oldcw   dw     0                       ; old control word
newcw   dw     0                       ; new control word

temp    dw     0                       ; scratch storage

cctab   db     0,4,1,5,2,6,3,7         ; relates condition code
                                       ; bits to octant numbers

fsintab label  word                    ; sine dispatch table
        dw     fsin0                   ; octant 0
        dw     fsin1                   ; octant 1
        dw     fsin2                   ; octant 2
        dw     fsin3                   ; octant 3
        dw     fsin4                   ; octant 4
        dw     fsin5                   ; octant 5
        dw     fsin6                   ; octant 6
        dw     fsin7                   ; octant 7
```

Figure 13-19.   (continued)

FTRIG.ASM, the source code for generalized sine, cosine, and tangent functions.

Figure 13-19. *continued*

```
ftantab label    word                  ; tangent dispatch table
                                        ; for reduced angle <> 0
         dw      ftan0                  ; octant 0
         dw      ftan1                  ; octant 1
         dw      ftan2                  ; octant 2
         dw      ftan3                  ; octant 3
         dw      ftan4                  ; octant 4
         dw      ftan5                  ; octant 5
         dw      ftan6                  ; octant 6
         dw      ftan7                  ; octant 7

ftanztab label   word                  ; tangent dispatch table
                                        ; for reduced angle = 0
         dw      ftanz0                 ; octant 0
         dw      ftanz1                 ; octant 1
         dw      ftanz2                 ; octant 2
         dw      ftanz3                 ; octant 3
         dw      ftanz4                 ; octant 4
         dw      ftanz5                 ; octant 5
         dw      ftanz6                 ; octant 6
         dw      ftanz7                 ; octant 7

_DATA    ends

_TEXT    segment word public 'CODE'

         assume  cs:_TEXT,ds:_DATA

         public  fsin
fsin     proc    near                  ; calculate sine of ST(0)

         call    octant                ; reduce angle, find octant
         shl     bx,1                  ; form index to jump table
         jmp     [bx+fsintab]          ; branch to correct sequence

fsin0:   call    psin                  ; octant 0
         ret                           ; sin(x) = psin(x)

fsin1:   fsubr   piby4                 ; octant 1
         call    pcos                  ; sin(x) = pcos((pi / 4) - x)
         ret

fsin2:   call    pcos                  ; octant 2
         ret                           ; sin(x) = pcos(x)

fsin3:   fsubr   piby4                 ; octant 3
         call    psin                  ; sin(x) = psin((pi / 4) - x)
         ret
```

(continued)

Figure 13-19. *continued*

```
fsin4:   call    psin                    ; octant 4
         fchs                            ; sin(x) = -(psin(x))
         ret

fsin5:   fsubr   piby4                   ; octant 5
         call    pcos                    ; sin(x) = -(pcos)((pi / 4) - x))
         fchs
         ret

fsin6:   call    pcos                    ; octant 6
         fchs                            ; sin(x) = -(pcos(x))
         ret

fsin7:   fsubr   piby4                   ; octant 7
         call    psin                    ; sin(x) = -(psin((pi / 4) - x))
         fchs
         ret

fsin     endp

         public  fcos
fcos     proc    near                    ; calculate cosine of ST(0)

         call    octant                  ; reduce angle, find octant
         add     bx,2                    ; add pi / 2 (90 degrees) and
         and     bx,7                    ; then use sine routines
         shl     bx,1                    ; form index to jump table
         jmp     [bx+fsintab]            ; branch to correct sequence

fcos     endp

         public  ftan
ftan     proc    near                    ; calculate tangent of ST(0)

         call    octant                  ; reduce angle, find octant
         shl     bx,1                    ; form index for jump table
         ftst                            ; is reduced angle = 0?
         fstsw   temp
         fwait
         mov     ax,temp
         sahf
         je      ftanz                   ; reduced angle = 0
         jmp     [bx+ftantab]            ; reduced angle <> 0

ftan0:                                   ; octant 0
ftan4:                                   ; octant 4
         fptan                           ; get y / x
         fdivp   st(1),st(0)
         ret
```

(continued)

Figure 13-19. *continued*

```
ftan1:                              ; octant 1
ftan5:                              ; octant 5
        fsubr   piby4               ; (pi / 4) - angle
        fptan                       ; get (y / x)
        fdivp   st(1),st(0)         ; 1 / (y / x)
        fld1
        fdivrp  st(1),st(0)
        ret


ftan2:                              ; octant 2
ftan6:                              ; octant 6
        fptan                       ; get y / x
        fdivp   st(1),st(0)
        fld1                        ; -(1 / (y / x))
        fdivrp  st(1),st(0)
        fchs
        ret


ftan3:                              ; octant 3
ftan7:                              ; octant 7
        fsubr   piby4               ; (pi / 4) - angle
        fptan                       ; get y / x
        fdivp   st(1),st(0)         ; -(y / x)
        fchs
        ret


ftanz:                              ; reduced angle = 0
        fstp    st(0)               ; discard angle and
        jmp     [bx+ftanztab]       ; go load special value

ftanz0: fldz                        ; 0 degrees
        ret                         ; load constant 0

ftanz1: fld1                        ; 45 degrees
        ret                         ; load constant 1

ftanz2: fld     plusinf             ; 90 degrees
        ret                         ; load constant +infinity

ftanz3: fld1                        ; 135 degrees
        fchs                        ; load constant -1
        ret

ftanz4: fldz                        ; 180 degrees
        ret                         ; load constant 0

ftanz5: fld1                        ; 225 degrees
        ret                         ; load constant 1
```

(continued)

Figure 13-19. *continued*

```
ftanz6: fld     neginf                  ; 270 degrees
        ret                             ; load constant -infinity

ftanz7: fld1                            ; 315 degrees
        fchs                            ; load constant -1
        ret

ftan    endp


;
; PSIN:         Partial sine
;
; Call with:    ST(0) = angle in range 0 <= x < pi / 4
;
; Returns:      ST(0) = sine
;
psin    proc    near

        fptan                           ; get fraction y / x
        fld     st(1)                   ; sin = y / sqrt(x * x + y * y)
        fmul    st(0),st(0)
        fxch    st(1)
        fmul    st(0),st(0)
        faddp   st(1),st(0)
        fsqrt
        fdivp   st(1),st(0)
        ret                             ; leave divide running

psin    endp

;
; PCOS:         Partial cosine
;
; Call with:    ST(0) = angle in range 0 <= x < pi / 4
;
; Returns:      ST(0) = cosine
;
pcos    proc    near

        fptan                           ; get fraction y / x
        fxch    st(1)                   ; cos = x / sqrt(x * x + y * y)
        fld     st(1)
        fmul    st(0),st(0)
        fxch    st(1)
        fmul    st(0),st(0)
        faddp   st(1),st(0)
        fsqrt
        fdivp   st(1),st(0)
        ret                             ; leave divide running
```

(continued)

Figure 13-19. *continued*

```
pcos    endp

;
; OCTANT:       Finds octant occupied by angle
;
; Call with:    ST(0) = angle in radians
;
; Returns:      ST(0) = reduced angle, 0 <= angle < pi / 4
;               BX    = octant(0-7)
;
octant  proc    near

        push    ax                      ; save register
        ftst                            ; test sign of angle
        fstsw   temp                    ; unload FTST status
        fabs                            ; force angle positive
        push    temp                    ; save FTST status
        fld     piby4                   ; load constant pi / 4
        fxch    st(1)                   ; put angle on top
        fprem                           ; reduce to 0 <= angle < pi / 4
        fstsw   temp                    ; unload FPREM status
        fwait                           ; wait until it arrives
        mov     bx,temp                 ; retrieve status word
        and     bx,4300h                ; shift C3, C1, C0 status
        rol     bx,1                    ; bits (which contain
        rol     bx,1                    ; low 3 bits of quotient
        shl     bh,1                    ; from FPREM) to form
        shl     bh,1                    ; index in range 0-7
        shl     bh,1                    ; then look up octant
        shl     bh,1
        rol     bx,1
        rol     bx,1
        mov     bl,[bx+cctab]           ; now BX = actual octant
        pop     ax                      ; get back FTST status
        sahf                            ; force CPU flags
        jae     oct1                    ; jump, orig angle >= 0
        fsubr   st(0),st(1)             ; angle was negative
        sub     bx,7                    ; adjust reduced angle
        neg     bx                      ; and octant

oct1:   fstp    st(1)                   ; discard pi / 4 constant
        pop     ax                      ; restore register, return
        ret                             ; BX = octant, ST(0) = angle

octant  endp

_TEXT   ends

        end
```

Calculating the inverse trigonometric functions is much less painful. The partial arctangent instruction (FPATAN) requires only that both its arguments be nonnegative and that the argument on top of the stack be larger than the one that is next on the stack. Thus, to obtain a generalized arctangent, you simply load the angle and the constant 1 and execute a possible swap before FPATAN is executed. Arcsine and arc-cosine are easily derived from the generalized arctangent using standard trigonometric relationships:

$$\arcsin(x) \; = \; \arctan(\frac{x}{\sqrt{1-x^2}})$$

$$\arccos(x) \; = \; \frac{\pi}{2} \; - \; \arcsin(x)$$

The hyperbolic functions and their inverses are also obtained readily with the aid of natural logs, antilogs, and the square root instruction:

$$\sinh(x) \; = \; \frac{e^x - e^{-x}}{2}$$

$$\cosh(x) \; = \; \frac{e^x + e^{-x}}{2}$$

$$\tanh(x) \; = \; \frac{\sinh(x)}{\cosh(x)}$$

When an 80387 or 80486 is available, most of these trigonometric shenanigans are not needed. These two numeric coprocessors support generalized forms of the FPTAN and FPATAN instructions that can accept any angle without prior reduction, and they also provide generalized FSIN, FCOS, and FSINCOS instructions that make complicated procedures such as those in Figure 13-19 unnecessary. For example, to take the sine of a number, you could write the following:

```
        .387
        .
        .
        .
myvar   dd      0
        .
        .
        .
        fld     myvar
        fsin
        fstp    myvar
        fwait
```

Input and Output

The most untidy job involved in using the numeric coprocessors is input and output: converting ASCII strings to floating-point numbers and vice versa. Floating-point numbers are expressed as fractions in base 2 times a power of 2 for the convenience of the computer, but these numbers do not transform neatly into human-friendly fractions of 10 times a power of 10. Consequently, writing robust, efficient conversion routines requires more extensive use of the coprocessor's capabilities and instruction set than anything we have covered so far.

Figure 13-20 contains the source code for the procedure ATOF, which converts an ASCII string to a 64-bit floating-point number. The basic strategy ATOF uses is to convert the mantissa and the exponent to binary numbers separately, update the exponent by the number of digits found after the decimal point in the mantissa, raise 10 to the power of the exponent, and then multiply that result by the mantissa. ATOF is called with DS:SI pointing to a floating-point number in this form:

[*sign*][*digits*][[.*digits*]][E|e[*sign*][*exp*]]

ATOF stops converting the string when it hits the first invalid digit; terminating the string with a null byte ensures that conversion stops at the proper place. Upon return from ATOF, the converted binary floating-point value is on the top of the coprocessor stack.

```
;
; ATOF.ASM -- Converts ASCII string to floating-point
;             number on 80x87 stack.
;             (Also requires FALOG from FALOG.ASM)
;
; Copyright (C) 1991 Ray Duncan
;
; Call with:   DS:SI = address of string in the form
;                      [sign][digits][.[digits]][E|e[sign][exp]]
;                      leading blanks or tabs ignored
;
; Returns:     ST(0) = floating-point value
;              DS:SI = address + 1 of terminator
;
; Uses:        Nothing
;
; This routine gives no warning in the event of
; overflow and terminates on the first invalid character.
;
; Be sure coprocessor has been properly initialized
; with a previous call to INIT87!
```

Figure 13-20.   *(continued)*

ATOF.ASM, the source code for a routine converting an ASCII string to a floating-point number.

Figure 13-20. *continued*

```
blank    equ     20h             ; ASCII blank character
tab      equ     09h             ; ASCII tab character

_DATA    segment word public 'DATA'

int10    dw      10              ; integer constant 10
digit    dw      0               ; current converted digit
places   dw      0               ; number of decimal places

_DATA    ends

_TEXT    segment word public 'CODE'

         assume  cs:_TEXT,ds:_DATA

         extrn   falog:near      ; we need FALOG routine

         public  atof
atof     proc    near            ; ASCII to floating-point

         push    ax              ; save registers
         push    cx
         push    dx

         call    convert         ; convert mantissa

         neg     dx              ; save -1 * decimal places
         mov     places,dx

         or      al,20h          ; fold char to lowercase
         cmp     al,'e'          ; is exponent present?
         je      atof1           ; yes, jump

         fldz                    ; assume zero exponent
         jmp     atof2

atof1:   call    convert         ; convert exponent

atof2:   fiadd   places          ; adjust exponent for
                                 ; dec places in mantissa

         call    falog           ; raise 10 to power
         fmul                    ; exponent * mantissa

         pop     dx              ; restore registers
         pop     cx
         pop     ax
         ret                     ; return ST(0) = result
```

(continued)

Figure 13-20. *continued*

```
atof    endp

;
; CONVERT:      Called by ATOF to convert ASCII number
;               with possible sign and/or decimal point
;
; Call with:    DS:SI = address of string
;
; Returns:      ST(0) = result
;               AL    = first nonconvertible character
;               DX    = number of digits after decimal point
;               DS:SI = address + 1 of character in AL
;
; Uses:         AH, CX
;
convert proc    near                ; convert numeric field

        fldz                        ; initialize result
        xor     cx,cx               ; initialize sign
        mov     dx,-1               ; initialize decimal count

conv1:  lodsb                       ; scan off white space
        cmp     al,blank            ; ignore leading blanks
        je      conv1
        cmp     al,tab              ; ignore leading tabs
        je      conv1

        cmp     al,'+'              ; if plus sign proceed
        je      conv2
        cmp     al,'-'              ; is it minus sign?
        jne     conv3               ; no, test if numeric
        dec     cx                  ; yes, set flag

conv2:  lodsb                       ; get next character

conv3:  cmp     al,'0'              ; is character valid?
        jb      conv4               ; jump if not >= 9
        cmp     al,'9'
        ja      conv4               ; jump if not <= 9

        and     ax,0fh              ; isolate lower 4 bits
        mov     digit,ax            ; and save digit value
        fimul   int10               ; previous value * 10
        fiadd   digit               ; accumulate new digit

        or      dx,dx               ; past decimal point?
        js      conv2               ; no, convert next digit
        inc     dx                  ; yes, count digits
        jmp     conv2               ; convert next digit
```

(continued)

Figure 13-20. *continued*

```
conv4:  cmp     al,'.'          ; is it decimal point?
        jne     conv5           ; no, proceed
        inc     dx              ; indicate decimal found
        jmp     conv2           ; convert more digits

conv5:  jcxz    conv6           ; jump if result positive
        fchs                    ; make result negative

conv6:  or      dx,dx           ; decimal point found?
        jns     conv7           ; yes, jump
        xor     dx,dx           ; no, return zero places

conv7:  ret                     ; return ST(0) = result

convert endp

_TEXT   ends

        end
```

Here is an example of how ATOF could be used:

```
mystr   db      '3.1415e0',0
        .
        .
        .
        mov     si,seg mystr
        mov     ds,si
        mov     si,offset mystr
        call    atof
```

The source code for the inverse procedure FTOA, which converts a floating-point number to an ASCII string, is found in Figure 13-21 on the following page. To keep this routine reasonably simple, the strings are always generated in this form:

```
+0.00000000000000000E+000
```

The overall approach in FTOA is to use the FXTRACT instruction to pick apart the mantissa and the binary exponent, convert the binary exponent to a power of 10, scale the mantissa (while adjusting the exponent) until it is an integer, and then bring the integer off the coprocessor as an 18-digit BCD value that can be transformed directly to ASCII characters. FTOA is called with the floating-point number on top of the stack and the address of the buffer to receive the converted string in registers DS:SI. The routine returns with DS:SI pointing to the converted string and AX containing the length of the string. FTOA uses the routine FALOG, which was previously shown in Figure 13-18.

```
;
; FTOA.ASM -- Converts floating-point number
;             on 80x87 stack to ASCII.
;             (Also requires FALOG from FALOG.ASM)
;
; Copyright (C) 1991 Ray Duncan
;
; Call with:    ST(0) = floating-point number
;               DS:SI = buffer to receive string
;
; Returns:      DS:SI = address of converted string
;               AX    = length of string
;               Coprocessor stack popped
;
; Uses:         Nothing
;
; Be sure coprocessor has been properly initialized
; with a previous call to INIT87!

_DATA   segment word public 'DATA'

sign     dw      0                                ; receives FXAM status
oldcw    dw      0                                ; previous rounding mode
newcw    dw      0                                ; new rounding mode
exp      dw      0                                ; extracted power of 10
status   dw      0                                ; receives FCOM status
mant     dt      0                                ; mantissa as BCD value

fp1e17   dq      1.0e17                           ; constant for scaling
fp1e18   dq      1.0e18                           ; constant for scaling
int10    dw      10                               ; constant for scaling

pzstr    db      '+0.000000000000000000E+000'     ; displayed if
pz_len   equ     $-pzstr                          ; ST(0) = +0

mzstr    db      '-0.000000000000000000E+000'     ; displayed if
mz_len   equ     $-mzstr                          ; ST(0) = -0

pistr    db      '<+infinity>'                    ; displayed if ST(0)
pi_len   equ     $-pistr                          ; is positive infinity

mistr    db      '<+infinity>'                    ; displayed if ST(0)
mi_len   equ     $-mistr                          ; is negative infinity

nanstr   db      '<NaN>'                          ; displayed if ST(0)
nan_len  equ     $-nanstr                         ; contains NaN

unstr    db      '<unnormal>'                     ; displayed for positive
```

Figure 13-21.   *(continued)*

FTOA.ASM, the source code for a routine converting a floating-point number to an ASCII string.

Figure 13-21. *continued*

```
un_len   equ      $-unstr               ; or negative unnormals

destr    db       '<denormal>'          ; displayed for positive
de_len   equ      $-destr               ; or negative denormals

empstr   db       '<empty>'             ; displayed if ST(0)
emp_len  equ      $-empstr              ; is tagged "empty"

                                        ; number types from
                                        ; condition code bits
typetab dw        ftoa14                ; 0000 +unnormal
        dw        ftoa15                ; 0001 +NaN
        dw        ftoa14                ; 0010 -unnormal
        dw        ftoa15                ; 0011 -NaN
        dw        ftoa1                 ; 0100 +normal
        dw        ftoa16                ; 0101 +infinity
        dw        ftoa1                 ; 0110 -normal
        dw        ftoa17                ; 0111 -infinity
        dw        ftoa10                ; 1000 +zero
        dw        ftoa12                ; 1001 empty
        dw        ftoa11                ; 1010 -zero
        dw        ftoa12                ; 1011 empty
        dw        ftoa13                ; 1100 +denormal
        dw        ftoa12                ; 1101 empty
        dw        ftoa13                ; 1110 -denormal
        dw        ftoa12                ; 1111 empty


_DATA   ends

_TEXT   segment word public 'CODE'

        assume  cs:_TEXT,ds:_DATA

        extrn   falog:near            ; we need FALOG routine

        public  ftoa
ftoa    proc    near                 ; floating-point to ASCII

        push    bx                   ; save registers
        push    cx
        push    dx
        push    di
        push    es

        push    ds                   ; let ES point to _DATA
        pop     es

        fxam                         ; test type of number
```

(continued)

Figure 13-21. *continued*

```
        fstsw   sign                    ; unload FXAM status
        fwait
        mov     bx,sign                 ; retrieve status and
        and     bx,4700h                ; shift C3, C2, C1, C0
        rol     bx,1                    ; status bits to form
        rol     bx,1                    ; value 0-15, then
        shl     bh,1                    ; * 2 for jump index
        shl     bh,1
        shl     bh,1
        rol     bx,1
        rol     bx,1
        rol     bx,1
        shl     bx,1
        jmp     [typetab+bx]            ; branch by number type

ftoa1:  fabs                            ; force number positive
        fxtract                         ; extract exponent
        fxch    st(1)                   ; put exponent on top
        fldlg2                          ; form power of 10
        fmulp   st(1),st(0)
        fstcw   oldcw                   ; save current rounding mode
        fwait
        mov     ax,oldcw                ; set bit field for rounding
        or      ax,0c00h                ; mode to "chop"
        mov     newcw,ax
        fldcw   newcw                   ; force new rounding mode
        fld     st(0)                   ; duplicate power of 10
        frndint                         ; find integer part of
        fist    exp                     ; exponent and save it
        fldcw   oldcw                   ; restore old rounding mode
        fsubp   st(1),st(0)             ; find fractional part of
        call    falog                   ; power of 10
        fmulp   st(1),st(0)             ; then times mantissa
        fmul    fp1e18                  ; scale mantissa for BCD
        frndint                         ; zap any remaining fraction

ftoa2:  fcom    fp1e17                  ; is mantissa < 1.0e17?
        fstsw   status
        fwait
        mov     ax,status
        sahf
        jae     ftoa3                   ; no, proceed
        fimul   int10                   ; yes, mantissa * 10
        dec     exp                     ; and decrement exponent
        jmp     ftoa2

ftoa3:  fcom    fp1e18                  ; is mantissa < 1.0e18?
        fstsw   status
        fwait
```

(continued)

Figure 13-21. *continued*

```
          mov     ax,status
          sahf
          jb      ftoa4                    ; yes, proceed
          fidiv   int10                    ; no, mantissa / 10
          inc     exp                      ; and increment exponent
          jmp     ftoa3

ftoa4:    fbstp   mant                     ; unload mantissa in BCD
          fwait
          mov     di,si                    ; address for ASCII string
          mov     al,'+'                   ; assume positive
          test    sign,200h                ; check FXAM flags
          jz      ftoa5                    ; jump, value was positive
          mov     al,'-'

ftoa5:    stosb                            ; store plus or minus sign
          mov     al,'0'                   ; store leading zero
          stosb
          mov     al,'.'                   ; store decimal point
          stosb
          mov     bx,8                     ; point to last BCD digits

ftoa6:    mov     al,byte ptr [bx+mant]    ; convert BCD byte to
          shr     al,1                     ; two ASCII digits
          shr     al,1
          shr     al,1
          shr     al,1
          call    digit                    ; convert high nibble
          mov     al,byte ptr [bx+mant]
          call    digit                    ; convert low nibble
          dec     bx                       ; back up through BCD value
          jns     ftoa6                    ; until 18 digits converted

          mov     al,'E'                   ; store E for exponent
          stosb
          mov     bx,exp                   ; test sign of exponent
          mov     al,'+'
          or      bx,bx
          jns     ftoa7                    ; jump, exponent positive
          mov     al,'-'
          neg     bx                       ; abs value of exponent

ftoa7:    stosb                            ; store sign of exponent

          mov     ax,bx                    ; convert exponent to
          cwd                              ; three ASCII digits
          mov     cx,100
          div     cx
          call    digit                    ; exponent hundreds digit
```

(continued)

Figure 13-21. *continued*

```
        mov     ax,dx
        cwd
        mov     cx,10
        div     cx
        call    digit               ; exponent tens digit
        mov     ax,dx
        call    digit               ; exponent ones digit

ftoa8:  mov     ax,di               ; return AX = string length
        sub     ax,si               ; and DS:SI = string address

        pop     es                  ; restore registers
        pop     di
        pop     dx
        pop     cx
        pop     bx
        ret

ftoa10: mov     di,offset pzstr     ; +zero value
        mov     cx,pz_len
        jmp     ftoa20

ftoa11: mov     di,offset mzstr     ; -zero value
        mov     cx,mz_len
        jmp     ftoa20

ftoa12: mov     di,offset empstr    ; empty value
        mov     cx,emp_len
        jmp     ftoa20

ftoa13: mov     di,offset destr     ; denormal value
        mov     cx,de_len
        jmp     ftoa20

ftoa14: mov     di,offset unstr     ; unnormal value
        mov     cx,un_len
        jmp     ftoa20

ftoa15: mov     di,offset nanstr    ; NaN value
        mov     cx,nan_len
        jmp     ftoa20

ftoa16: mov     di,offset pistr     ; +infinity value
        mov     cx,pi_len
        jmp     ftoa20

ftoa17: mov     di,offset mistr     ; -infinity value
        mov     cx,mi_len
```

(continued)

Figure 13-21. *continued*

```
ftoa20: xchg    si,di               ; SI = canned string
        push    di                  ; DI = caller's buffer
        rep movsb                   ; copy canned string
        pop     si                  ; restore SI
        fstp    st(0)               ; discard original value
        jmp     ftoa8               ; go to common exit point

ftoa    endp

;
; DIGIT:         Converts low nibble of AL to ASCII digit
;                and stores at address given by DS:DI
;
; Call with:     AL    = value to be converted in bits 0-3
;                ES:DI = address to store ASCII character
;
; Returns:       AL    = unchanged
;                ES:DI = address + 1
;
digit   proc    near                ; nibble to ASCII digit

        push    ax                  ; save register
        and     al,0fh              ; isolate nibble
        add     al,'0'              ; convert to ASCII char
        stosb                       ; store character
        pop     ax                  ; restore register
        ret

digit   endp

_TEXT   ends

        end
```

A typical call to FTOA would be coded as follows:

```
mybuff  db      26 dup (?)
              .
              .
              .
        mov     si,seg mybuff
        mov     ds,si
        mov     si,offset mybuff
        call    ftoa
```

ATOF and FTOA are only simple models of conversion routines, and they do trade some accuracy and speed in favor of simplicity. When you understand how ATOF and FTOA work, you can refer to the Intel coprocessor manuals for examples of more complex and precise conversion routines.

PROCEDURES INTRODUCED IN THIS CHAPTER

Procedure Name	Action	Parameters	Results
ATOF	Converts ASCII string to floating-point value	DS:SI = segment:offset of string	ST(0) = binary value DS:SI = segment:offset of string terminator
DIDIV87	Double-precision (64 x 32) signed division	DX:CX: BX:AX = dividend SI:DI = divisor	DX:AX = quotient CX:BX = remainder
DIMUL87	Double-precision (32 x 32) signed multiplication	DX:AX = *value1* CX:BX = *value2*	DX:CX: BX:AX = product
FALOG	Common (base 10) antilog	ST(0) = argument	ST(0) = result
FCOS	Cosine	ST(0) = value	ST(0) = result
FSIN	Sine	ST(0) = value	ST(0) = result
FTAN	Tangent	ST(0) = value	ST(0) = result
FTOA	Converts floating-point value to ASCII string	ST(0) = value DS:SI = segment:offset of buffer to receive string	DS:SI = segment:offset of string AX = length of string
INIT87	Initializes numeric coprocessor if it is present	AX = coprocessor control word	If coprocessor present: Zero flag = true (1) If coprocessor not found or not initializable: Zero flag = false (0)

Companion Disk

The companion disk directory \CH13 contains the programs and modules that are listed below.

Routines Presented in This Chapter

ATOF.ASM	Converts an ASCII string to a floating-point number
DIDIV87.ASM	Double-precision signed division using a numeric coprocessor
DIMUL87.ASM	Double-precision signed multiplication using a numeric coprocessor
FALOG.ASM	Floating-point common antilog using a numeric coprocessor
FTOA.ASM	Converts a floating-point number to an ASCII string
FTRIG.ASM	Floating-point sine, cosine, and tangent
INIT87.ASM	Tests for the existence of a numeric coprocessor and initializes it if it is present

Routines Previously Discussed

HTOL.ASM	Converts a hexadecimal ASCII string to a double-precision (32-bit) unsigned integer
HTOQ.ASM	Converts a hexadecimal ASCII string to a quad-precision (64-bit) unsigned integer
ITOH.ASM	Converts a single-precision (16-bit) unsigned integer to a hexadecimal ASCII string

Interactive Demonstration Programs

TRYDIMUL	MAKE file for TRYDIMUL.EXE
TRYDIMUL.ASM	Interactive demonstration program
TRYDIDIV	MAKE file for TRYDIDIV.EXE
TRYDIDIV.ASM	Interactive demonstration program
TRYFTRIG	MAKE file for TRYFTRIG.EXE
TRYFTRIG.ASM	Interactive demonstration program

The interactive program TRYDIMUL.ASM demonstrates use of the routines in INIT87.ASM, DIMUL87.ASM, ITOH.ASM, and HTOL.ASM. To build TRYDIMUL.EXE, enter this command:

```
C>MAKE TRYDIMUL  <Enter>
```

When you run TRYDIMUL.EXE, it prompts you for two 32-bit hex integers, converts the ASCII strings to their binary equivalents, uses the coprocessor to multiply the arguments together, and then displays the 64-bit result in hexadecimal. Press the Enter key at any prompt to exit the program.

Similarly, the interactive program TRYDIDIV.ASM demonstrates use of the routines in INIT87.ASM, DIDIV87.ASM, ITOH.ASM, HTOL.ASM, and HTOQ.ASM. To build TRYDIDIV.EXE, enter this command:

```
C>MAKE TRYDIDIV  <Enter>
```

When you execute TRYDIDIV.EXE, it prompts you for a 64-bit hex dividend and a 32-bit hex divisor, converts the ASCII strings to their binary equivalents, carries out the division operation on the coprocessor, and then displays the 32-bit quotient and remainder in hex ASCII. Press the Enter key at any prompt to exit the program.

The demonstration program TRYFTRIG.ASM is considerably more complex; it illustrates use of the routines in ATOF.ASM, FTOA.ASM, FALOG.ASM, FTRIG.ASM, and INIT87.ASM. To build TRYFTRIG.EXE, enter this command:

```
C>MAKE TRYFTRIG  <Enter>
```

The TRYFTRIG program prompts you for an angle in degrees; converts the ASCII string to a floating-point number; calculates the sine, cosine, and tangent of the angle; and then displays the angle in degrees, the angle in radians, and the sine, cosine, and tangent. Press the Enter key at any prompt to exit the program.

14

Optimizing Assembly-Language Programs

In spite of the increasing dominance of high-level languages and integrated development environments, the optimization of assembly-language code is still a fashionable subject for online debates. For example, the Programming Forum on PC MagNet has been the "level playing field" for many coding challenges—a member describes a small but interesting programming problem and then sits back to see who can do it in the fewest number of bytes. Similarly, on BIX, the *assembler/cpu8088* conference has been the venue for many deliberations on obscure assembly-language optimization issues.

Despite grass-roots interest, the literature on Intel 80x86 assembly-language optimization is surprisingly sparse. While preparing a talk on this subject for a Software Development conference a couple of years ago, I searched the back issues of the major programming magazines and found only a handful of articles. The literature on code optimization for high-level language compilers, in contrast, is extensive, and many of the concepts developed in this literature are useful in assembly-language coding as well. A Bibliography is included at the end of this book for those of you who want to explore this subject further; in the meantime, let's survey some of the more common optimization techniques and then turn to the larger questions of when and where to optimize.

Optimizing for Speed

When you decide that a program isn't running fast enough, you should first check to be sure that you are using the best algorithms and data representations for the job. Switching from an inappropriate or primitive algorithm to a more appropriate or clever algorithm might well speed up your program by an order of magnitude or more. Thus, time spent perusing Knuth or Sedgewick for an algorithm that you would not be likely to think of on your own is time well invested. Similarly, changing from an "obvious" but simple data structure (such as a linked list) to a more sophisticated structure (such as a B-tree) could yield results far out of proportion to the programming effort involved.

When you're satisfied that you're using the appropriate algorithms and data structures, look next at the program's use of mass storage. Because even the fastest disk devices used on personal computers are abominably slow compared to the computing horsepower of an 80386 or 80486, you want to minimize or eliminate disk I/O whenever possible. Become familiar with all the types of memory available to an MS-DOS program—extended memory, expanded memory, upper memory blocks, and the high memory area—and fully exploit this memory to keep your program's data in RAM, where you can access it quickly. You might even want to look into data compression techniques because it will almost always be faster to squeeze and unsqueeze data than to read it several times from disk.

Another important consideration is reducing your program's calculation burden. The compiler writers have fancy terms—"common subexpression elimination," "constant folding," "constant propagation"—for variations on the basic rule that your program should never calculate the same value twice at runtime; instead, it should calculate the value once and save it for reuse. An even better solution is to move calculations from runtime to assembly time whenever the mathematical capabilities of MASM allow. Along the same lines, you might be able to enhance a program's performance drastically by converting calculations to table lookups and making use of tables that are generated and stored on disk ahead of time by a separate program. (See Example #1: Table Lookups, later in this chapter.)

After you've done whatever can be done at these more abstract levels, you're essentially reduced to classic code-hacking and cycle-shaving to improve your program's performance—particularly if your program is heavily display-oriented and performs its own memory-mapped video output. Some of the more common optimizations in this category are the following:

- Substituting fast special-case sequences of instructions for more generalized, complex instructions—for example, replacing a hardware multiply by a power of 2 with a shift or series of shift instructions (see Example #2: Strength Reduction) or replacing a loop that moves, initializes, or compares strings with one of the Intel 80x86 string instructions (Chapter 5).

- Reducing the overhead of jumps and calls by converting subroutines to macros and assembling them in-line, changing the sense of conditional jumps so that the jumps are taken on the less common condition, moving common cases to the front of multiway jumps, converting calls followed immediately by returns into jumps (tail merging and tail recursion optimization), and so on. (See Example #3: Jump and Call Optimizations.)

- Using loop optimizations, including moving the calculations of invariant values outside loops, simplifying calculations inside loops, unrolling loops, and consolidating separate loops that are executed the same number of times into a single loop (loop jamming). (See Example #4: Loop Optimizations.)

- Taking maximum advantage of the available registers by keeping working values in registers whenever possible to minimize memory accesses, packing multiple values or flags into registers, and eliminating unnecessary stack pushes and pops (especially at subroutine entries and exits).

- Exploiting CPU-specific instructions such as the push immediate value instruction that is available on the 80286 or later CPUs and the doubleword string, 32-bit by 32-bit multiply, 64-bit by 32-bit divide, and multiply by immediate value instructions that are available on the 80386 and 80486 CPUs. (See Example #5: CPU-Specific Optimizations.) Of course, your program must first determine which CPU it is running on (see Figure 14-1 on page 354).

You might also be able to improve execution speed slightly by aligning data items and the targets of jump instructions on appropriate boundaries. With the 8086 and 80286, which are 16-bit CPUs, you want to align on 16-bit (word) boundaries. The 80386 prefers 32-bit (doubleword) alignment, and the 80486 performs best with paragraph (16-byte) alignment because of its internal cache design.

If all else fails, and if you are writing a specialized application rather than a mass-market software package, you can usually trump your performance problems with hardware. At today's mail-order prices, the cost of replacing the machine your application runs on with a new, much faster machine could be considerably less than the cost of the time required for you to painstakingly redesign, optimize, and re-debug the application.

Optimizing for Size

If your program is too big rather than too slow, you must fall back on optimization strategies that are in most ways the inverse of the tricks you use for speed. You must first examine the program carefully and determine whether the primary problem is code size or data size.

If the problem is data size, sophisticated data structures might help, although you would probably reap more short-term benefits from eliminating fast but sparse arrays or tables in favor of more compact structures such as linked lists and the packing of data using bit fields. Using brute-force compression and decompression of tables or structures as they are needed is rarely useful because it is typically necessary to decompress all the data simply to access one item. In addition, the compression/decompression routines themselves occupy considerable memory.

Large lookup tables and arrays can be built in a disk file and read into memory in small chunks when needed, although this approach can have a crushing effect on throughput if the data is randomly accessed. Lookup tables can often be completely eliminated in favor of recomputing values as they are needed. You must also search for and remove constants and variables that are never actually used by the program because they have been superseded by other constants and variables during development and debugging. Again, it's extremely important to learn how to access all the available types of memory and to make your program flexible enough to use them.

Optimizing a program's code for size is quite a different ballgame than optimizing it for speed. First, you must inspect every line of source code and eliminate all statements or procedures that are never executed or cannot be reached from any point in the main line of execution ("dead code"). If you have a large application that has gone through a prolonged development cycle involving several programmers, you might be surprised at the number of lines that can be excised in this way.

Second, you must analyze the program again and consolidate all identical or functionally similar code sequences into subroutines that can be called from any point in the program. The more general you can make the subroutines, the more likely it is that their code can be reused. When carried to an extreme, this approach leads to a highly modular and compact program that consists mostly of calls.

At this point, if memory shortage is still a problem, your efforts might diverge in several directions. You can decompose your program into relatively independent modules that can be read into memory separately as overlays. You can encode the program's functionality in tables that "drive" its execution. You can resort to threaded-code or pseudocode techniques that represent your program's logic in considerably less memory at some cost in performance. Or you can pull out all the technological stops and implement a custom interpreter or compiler for a "little language" that in turn serves as the virtual machine for your application. Microsoft QuickBasic, Microsoft Excel, and BRIEF are everyday examples of the threaded-code, pseudocode, and little-language strategies, respectively.

Finally, if you are writing a special-purpose application, you might be able (again) to simply trump your memory problems with hardware or software. The many possibilities include upgrading to MS-DOS 5 or OS/2 2.0 to make more memory available below 640 KB, plugging in yet another EMS board, switching to an 80386 or 80486 machine that will support more extended memory than your 8086 or 80286 machine will support, or porting your program to run on a DOS extender.

When to Optimize, When to Punt

Code optimization in any language always requires trade-offs:

- Trading speed for memory
- Trading code maintainability and readability for code performance
- Trading development time for execution time

These trade-offs seem straightforward, but often they are not nearly as simple as they appear. A classic example is the following two instructions, either of which can be used to transfer a value from register DX into AX (with different side effects):

```
xchg   ax,dx
mov    ax,dx
```

On an Intel 8088, the MOV instruction is 2 bytes and requires 2 CPU clocks, whereas the XCHG instruction is 1 byte but requires 3 CPU clocks—so far, a clear-cut trade of speed for memory. But the actual performance of the instructions is highly dependent on context, the size of the CPU's prefetch queue, the size and characteristics of system caches, and so on, while even the number of clock cycles required to execute the instructions varies from one model of Intel CPU to another. As it turns out, it's nearly impossible to predict the performance of a nontrivial sequence of instructions on an Intel processor, especially on the later CPUs such as the 80386 and 80486, which make more extensive use of pipelining. You simply have to benchmark the various possibilities *in vivo* and see how they perform.

Similarly, the trade of development time for execution time and the trade of code maintainability for performance are seldom as well ordered as we would like, and the long-term impact of wrong decisions can be enormous. By far the most important thing to understand about optimization is when to do it and when to leave well enough alone; as Donald Knuth says, "Premature optimization is the root of much programming evil." Before you even think about tuning up your program, you should first be sure that it is logically correct and complete, that you're using the right algorithm for the job, and that you've written the cleanest, most straightforward, most structured code you possibly can.

If your program meets those criteria, its performance and size will be fine, most of the time, without any further attention. Remember that merely by using assembly language at all you're gaining a two-fold or three-fold speed and size advantage over the programmer using a high-level language. Additionally, many of the characteristics that make a program easy to read and maintain also tend to make it fast—for example, the avoidance of spaghetti code with its many unnecessary jumps and calls (which have a severe penalty on the Intel 80x86 architecture because they dump the instruction prefetch queue) and the use of simple, straightforward machine instructions rather than complex instructions.

Nevertheless, the user's perception of your program's performance is your overriding concern. As Michael Abrash observes, "Any optimization that is perceptible to the user is an optimization worth doing." Conversely, if users perceive your program as pudgy and pokey, it's likely to remain unappreciated. It is important that your program appear to be instantly responsive, even when it is occupied with time-consuming calculations or disk operations. It should keep the screen alive with progress indicators such as dials or thermometers and should allow the user to interrupt lengthy operations safely.

If you must resort to the code-hacking and cycle-shaving tricks mentioned earlier, avoid misdirection of your limited time and energy. Bear in mind the natural hierarchy of time scales—register/register operations, memory operations, disk operations, and user interactions—each of which is an order of magnitude (or more) slower than its predecessor. For example, don't waste effort trying to save a few machine cycles in a routine if your program's speed is limited by its access to disk files; instead, try to identify ways to reduce disk I/O. It's vital to employ profiling tools to identify the hot spots in your program and concentrate your attention in those areas. And after you make each presumptive optimization, time the results carefully and test, test, test.

In his superb book *Writing Efficient Programs,* Jon Bentley relates a horror story from Bell Labs that we should all take to heart:

> "Victor Vyssotsky enhanced a FORTRAN compiler in the early 1960s under the design constraint that compilation time could not be noticeably slower. A particular routine was executed rarely (he estimated during design that it would be called in about one percent of compilations, and just once in each of those) but was very slow, so Vyssotsky spent a week squeezing every last cycle out of the routine. The modified compiler was fast enough. After two years of extensive use, the compiler reported an internal error during compilation of a program. When Vyssotsky inspected the code, he found that the error occurred in the prologue of the 'critical' routine, and that the routine had contained this bug for its entire production life."

Vyssotsky made three important errors: He failed to profile the program before he optimized it and thus wasted time optimizing a routine that had no impact on performance; he failed to implement the optimized routine correctly; and he failed to test the optimized routine to see if it worked according to specification. Now, it is not my intent to pick on Mr. Vyssotsky; I've made far worse blunders in my day, which fortunately have not been immortalized in Jon Bentley's books. But Vyssotsky's experience is a good example of how time and energy can be wasted in the holy cause of optimization and how a failure to methodically cover all the bases of profiling and validation during optimization usually comes home to roost sooner or later.

The remainder of this chapter presents five in-depth examples of the optimization strategies we've discussed.

Example #1: Table Lookups

One of the most powerful types of optimization is to move calculations from the program's execution time to its compile or assembly time or to perform the calculations in another, specialized program and write the results into an intermediate file where they can be retrieved when needed. An especially useful category of this type of optimization is known as *table lookup*.

Let's consider an application in which table lookup might be extremely profitable. Imagine a graphics program that needs to rotate and translate line segments in order to provide the user with the illusion of three-dimensional projections and thus must be able to determine the sines and cosines of angles. The calculation of sines and cosines is typically implemented with polynomial expansions in floating-point arithmetic and involves a series of multiply and divide operations that are extremely expensive. Moreover, the sines and cosines obtained in this way are far more precise than necessary for ordinary PC graphics adapters; even single-precision (32-bit) floating-point sines and cosines are calculated to at least eight digits of precision, although only four or five digits are needed (because typical PC graphics adapters have at best 1024 by 768 resolution).

You could, however, use table lookups to obtain the sines of angles in increments of 1 degree to four-digit precision. First, you need to create a data structure in which each slot corresponds to an angle in degrees and contains the sine of that angle multiplied by 10,000:

```
table   dw    0     ; sin(0)
        dw    175   ; sin(1)
        dw    349   ; sin(2)
          .
          .
          .
```

With the table in hand, you can easily write a short routine that accepts an angle of 0 through 359 degrees in register AX and returns the sine of that angle in AX:

```
; Function SINE
; Call    AX = degrees
; Return AX = sine * 10000
sine      proc near
          push  bx
          mov   bx,ax
          add   bx,bx
          mov   ax,[bx+table]
          pop   bx
          ret
sine      endp
```

To make the procedure even faster, you can convert it to a macro and expand it in-line wherever it is needed. You can also use elementary trigonometric identities to shorten the table (only the data for 0 through 90 degrees is needed) and to calculate cosines from the same table by adding 90 degrees and calling the sine routine.

Table lookup techniques can sometimes be used effectively in places that might not ordinarily occur to you. For example, if you were given the job of writing a routine that returns the number of nonzero bits in a byte, your first impulse might be to use shifts and a loop to count the nonzero bits one by one. But a much faster approach would be to build a byte table whose positions correspond to each of the possible values of a byte, from 0 through 255, with the number of nonzero bits for a particular value in the table's byte at that position:

```
table   db    0     ; bits set in 00H
        db    1     ; bits set in 01H
        db    1     ; bits set in 02H
        db    2     ; bits set in 03H
         .
         .
         .

; Function BITS
; Call   AL = byte value
; Return AL = number of nonzero bits
bits    proc  near
        push  bx
        mov   bl,al
        xor   bh,bh
        mov   al,[table+bx]
        pop   bx
        ret
bits    endp
```

Again, for even more speed, you can convert this procedure to a macro and assemble it in-line wherever it is needed. For byte tables, you might get better performance by replacing the MOV instruction with the special string instruction XLAT. But this technique is hardly limited to byte tables. I have seen an ingenious word-counting utility in which the author used a 64-KB lookup table to inspect each possible two-character sequence for word breaks. Gordon Letwin reportedly used a similar technique to scan freespace bitmaps for collections of free sectors in OS/2's High Performance File System (HPFS).

Example #2: Strength Reduction

Multiplication and division operations are expensive on just about any CPU because they must be implemented (at some level) in terms of shifts and adds or shifts and subtracts, respectively. The original 4-bit and 8-bit microprocessors didn't have any machine instructions for multiplication or division, so programs had to carry out those operations in lengthy subroutines that performed the shifts and adds or subtracts explicitly. The early 16-bit microprocessors such as the 8086 and the 68000 did offer multiplication and division in hardware, unlike their 8-bit predecessors, but the instructions were unbelievably slow—a 32-bit by 16-bit division on the 8086, for instance, required approximately 150 machine cycles.

Consequently, the little tricks for speeding up or eliminating multiplication and division operations were, and still are, among the first learned by any performance-minded programmer. Most of these tricks fall into a category of techniques known as *strength reduction*—the replacement of general-purpose multiply or divide instructions (or subroutine calls) with specialized sequences of shifts and adds or subtracts.

Let's look at the simplest optimizations for multiplication first. To multiply a number by a power of 2, you merely shift it left by the appropriate number of bit positions. For example, here is some generalized but pokey code that multiplies the value in the variable *myvar* by 8:

```
mov     ax,myvar
mov     bx,8
mul     bx
mov     myvar,ax
```

This code can be transformed (on 8086/8088 processors) into a sleeker sequence:

```
mov     ax,myvar
shl     ax,1     ;  * 2
shl     ax,1     ;  * 4
shl     ax,1     ;  * 8
mov     myvar,ax
```

Alternatively, you could use the following:

```
shl     myvar,1
shl     myvar,1
shl     myvar,1
```

If you are merely shifting the value one or two positions, it's usually cheaper to shift the value in memory. If you need to shift the value many positions, the increased speed of in-register shifting compensates for the additional instructions required to load the value into a register first and then store it back afterward. But even this simple optimization is not as straightforward as it first appears. The 80x86's instruction prefetch queue, the particular model of Intel CPU you are running on, and the presence or absence of cache can interact in strange and wonderful ways. At some point and on some CPUs, it becomes worthwhile to use the "shift by count in CL" variant of the instruction:

```
mov     ax,myvar
mov     cl,3
shl     ax,cl
mov     myvar,ax
```

The 80186 and later CPUs have a "shift by immediate count" variant, which is even more convenient:

```
shl     myvar,3
```

If you need to multiply values that are larger than 16 bits by powers of 2, you can use the CPU's carry flag to propagate the shift through multiple registers. For example, to multiply the 32-bit value in DX:AX by 4, you could write the following:

```
shl     ax,1    ; * 2
rcl     dx,1
shl     ax,1    ; * 4
rcl     dx,1
```

With some creative combinations of shifts and adds, you can perform fast special-case multiplication by almost any value. The following code multiplies the value in register AX by 10:

```
mov     bx,ax   ; save copy
shl     ax,1    ; * 2
shl     ax,1    ; * 4
add     ax,bx   ; * 5
shl     ax,1    ; * 10
```

The application of strength reduction to division is somewhat more limited. Dividing by powers of 2 is, of course, very easy. You merely shift the value right, being sure to choose the appropriate shift instruction for the type of division (signed or unsigned). For example, to perform an unsigned division of the value in AX by 4, you would write the following:

```
shr     ax,1
shr     ax,1
```

On 80186 and later CPUs, you could use this instead:

```
shr     ax,2
```

To perform a signed division by 4, you would write this code:

```
sar     ax,1
sar     ax,1
```

Or, on 80186 and later CPUs, you could use the following:

```
sar     ax,2
```

The only difference between the logical (or unsigned) shift instruction SHR and the arithmetic (or signed) instruction SAR is that SHR copies the most significant bit into the next lower bit and then replaces the most significant bit with 0, whereas SAR copies the most significant bit into the next lower bit but leaves the most significant bit unchanged. Selecting the correct shift instruction for fast division is very important, particularly when you are dealing with addresses. If you accidentally use signed arithmetic on an address when you meant to use unsigned, the bug may bite you immediately—but it can also remain latent until some change in the size or linking order of the application unmasks the error at a later date. (Incidentally, parallel SHL and SAL mnemonics exist, but they assemble into the same machine instruction; think about it.)

Multiple-precision division by powers of 2 with shifts can be accomplished with the aid of the carry flag and is no more difficult than multiple-precision multiplication. For example, to perform a signed divide of the value in DX:AX by 8, you could code as follows:

```
sar     dx,1     ; / 2
rcr     ax,1
sar     dx,1     ; / 4
rcr     ax,1
sar     dx,1     ; / 8
rcr     ax,1
```

But, unlike multiplication, fast division by arbitrary values such as 3 or 10 rather than powers of 2 using shifts is surprisingly messy. When I was first dabbling in programming on a Raytheon 703 minicomputer, I tried to throw together a fast divide-by-10 sequence that was analogous to the multiply-by-10 method shown above. If you take the trouble to implement such a sequence, you'll find that you've got a lengthy, slow chunk of code and, furthermore, that you've done 90 percent of the work for a generalized software division routine using shifts and subtracts. It's usually more profitable to rethink the whole situation and transform the algorithm or data structure so that division by odd values is not necessary.

Here I must mention a nifty optimization that is attributed to Mark Zbikowski, one of the authors of MS-DOS versions 2.x and 3.x. The code below divides the value in register AX by 512:

```
shr     ax,1
xchg    ah,al
cbw
```

This clever sequence, once you've seen it, naturally leads the mind to all sorts of special-purpose sequences of XCHG or MOV instructions that yield multiplication or division by relatively large powers of 2—256, 512, and so on.

Example #3: Jump and Call Optimizations

Spaghetti code—code that is poorly organized and infested with branches in all directions—is always undesirable, but it carries a particularly harsh penalty on Intel 80x86 CPUs. Although this does provide a powerful incentive for assembly-language programmers and the designers of optimizing compilers to structure their code properly, it also introduces some interesting problems. Before we discuss jump and call optimizations, let's review some of the characteristics of Intel hardware.

The Intel architecture relies for much of its performance on a simple pipelining scheme with three components: a bus interface unit (BIU), a prefetch queue, and an execution unit (EU). Whenever the memory bus is idle (for example, during the execution of a multicycle instruction whose operands are in registers), the BIU fetches instruction bytes from memory and places them in the prefetch queue, working forward sequentially from the current value of the CPU's instruction pointer (IP). As the EU completes each instruction, it looks in the prefetch queue for the next instruction; if the instruction is in the queue, the EU can proceed immediately to decode the instruction without waiting for a memory access.

How do jumps and calls interact with this simple implementation of pipelining? Whenever the EU decodes a jump or call instruction, it invalidates the complete contents of the prefetch queue and reloads the IP. The BIU must then start from scratch to fetch instruction bytes from the new execution address and load them into the prefetch queue, while the EU must "stall" until a complete instruction has been retrieved. Then, any memory accesses involved in the execution of that first instruction at the new address will interfere with the BIU's ability to prefetch the subsequent instruction, and so on. It could be quite a while before the BIU can completely fill the prefetch queue again so that the EU can run at its maximum speed.

To further complicate the situation, the size of the prefetch queue varies from one CPU model to another. It's as small as 6 bytes on early models and as large as 32 bytes on recent models. This variation is one of the factors that make prediction of execution times for particular sequences of instructions, based on instruction cycle counts and byte lengths, quite difficult. Additionally, the dependence of the prefetch queue on instruction alignment varies among the CPU models. The BIU must fetch instructions on address boundaries and in multiples of bytes that are dictated by the width of the CPU's external memory bus, and the performance of the prefetch queue can be significantly impaired when the targets of calls or jumps lie at the "wrong" addresses. For example, on an 8086 CPU with a 16-bit memory bus, the CPU always fetches instructions from memory 16 bits at a time. Thus, if the instruction that is the target of a jump or call begins on an odd address, one-half of the first memory access to fetch the instruction at that address is wasted.

This brings us to the first guideline for optimizing jumps and calls: Be sure that their destinations fall on the proper address boundaries for the type of CPU your application will run on most often. You do this by adding the appropriate alignment attribute (WORD or DWORD) to your segment declarations and inserting ALIGN directives before each label. Because the 8088 has an 8-bit external bus, it is not sensitive to alignment; if your program's market is primarily 8088-based PCs, you should avoid alignment altogether because it will simply waste memory without affecting performance. But if your program will run primarily on 8086 or 80286 CPUs, you should use WORD alignment; and, if your program is specific to 80386DX or 80486DX CPUs, you should use DWORD alignment. (The 80486 actually prefers that items lie on 16-byte boundaries because of the structure of its internal cache, but wasting an average of 8 bytes at each instruction label for the sake of alignment seems like a lot to give away.)

The next rule of thumb for jumps and calls is simply to eliminate them whenever possible, at least in those parts of your program that are CPU-bound. Toward this end, you want to organize your code so that it executes in a straightforward, sequential manner with the minimum number of decision points. Such organization tends to keep the prefetch queue full and also makes your code easier to read, maintain, and debug. After you've obtained as much improvement as you can with "good" code structuring, you must decide whether to go further and introduce "bad" structure in the name of performance, such as converting jumps to a common subroutine exit point into multiple exits. In extreme cases, short subroutines can be converted to macros and expanded in-line to avoid the overhead of a call and return.

When your code needs to make a conditional jump, analyze the decision point and structure the code so that the jump is taken on the less common case, thus minimizing the number of times that the prefetch queue must be dumped. For example, if your code is checking a variable for a negative value but the value would be negative only under unusual circumstances, design your code to "fall through" the branch when the value is positive:

```
cmp     balance,0
jl      in_the_red   ; rarely happens
```

Similarly, if you have a value that can trigger many different actions and you're making multiple comparisons followed by conditional branches based on this value, try to move the comparisons for the most common cases to the front:

```
        cmp     ax,most_common_value
        jne     L1
        .
        .
        .
        jmp     L3
L1:     cmp     ax,less_common_value
        jne     L2
        .
        .
        .
        jmp     L3
L2:     cmp     ax,least_common_value
        jne     L3
        .
        .
        .
L3:
```

If many sparsely arranged values must be tested for, you can implement the multiway comparison much as you implement a binary search: First bisect the range of possible values by checking whether the value being tested is the same as, greater than, or less than the middle value; then (if it was less or greater) bisect the remaining range with another comparison; and so on. This strategy is extremely efficient if the frequencies of the various possible values are fairly uniform.

If the values are not sparse, the best solution is often a jump table. For example, imagine that you have an ASCII character in AL and an assortment of routines that perform special processing for certain character values and, further, that you want to get to those routines quickly without explicitly comparing for each character value. You could first construct a table that contains the address of the appropriate routine in the slot corresponding to the character's ASCII code and then branch "through" the table as follows:

```
table   dw      routine_00
        dw      routine_01
        .
        .
        .
        dw      routine_FE
        dw      routine_FF
        .
        .
        .
        mov     bl,al   ; copy char to BL
        xor     bh,bh   ; form index to table
        shl     bx,1    ; and jump "through" table
        jmp     [table+bx]
```

Two more optimizations that are related to jumps and calls and that require a certain amount of destructuring of an otherwise valid program are *tail merging* and *tail recursion elimination*. Both involve the transformation of calls into jumps; calls are inherently more expensive than jumps because they push a return address onto the stack and thus involve more memory accesses. Tail merging is simply the conversion of a CALL instruction followed immediately by a RET instruction into a JMP instruction—that is, a sequence such as the following:

```
proc1   proc  near
        .
        .
        .
        call  proc2
        ret
proc1   endp

proc2   proc  near
        .
        .
        .
        ret
proc2   endp
```

is converted to this faster sequence:

```
proc1   proc  near
        .
        .
        .
        jmp   proc2
proc1   endp
```

```
proc2   proc  near
        .
        .
        .
        ret
proc2   endp
```

After this optimization, because the return address of the caller of PROC1 is on the stack at entry to PROC2, the PROC2 procedure returns directly to the original caller, eliminating the overhead of an extra CALL and RET. If the code for PROC2 physically follows the code for PROC1, even the JMP PROC2 can be excised and the execution of PROC1 can simply "fall through" into PROC2.

Tail recursion elimination is much like tail merging. When a routine calls itself recursively and this call is located just before the routine's final return, the call can be converted to a jump, thereby both increasing speed and reducing the amount of stack space needed. For example, the following code

```
proc1   proc  near
        .
        .
        .
        cmp   ax,some_value
        je    exit
        call  proc1
exit:   ret
proc1   endp
```

can be transformed into this code:

```
proc1   proc  near
        .
        .
        .
        cmp   ax,some_value
        jne   proc1
        ret
proc1   endp
```

Such recursive routines can often be optimized even further by converting the recursion to a loop.

Example #4: Loop Optimizations

The compiler literature bulges with all manner of loop optimizations, under such picturesque names as "code hoisting," "loop-invariant code motion," "induction variable elimination," "loop jamming," "loop unrolling," and the like. But we can boil down the principles behind all these optimizations into two basic rules:

Rule #1. Never do anything inside a loop that you can do somewhere else.

Rule #2. Eliminate the jumps that control loops whenever possible.

Rule #1 is a corollary to the adage that 90 percent of a program's execution time is spent in 10 percent of the code. If you look to see where that 10 percent of the code is located, it's usually inside loops of some sort. So when you're trying to speed up a program, you should be sure to profile it, identify the hot spots, and inspect each one for a loop that is a possible target for optimization. A loop construct might not always jump out at you as a nice series of instructions ending with a LOOP, LOOPZ, or LOOPNZ (especially if someone else has written the code!), but any sequence that is executed repetitively based on the value of some controlling variable or flag qualifies for our purposes here.

In general, the loops will fall into two categories: loops whose speed is constrained by some external synchronization mechanism, and loops that are CPU-bound. An example of a loop in the first category might be one that sends a string of characters out to the parallel port; your code can't run any faster than the parallel port can accept characters, and the parallel port is at least a couple of orders of magnitude slower than any reasonable sequence of machine instructions that might be used to drive it. You can optimize such externally constrained loops for your own entertainment, but you could probably put the effort to better use elsewhere. Instead, the loops in the second category, which are basically free-running, are the ones you want to concentrate on.

In order to fully optimize your program's loops, you must approach the problem methodically. Inspect each loop for operations that don't depend on the loop's control variable, and "hoist" those operations out of the loop (typically by moving them ahead of the loop). Analyze whatever code remains, and simplify it wherever possible by using table lookups, CPU-specific instructions, strength reduction, and any other tricks you have at your command to shorten the code and eliminate expensive instructions. If certain calculations depend on the current value of the loop variable, try to rearrange the code to turn this situation on its head so that the calculations are done outside the loop instead and the starting and ending values for the loop variable depend on the results. For example, imagine a poorly coded loop that sums every fifth value in an array of single-precision integers, leaving the result in AX:

```
items   equ    100
array   dw     items dup (?)
        .
        .
        .
        xor    cx,cx    ; init counter
        xor    ax,ax    ; init sum
L1:     mov    bx,cx    ; form pointer
        add    bx,bx    ; * 2
        add    bx,bx    ; * 4
        add    bx,cx    ; * 5
        add    bx,bx    ; * 10
        add    ax,[bx+array]
        inc    cx
        cmp    cx,(items/5)
        jne    L1
```

After simplifying the loop, you have the following:

```
items    equ    100
array    dw     items dup (?)
         .
         .
         .
         xor    ax,ax    ; init sum
         mov    bx,offset array
L1:      add    ax,[bx]
         add    bx,10
         cmp    bx,offset array+(items*2)
         jb     L1
```

After you've optimized the contents of your loops as much as possible, you need to take a bird's-eye view of your program to see if you can eliminate the compares and conditional jumps that are controlling loops. The motive for doing so is the same as for the jump and call optimizations that we discussed earlier. Remember that the performance of Intel 80x86 CPUs relies heavily on a pipelining system consisting of a bus interface unit (BIU), a prefetch queue that is filled from memory with instructions by the BIU, and an execution unit (EU) that takes instructions out of the prefetch queue and decodes them. Whenever a jump or call is executed, the prefetch queue is invalidated, the memory cycles that were used to put instructions beyond the jump into the queue are wasted, and the EU must stall until the BIU gets it some instructions to work on from the new execution address. Consequently, jumps and calls are far more costly in practice than they seem to be if you merely count machine cycles according to the Intel databooks.

One way to get rid of compares and conditional jumps is *loop jamming,* or *loop fusion*—that is, rearranging your code so that two or more loops that execute the same number of times are combined into a single loop. For example, two loops of the form

```
         mov    cx,100
L1:      ; do something here
         loop   L1
         mov    cx,100
L2:      ; do something else here
         loop   L2
```

can often be combined into a single loop that looks like this:

```
         mov    cx,100
L1:      ; do something here
         ; do something else here
         loop   L1
```

The other way to get rid of loops is *loop unrolling*—eliminating the overhead of loop control structures by simply duplicating the contents of the loop an appropriate number of times. This works especially well when the time required to execute the contents of the loop is swamped by the time required to execute the jump that controls the loop.

For example, a loop of the form

```
        mov     cx,3
L1:     add     ax,[bx]
        add     bx,2
        loop    L1
```

might be rewritten as follows:

```
        add     ax,[bx]
        add     bx,2
        add     ax,[bx]
        add     bx,2
        add     ax,[bx]
```

and then like this:

```
        add     ax,[bx]
        add     ax,[bx+2]
        add     ax,[bx+4]
```

Unrolling loops is a classic trade-off of speed for memory. Each time you evaluate a loop for unrolling, you must decide whether the size of the loop and the number of iterations make it a reasonable candidate for this optimization, based on your program's overall size and the machine resources available. Sometimes unrolling pays off in funny places. For example, all of us who write 80x86 assembly code have learned to be alert for situations in which we can use the special string instructions. We often write little sequences of code like this:

```
        mov     cx,3
        mov     si,offset string1
        mov     di,offset string2
        rep movsw
```

The loop here is implicit: Processing of the REP prefix involves some setup time, and the effect of the REP is exactly as though we had written this instead:

```
L1:     movsw
        loop L1
```

On some Intel CPUs, for small numbers of iterations of string instructions, it's faster to eliminate the REP prefix and write the string instructions out linearly:

```
        movsw
        movsw
        movsw
```

But in this kind of optimization you must benchmark the alternatives in the context of your program to locate the payoff point. The speed of one of these snippets of code is not strictly predictable by counting machine cycles and opcode bytes because it depends on the code's context, the bandwidth of the memory bus, the differing sizes of the prefetch queue on the various CPUs, the presence (and size) or absence of an off-CPU cache, and so on.

Example #5: CPU-Specific Optimizations

If your program is going to run on a specific model of Intel CPU, or if you think it's worth the trouble to have a version of the program for each possible type of CPU it might be used on, you can take advantage of the machine instructions that are unique to each CPU type when you do your local optimizations. (The routine in Figure 14-1, which appears at the end of this discussion, can be used to determine which CPU the program is running on.)

Compared to the 8086 and 8088, the 80286 has quite a few additional instructions that can help performance:

- Shifts and rotates by literal counts other than 1
- PUSH literal value
- IMUL by literal value
- String input and output instructions
- PUSHA (push all) and POPA (pop all)
- ENTER and LEAVE to set up and destroy stack frames
- BOUND instruction to check array indices

If your program will run only on an 80286 or higher, you should also word-align all data items and the targets of jump or call instructions. This could give you a small improvement in performance at a relatively trivial cost in memory. (The 8086 also benefits from word alignment, although the 8088 does not, because of its 8-bit external data bus.)

On the 80386DX and its clones, you can improve performance of 16-bit programs by using any of the already-mentioned 80286 instructions, by aligning data items and the destinations of jumps or calls on 32-bit boundaries, and by exploiting the following additional features:

- 32-bit registers (which must be used cautiously because they are not preserved by some DOS emulators such as the MS-DOS compatibility box in OS/2 versions earlier than 1.3)
- Move with zero-extension or sign-extension (MOVZX or MOVSX)
- 64-bit (double-register) shifts (SHLD and SHRD)
- Set byte to true or false according to CPU flags, eliminating the need for a conditional jump (SETZ, SETC, and so on)
- Bit test, clear, set, and scan instructions (BT, BTC, BTR, BTS, BSF, BSR)
- Generalized indexed addressing and scaled indexed addressing modes
- Fast multiplication with LEA via scaled indexed addressing
- "Long" conditional jumps

- 32-bit by 32-bit multiply and 64-bit by 32-bit divide
- Additional segment registers (FS and GS)

Of course, the way to get the most mileage out of the 80386 architecture is to use a DOS extender or OS/2 2.0 and port your application to 32-bit protected mode. You will then have full access to the 80386's 32-bit registers, improved addressing, and 4-GB linear address space.

The 80486 offers only three additional instructions not present on the 80386 that might be used by an application program:

- BSWAP (convert "Little-Endian" to "Big-Endian" data format and vice versa)
- CMPXCHG (compare and exchange, for maintenance of semaphores)
- XADD (exchange and add, also for maintenance of semaphores)

The instruction cycle counts on the 80486, however, are quite different from those on the 80386 and 80286. In general, the simpler instructions have been speeded up at the expense of the more complex instructions, meaning that code originally written for an 8088 often runs faster on an 80486 than code written for an 80286 or 80386. Other considerations for the 80486DX are its 8-KB internal cache, which prefers alignment on 16-byte (paragraph) boundaries, and its built-in numeric coprocessor. Unfortunately, Intel's recent release of the 80486SX without a (functional) numeric coprocessor means that we still cannot take hardware floating-point support for granted on high-end PCs.

```
        .486
;
; CPUTYPE.ASM -- Returns Intel CPU type (adapted from
;                 source code distributed to ISVs by Intel Corp.).
;
; Copyright (C) 1991 Ray Duncan
;
; Call with:    N/A
;
; Returns:      AX = CPU type
;                 0086H = 8086 or 8088
;                 0286H = 80286
;                 0386H = 80386SX or 80386DX
;                 0486H = 80486SX or 80486DX
;
; Destroys:     Upper 16 bits of EAX and ECX on 386/486
```

Figure 14-1. *(continued)*

CPUTYPE.ASM, a routine that returns a code indicating whether the host CPU is an 8088, 8086, 80286, 80386, or 80486 (adapted from code distributed by Intel). When a program is running on an 80286, 80386, or 80486 CPU, many CPU-specific instructions can be exploited to improve performance. First, however, the program must be able to determine the CPU type so that it can adapt itself accordingly.

Figure 14-1. *continued*

```
_TEXT    segment word use16 public 'CODE'

         assume  cs:_TEXT

         public  cputype
cputype proc    near

         pushf                           ; save copy of flags and
         push    bx                      ; other affected registers
         push    cx
         pushf                           ; now try to clear bits 12-15
         pop     ax                      ; of CPU flags
         and     ax,0fffh
         push    ax                      ; set modified CPU flags
         popf
         pushf
         pop     ax                      ; get flags again
         and     ax,0f000h               ; if bits 12-15 are still
         cmp     ax,0f000h               ; set, this is 8086/88
         jne     cpu1                    ; jump, not 8086/88
         mov     ax,0086h                ; set AX = 86/88 CPU type
         jmp     cpux                    ; and exit

cpu1:    or      ax,0f000h               ; must be 286 or later
         push    ax                      ; now try to set bits 12-15
         popf                            ; of CPU flags
         pushf
         pop     ax                      ; if bits 12-15 can't be
         and     ax,0f000h               ; set, this is a 286
         jnz     cpu2                    ; jump, not 80286
         mov     ax,286h                 ; set AX = 286 CPU type
         jmp     cpux                    ; and exit

cpu2:    mov     bx,sp                   ; 386 or later, save SP
         and     sp,not 3                ; avoid stack alignment fault
         pushfd                          ; get value of EFLAGS
         pop     eax
         mov     ecx,eax                 ; save copy of EFLAGS
         xor     eax,40000h              ; flip AC bit in EFLAGS
         push    eax                     ; try to force EFLAGS
         popfd
         pushfd                          ; get back EFLAGS value
         pop     eax
         mov     sp,bx                   ; restore old stack pointer
         xor     eax,ecx                 ; can AC bit be changed?
         jnz     cpu3                    ; no, jump, not a 386
         mov     ax,0386h                ; set AX = 386 CPU type
         jmp     cpux                    ; and exit
```

(continued)

Figure 14-1. *continued*

```
cpu3:   mov     ax,0486h            ; set AX = 486 CPU type

cpux:   pop     cx                  ; restore registers
        pop     bx
        popf                        ; restore original flags
        ret                         ; return with AX = cpu type

cputype endp

_TEXT   ends

        end
```

Companion Disk

The companion disk directory \CH14 contains the programs and modules that are listed below.

Routine Presented in This Chapter

CPUTYPE.ASM   Returns a code indicating the CPU type: 8086/8088, 80286, 80386, or 80486

Demonstration Program

CHECKCPU   MAKE file for CHECKCPU.EXE

CHECKCPU.ASM   Demonstration program for CPUTYPE.ASM

The program CHECKCPU.ASM demonstrates use of the routine CPUTYPE.ASM. To build CHECKCPU.EXE, enter this command:

```
C>MAKE CHECKCPU   <Enter>
```

When you run CHECKCPU.EXE, it calls CPUTYPE to determine the CPU type and then displays the type on the standard output device.

Bibliography

MS-DOS and IBM PC Programming

Duncan, Ray. 1988. *Advanced MS-DOS Programming*. 2d ed. Redmond, Wash.: Microsoft Press. ISBN 1-55615-157-8.

Microsoft Corporation. 1991. *Microsoft MS-DOS Programmer's Reference*. Redmond, Wash.: Microsoft Press. ISBN 1-55615-329-5.

Microsoft Press. 1988. *The MS-DOS Encyclopedia*. Redmond, Wash.: Microsoft Press. ISBN 1-55615-049-0.

Phoenix Technologies Ltd. 1991. *System BIOS for IBM PCs, Compatibles, and EISA Computers*. 2d ed. Reading, Mass.: Addison-Wesley. ISBN 0-201-57760-7.

Sargent, Murray, III, and Richard L. Shoemaker. 1986. *The IBM PC from the Inside Out*. Rev. ed. Reading, Mass.: Addison-Wesley. ISBN 0-201-06918-0.

Schulman, Andrew. 1990. *Undocumented DOS*. Reading, Mass.: Addison-Wesley. ISBN 0-201-57064-5.

Intel 80x86 Architecture and Assembly Language

Agarwal, Rakesh. 1991. *80x86 Architecture and Programming*. Englewood Cliffs, N.J.: Prentice-Hall. ISBN 0-13-245432-7.

Crawford, John, and Patric Gelsinger. 1987. *Programming the 80386*. Alameda, Calif.: Sybex. ISBN 0-89588-381-3.

Duntemann, Jeff. 1990. *Assembly Language from Square One*. Glenview, Ill.: Scott, Foresman. ISBN 0-673-38590-6.

Intel Corporation. *80286/80287 Programmer's Reference Manual*. Order no. 210498. Santa Clara, Calif.: Intel Corporation. Phone (800) 548-4725.

Intel Corporation. *80386DX Programmer's Reference Manual*. Order no. 230985. Santa Clara, Calif.: Intel Corporation. Phone (800) 548-4725.

Intel Corporation. *86/88 186/188 Programmer's Reference Manual*. Order no. 210911. Santa Clara, Calif.: Intel Corporation. Phone (800) 548-4725.

Intel Corporation. 1990. *i486 Microprocessor Programmer's Reference Manual*. Berkeley, Calif.: Osborne-McGraw Hill. ISBN 0-07-881674-2.

Microsoft Corporation. 1991. *Microsoft MASM Version 6.0 Programmer's Guide*. Redmond, Wash.: Microsoft Corporation.

Nelson, Ross P. 1991. *Microsoft's 80386/80486 Programming Guide*. 2d ed. Redmond, Wash.: Microsoft Press. ISBN 1-55615-343-0.

General Algorithms

Aho, Alfred, John Hopcroft, and Jeffrey Ullman. 1983. *Data Structures and Algorithms*. Reading, Mass.: Addison-Wesley. ISBN 0-201-00023-7.

Folk, Michael, and Bill Zoellick. 1987. *File Structures: A Conceptual Toolkit*. Reading, Mass.: Addison-Wesley. ISBN 0-201-12003-8.

Knuth, Donald. 1968. *Fundamental Algorithms*. Vol. 1 of *The Art of Computer Programming*. Reading, Mass.: Addison-Wesley. ISBN 0-201-03809-9.

Knuth, Donald. 1973. *Seminumerical Algorithms*. Vol. 2 of *The Art of Computer Programming*. Reading, Mass.: Addison-Wesley. ISBN 0-201-03822-6.

Knuth, Donald. 1981. *Sorting and Searching*. Vol. 3 of *The Art of Computer Programming*. Reading, Mass.: Addison-Wesley. ISBN 0-201-03803-x.

Polya, G. 1971. *How to Solve It*. Princeton, N.J.: Princeton University Press. ISBN 0-691-02356-5.

Sedgewick, Robert. 1988. *Algorithms*. 2d ed. Reading, Mass.: Addison-Wesley. ISBN 0-201-06673-4.

Sedgewick, Robert. 1990. *Algorithms in C*. Reading, Mass.: Addison-Wesley. ISBN 0-201-51425-7.

Graphics and User Interfaces

Foley, James D., Andries van Dam, Steven K. Feiner, and John F. Hughes. 1990. *Computer Graphics: Principles and Practice*. 2d ed. Reading, Mass.: Addison-Wesley. ISBN 0-201-12110-7.

Norman, Donald A. 1989. *The Design of Everyday Things*. New York: Doubleday. ISBN 0-385-26774-6.

Wilton, Richard. 1987. *Programmer's Guide to PC and PS/2 Video Systems*. Redmond, Wash.: Microsoft Press. ISBN 1-55615-103-9.

Multiple-Precision Arithmetic and Floating Point

Clinger, William. 1990. "How to Read Floating Point Numbers Accurately." *Proceedings of the ACM SIGPLAN '90 Conference on Programming Language Design and Implementation,* pp. 92–101.

Cody, William J., and William Waite. 1980. *Software Manual for the Elementary Functions*. Englewood Cliffs, N.J.: Prentice-Hall. ISBN 0-13-822064-6.

Goldberg, David. 1990. "Computer Arithmetic." Appendix A in *Computer Architecture: A Quantitative Approach,* by John L. Hennessy and David A. Patterson. San Mateo, Calif.: Morgan Kaufmann. ISBN 1-55880-069-8.

Goldberg, David. 1991. "What Every Computer Scientist Should Know About Floating Point Arithmetic." *ACM Computing Surveys* 23, no. 1 (March), pp. 5–48.

Grehan, Rick. 1988. "Floating Point Without a Coprocessor." Parts 1 and 2. *BYTE,* September, pp. 313–19; October, pp. 293–98.

Hart, John, et al. 1978. *Computer Approximations.* Malabar, Fla.: Robert E. Krieger. ISBN 0-88275-642-7.

Institute of Electrical and Electronics Engineers. 1987. *IEEE Standard for Radix-Independent Floating Point Arithmetic.* ANSI/IEEE Standard 854-1987. IEEE, 345 East 47th Street, New York, N.Y. 10017.

Intel Corporation. *80387 Programmer's Reference Manual.* Order no. 231917. Santa Clara, Calif.: Intel Corporation. Phone (800) 548-4725.

Knuth, Donald. 1973. Chapter 4 in *The Art of Computer Programming,* vol. 2, *Seminumerical Algorithms.* Reading, Mass.: Addison-Wesley. ISBN 0-201-03822-6.

Moshier, Stephen L. 1986. "Computer Approximations." *BYTE,* April, pp. 161–78.

Plauger, P. J. 1988. "Computer Arithmetic." *Computer Language,* February, pp. 17–23.

Plauger, P. J. 1988. "Do It Yourself Math Functions." *Computer Language,* June, pp. 17–22.

Plauger, P. J. 1988. "Properties of Floating Point Arithmetic." *Computer Language,* May, pp. 17–21.

Plauger, P. J. 1988. "Safe Math." *Computer Language,* March, pp. 17–22.

Steele, Guy, and Jon White. 1990. "How to Print Floating Point Numbers Accurately." *Proceedings of the ACM SIGPLAN '90 Conference on Programming Language Design and Implementation,* pp. 112–26.

Code Optimization

Abrash, Michael. 1986. "More Optimizing for Speed." *Programmer's Journal,* July/August, pp. 36–39.

Abrash, Michael. 1990. *The Zen of Assembly Language.* Glenview, Ill.: Scott, Foresman. ISBN 0-673-38602-3.

Abrash, Michael. 1991. "80x86 Optimization." *Dr. Dobb's Journal,* March, pp. 16–26.

Abrash, Michael. "Pushing the Envelope." Monthly column. *PC Techniques.*

Abrash, Michael, and Dan Illowsky. 1989. "Roll Your Own Mini-Languages with Mini-Interpreters." *Dr. Dobb's Journal,* September, pp. 52–62.

Barrenechea, Mark. 1990. "Peak Performance." *Programmer's Journal,* November/December, pp. 64–69.

Barrenechea, Mark. 1991. "Loop Unrolling." *Programmer's Journal,* July/August, pp. 66–72.

Barrenechea, Mark. 1991. "Optimania." *Programmer's Journal,* January/February, pp. 72–75.

Bentley, Jon. 1982. *Writing Efficient Programs.* Englewood Cliffs, N.J.: Prentice-Hall. ISBN 0-13-970244-x.

Bentley, Jon. 1986. Chapters 3, 5, 8, and 9 in *Programming Pearls.* Reading, Mass.: Addison-Wesley. ISBN 0-201-10331-1.

Bright, Walter. 1989. "Secrets of Compiler Optimization." *Micro Cornucopia,* January/February, pp. 26–33.

Disque, Tom. 1987. "8088 Assembly-Language Programming Techniques." *Dr. Dobb's Journal,* July, pp. 24–28.

Grappel, Robert. 1987. "Optimizing Integer Multiplications by Constant Multipliers." *Dr. Dobb's Journal,* March, pp. 34–37.

Hoyt, Michael. 1986. "Optimizing for Speed." *Programmer's Journal,* March/April, pp. 32–37.

Paterson, Tim. 1990. "Assembly Language Tricks of the Trade." *Dr. Dobb's Journal,* March, pp. 30–36.

Index

Note: References to program listings, tables, and illustrations are in italics.

5¹/₄-inch Low-Density Companion Disk

Upon request, you can replace the high-density disk included with this book with two 5¹/₄-inch low-density disks. Limit one set per customer. To request your replacement, send your name, street address (no P.O. boxes, please), city, state, ZIP, and daytime phone number to: Microsoft Press, Attn: MASM Companion Disk, One Microsoft Way, Redmond, WA 98052-6399. Allow 2-3 weeks for delivery. This offer is valid in the U.S. only.

3¹/₂-inch Companion Disk

The companion disk for *Power Programming with Microsoft Macro Assembler* is available in 3¹/₂-inch format. Cost per disk is $6.95 plus your local sales tax, and shipping charges of $5.00 per disk. To order, send your name, street address (no P.O. Boxes, please), city, state, ZIP, and daytime phone number, along with your check or money order (U.S. funds only) to: Microsoft Press, Attn: MASM Companion Disk, One Microsoft Way, Redmond, WA 98052-6399. Allow 2-3 weeks for delivery. This offer is valid in the U.S. only.